AF530782

RED ROSES AND SILVER WINGS

A WORLD WAR II MEMOIR

BY

KITTY STRICKLAND SHORE

RED ROSES AND SILVER WINGS, A WWII MEMOIR.

Printed in the United States of America.

Library of Congress Catalog Card #98-93772

ISBN 0-9667856-8-1

Published by A.A.M. Press
Chevy Chase, Maryland

Cover Design by Lynne Strickland Grace

Jack Strickland 1941

Jack Strickland 1941

Kitty Murray Strickland 1941

Kitty and Jack 1941

1st Lt. Jennis (Jack) Strickland
England 1944

B-24 Liberator

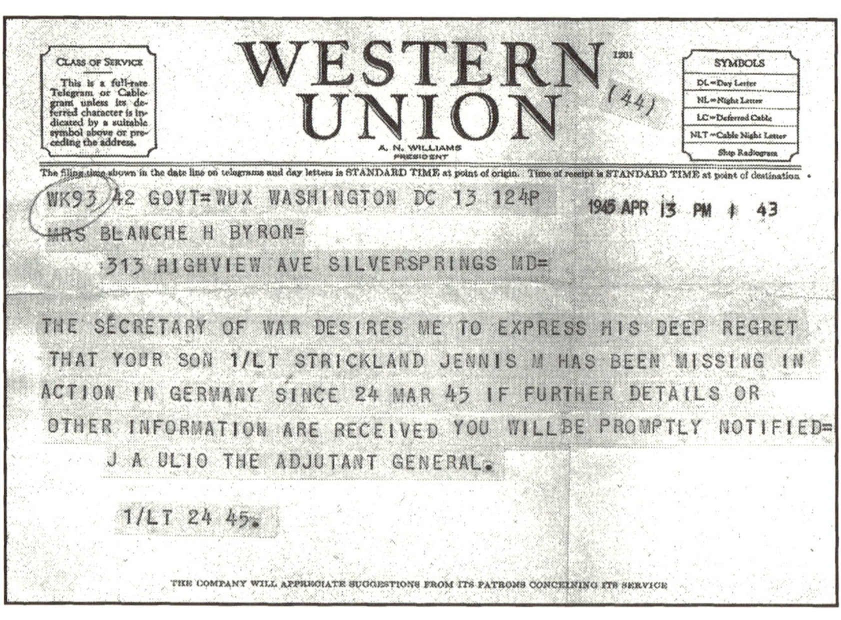

CLASS OF SERVICE

This is a full-rate Telegram or Cablegram unless its deferred character is indicated by a suitable symbol above or preceding the address.

WESTERN UNION 1201

A. N. WILLIAMS
PRESIDENT

SYMBOLS

DL = Day Letter
NL = Night Letter
LC = Deferred Cable
NLT = Cable Night Letter
Ship Radiogram

The filing time shown in the date line on telegrams and day letters is STANDARD TIME at point of origin. Time of receipt is STANDARD TIME at point of destination

(44)

WK93 42 GOVT=WUX WASHINGTON DC 13 124P 1945 APR 13 PM 1 43

MRS BLANCHE H BYRON=

313 HIGHVIEW AVE SILVERSPRINGS MD=

THE SECRETARY OF WAR DESIRES ME TO EXPRESS HIS DEEP REGRET THAT YOUR SON 1/LT STRICKLAND JENNIS M HAS BEEN MISSING IN ACTION IN GERMANY SINCE 24 MAR 45 IF FURTHER DETAILS OR OTHER INFORMATION ARE RECEIVED YOU WILLBE PROMPTLY NOTIFIED=

J A ULIO THE ADJUTANT GENERAL.

1/LT 24 45.

THE COMPANY WILL APPRECIATE SUGGESTIONS FROM ITS PATRONS CONCERNING ITS SERVICE

Telegram

Preface

As I climbed the attic stairs I hoped I could find the letters. It had been so many years since I had seen them. I have lived in this house for 40 years and am somewhat of a pack rat. Unfortunately all of my children take after their mother in that regard and the attic is chock full of old report cards, outgrown football cleats, well-worn toys, comics, semi-formal dresses from the '50s; you name it and it is probably in my attic.

I promised Cherie and Tim I would look for the letters and let them read them. Cherie is my granddaughter and Tim is her bridegroom. They live in England and recently sent me the most wonderful gift I have ever received. The two of them spent a year collecting all the information they could find about her grandfather–my husband, Jennis Strickland–who had served as a B-24 Bomber pilot in England during the Second World War. They located and photographed the airbase where he was stationed, found some of his flight orders, and visited and took pictures of the various memorials that the British have erected in honor of the Americans who served there. They even contacted some men who had served with him and remembered "Jack"–and many, many more things. These

Cherie and Tim put in a binder and sent to me. Among all this information was a letter that Jack had written to me and that Cherie's mother had kept. That's what reminded me that I had lots more somewhere in my attic. Thus, after all these years, the search into the past began.

I found the letters in an old trunk stuck in a corner, along with many other letters that had been written during the war years. I took them all downstairs and dumped them on the dining room table. For the next two weeks, as I reread them, I stepped back in time and was reliving my 14th to 21st years. The long-forgotten memories were as new and fresh as though they had happened yesterday.

Chapter One

First Date

I remembered the first time I ever saw Jack. We were in Blair High School in Silver Spring, Md. He was a class ahead of me and the best looking guy I had ever seen. He also was bashful and had never spoken to me. I had a good friend, Nell, who had an older sister who was the best friend of Jack's sister, Justine. We all went to the same church. The church was sponsoring a moonlight cruise down the Potomac River and Nell and I wanted to go. Knowing I had a "crush" on Jack, Nell's sister and Jack's older sister talked me into inviting him to go with me.

In those days nice girls did not ask boys out on dates but the older sisters dared me and I took the dare. I was scared to death when I made the phone call. Jack's mother answered the phone and said that Jack was not there. Greatly relieved, I started to hang up when Jack walked in his front door. Now I HAD to go through with it, so I asked him and after a pause, he said, "Wow"-another pause and, "Yes" and the date was on.

It was a lovely, soft spring night on the river when we

had our first date and fell in love. That night Jack, with his southern accent, told me that I needed a red rose for my "hay-uh."

The next day was a school day and I was in my first period class when the door opened and Jack walked in. The teacher stopped her lecture and Jack walked over and put a beautiful red rose on my desk, turned around and walked out. The teacher made no comment and resumed our lesson as though nothing had happened. This procedure was repeated every morning until the close of school that June.

Chapter Two

Rocky Mount

The summer of 1938 Jack and I spent every moment we could together. He had taken a summer job with a nice young couple who had an estate just outside of town. We found time to have long talks and he told me about his childhood, his family, his hopes, and his dreams.

Jack was born in Rocky Mount, N.C., in 1922. His father died when he was 6, leaving his mother, Blanche, with four children–Justine, Jack, Harold, and Doris. Doris was only 18 months old at the time. He didn't remember much about his father except that he was a baseball player in the Minor Leagues and apparently a GOOD one as he had just been offered a job in a Major League when he was in an accident that took his life. He was 27. Two of Jack's father's brothers, Uncle Matthew who lived in Nashville, N.C., and Uncle Richard who lived in Rocky Mount, took Jack under their wings, teaching him to hunt and fish and thoroughly appreciate Nature. He loved his uncles dearly but I think he missed his father all of his life. He used to say that had his father lived he might have taught

Jack to be more of a "Man." I don't think he realized how much more of a "Man" he was than any of his contemporaries. For example, being the oldest boy, he had a paternal attitude about his younger brothers and sisters and was always very protective of them.

Blanche's second marriage was to a man named Karl Byron. When Jack was 14, Karl got a job with the Government in Washington, D.C., and the family moved to Silver Spring, Md. (a suburb of D.C.). Jack had no desire to leave Rocky Mount so they let him stay with relatives until he was 16. But finally he had to join his family in Silver Spring.

Every once in a while Jack couldn't take another day of "city life." The lure of the south and home became irresistible and he would hitchhike back to Rocky Mount.

In the following two years I often went with him for a weekend. I never hitchhiked and I know we couldn't have afforded the train so I guess we went by bus. I really don't remember how we got there but I surely do remember BEING there. Jack wanted me to meet all his relatives and friends. His relations teased us a lot but they were all as kind as they could be to me.

Uncle Matthew and his wife, Aunt Beulah, lived on a farm. Aunt Beulah was a fabulous cook and every day at noon she cooked "dinner." There was a big table set up on the back porch and she would fill it to overflowing with at least two pies, cakes, fried chicken, coleslaw, vegetables, homemade bread, home churned butter and to top it off she offered us a glass of homemade scuppernong wine. They grew the grapes on their farm. I had never seen scuppernong grapes before. They were big, translucent, amber, and as sweet as honey. It was the best wine I have ever tasted.

And speaking of southern food, one of my fondest memories was of going to Bob Melton's in Rocky Mount. That man had to make the best BBQ in the world. It was made with pork, vinegar, and pepper and cooked over a slow fire all day. His "restaurant" (which was an old house with outdoor wooden tables and benches) was known for miles around. They would serve the BBQ and Brunswick stew in great big family sized bowls. (When Jack got his commission and we were in Louisiana he would arrange to fly to Rocky Mount whenever he could and would bring me back a shoebox full of Bob's barbecue. Heavenly!)

That summer Jack taught me to fish. I learned how to cast the line without causing a backlash in the reel and to jiggle the lure so the fish thought it was something alive. (I remember one lure was called a "Hawaiian Wiggler." I liked that one the best because it looked like it had a hula skirt.) We always ate what we caught but I convinced Jack that I couldn't clean fish. He used to look puzzled and say he couldn't understand how, since I was fairly intelligent and he had shown me repeatedly, I just never got the knack of it. That was probably the smartest thing I ever did.

He also taught me to shoot. We used .22 rifles. Our shooting was mostly at tin cans that we had placed on logs. I got to be a very good shot. Occasionally we shot squirrels. My parents, who also came from the south, liked squirrel meat, but I confess I never ate any, being perfectly happy to give them my share. (Nowadays I have squirrels who come to my window and demand peanuts which they will take out of my hand. Guess I'll always feel guilty about shooting them back then.)

We both wished that summer would never end but too soon it was time for school to start again.

Although Jack was a senior and I was a junior we did have one class together–first period algebra taught by Miss Aud. Now, Miss Aud was a very nice lady but would not have won any beauty contests. She was very serious and I'm sure she must have smiled from time to time but I don't remember seeing it happen. However, Jack had charmed all the teachers with his southern accent and southern manners. (The teachers in this suburb of Washington, D.C., were not used to being called "Ma'am" and "Sir.")

One day Jack was 20 minutes late in coming to class. When he did arrive, Miss Aud asked him why he was late. I will never forget him standing there in front of the class telling her how on his way to school he had to go through a wooded park area and had seen a flying squirrel. He gave her a brief rundown on the habits and nature of the flying squirrel and said he had never seen one this far north, so he sat himself down and watched it. Miss Aud nodded and told him to take his seat and we continued with the algebra lesson.

We had wooden desks in school. Occasionally I would sit at a desk on which Jack had previously carved his initials. He cleverly combined all three initials (JMS) so they looked like just one letter. The bottom left leg of the 'M' curved to the left to form a "J." The right leg of the 'M' curved to make an "S." Gradually I noticed that in all the "carvings" an 8 had been added to the bottom right of the "S." When I asked him about it, Jack said, "That's a message for you because there are eight letters in I LOVE YOU." I delighted in coming across these little "love letters" from time to time.

J.M. Strickland, Sr.
Second from left

Clockwise from upper left: Justine, Ma (Grandmother) Blanche, Jack (in helmet and goggles), Doris, and Harold

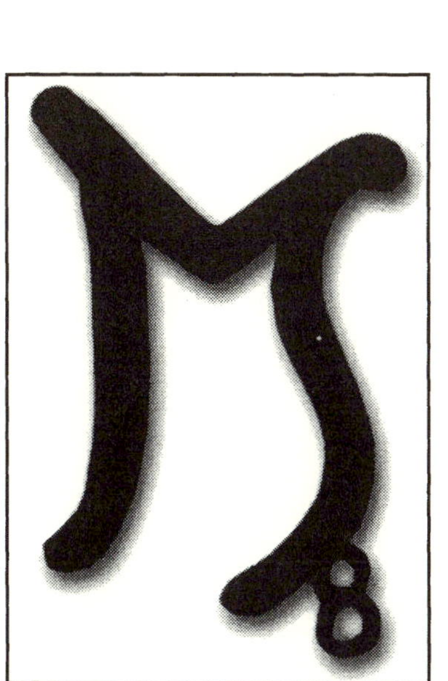

Carving on desks

Chapter Three

Friends and Baby Sisters

That school year was ideal. I was a serious student and ran for secretary of the Student Council. I was elected. Jack got passing grades but his heart was never in schoolwork. However, he campaigned to be representative for his class in order for us to be able to attend Student Council meetings together. He won his election easily.

We had a lot of friends and the most memorable were the Clements. They were a large family who lived in one of the original farmhouses built before Silver Spring began to be developed. It was a warm, loving group consisting of the mother (whom we called Aunt Grace), the father (Uncle Clarence) and five kids–Joe, Jane, Faith and Hope (twins), and Anne. All were close in age.

Every Friday night a bunch of us would congregate at the Clements' house to play records, dance, drink cokes, and have fun. During the week the fellows would spend their afternoons taking apart and putting together old cars and motorcycles in the Clements' yard. I certainly did not know then that these guys were mathematical geniuses. When Joe went to college, his math teachers told his parents, "You're wasting your money. Joe knows more about mathematics than we do." During the war Joe worked on the Manhattan Project with Dr. J. Robert Oppenheimer at Los Alamos, N.M., and helped design the detonating mechanism for the atomic bomb. As you can imagine, it was ultra hush-hush and neither his family nor any of his friends knew about it at the time.

Art Tool, another member of the group, worked on top-secret projects for the Naval Research Laboratory. He and Jane Clements celebrated their 50th wedding anniversary last year.

Another one of the fellows, Billy McKeever, served overseas in the Infantry. As you will see in Jack's wartime letters, he and Billy tried repeatedly to meet in London but much to Jack's disappointment they never managed to get together. Billy married Hope Clements.

I talked with Joe recently to get his permission to write about his work at Los Alamos. We began to reminisce and he laughingly said, "In those days I always thought my best pals were coming to the house to see me. When they all ended up marrying my sisters, it dawned on that I hadn't been the attraction."

Jack thought Jane Clements was one of the nicest people he had ever known and they were good friends. I must confess I did not want him liking any other girl that much. Let's face it–I was jealous. Later, during the war, Jane and I got to be good friends, too, and I had to agree with Jack–she WAS (and IS) a lovely human being.

Our closest friend was Harvey Holland whom Jack called "Harp." Jack and Harvey had become best buddies before I came into the picture. Adding another friend to a twosome quite often doesn't work out. Despite that fact and much to my delight, they let me become the third Musketeer.

We went everywhere together. Harp was an unusually nice guy with a great sense of humor and very attractive so he had little trouble getting dates to dances and parties. When he did, we would double date and if he didn't, the three of us would attend social events together.

Later on I'll tell you more about Harp because he plays a big part in this story.

I had a brother, Banks Murray, Jr., three and a half years older than I. Through odd circumstances (he had to repeat a grade and I skipped a grade) we ended up in high school together.

That fall our mother told us she was pregnant. Banks and I were delighted–I think my mother was embarrassed. She said that if the baby were a boy, Banks could name him and if a girl, I got the honor. In January Felicia Ann Murray was born. (I did get to name her.) Being so much older than our baby sister, Banks and I adored her. (I've often told her she was responsible for my having so many children. She was precious and I loved her dearly and knew that I wanted to have lots of babies of my own someday.)

Jack didn't have a car so he would borrow his stepfather Karl's car from time to time. Not too long after Felicia was born, we asked Karl if we could borrow his car and he said, "No," that he had to use it to go and see Blanche in the hospital.

This was scary news and we asked what was wrong with her. Karl laughed and told us Blanche had just given birth to a baby girl whom they named Betty. Jack, of course, lived with his mother and I was in and out of their house all the time. Neither of us had any idea she was pregnant. She had never said a word about it to any of us. She and Karl had had two sons, John and Donald, since they moved to Silver Spring. I don't know if she, like my mother, was embarrassed or didn't mention it because it was her nature to be interested in everyone else and not draw attention to herself. She was a remarkable woman and her children, rightly so, idolized her. I did, too.

Kitty and Jack
Skyline Drive
Fall of 1939

Jack and Kitty
on Sligo Creek Bridge
1939

Chapter Four

Aging 5 Months in a Day

Jack graduated from high school that June and got a job at a local hardware store.

On September 14, 1940, the United States approved the first peacetime draft.

School, without Jack, was not nearly as much fun for me that year. One interesting thing did happen to me. I ran for school president and lost by one vote to Ford Kelley, making me vice-president. Ford went on to become quite a war hero. He was a navigator in the Air Corps, went overseas, and won many medals. When he came home Silver Spring had a parade for him, bands and all. At our 50th high school reunion I asked him a question that I had wondered about for years. I asked him if he had voted for himself in that election. He laughed and said, "Of course!" Dumb me had voted for him, too.

I graduated from Blair in June of 1941. I had wanted to go to college but my father had some very old-fashioned ideas, one being "women didn't need an education because they got married and their husbands would support them." He offered me a proposition: He would pay for my tuition if I gave him my word that I wouldn't get married until a year after I graduated from college. Being in love, there was no way I could make that promise. I thanked him but no-thanked him and got a job, first with an insurance company and then with the Department of Justice in D.C.

Jack and I had agreed not to get married until we were a little older and more established. However, with college now out of the question and the draft breathing down Jack's neck we changed our minds. We knew we couldn't set up housekeeping until Jack had served his time in the army so we decided to be secretly married. We had heard that there was no waiting period required before you could get married in South Carolina. Therefore, we made plans.

One weekend when my parents were going to be out of town, we took off for Rocky Mount and then crossed the state line to the county court house in Florence, S.C.

We told the judge and the clerk that we wanted to get married. The clerk started filling out the necessary papers. When she asked my date of birth, I told her. She stopped writing and looked up at the judge and said, "Did you hear that?"

"Yes, I'm afraid I did." he answered.

The clerk said, "You have to be 18 to be married in South Carolina." She and the judge looked at each other and seemed to silently agree upon a solution. She said, "Do you think you could age 5 months between here and Marion–the next closest county seat?" I assured her that I could. So we drove to Marion, S.C., where, with a straight face, I said I was 18. Jack was 19. We were married there on September 1, 1941. We told Harp and I may have told a girl friend and also a few friends of Jack's in Rocky Mount. We went back home and I continued to live with my parents.

December 7, 1941, the Japanese bombed Pearl Harbor and the U.S. was in the war. Jack had not been drafted yet but, like most Americans, wanted to join the Service and help win the war. He enlisted in the U.S. Army Air Corps. He and Harp had had flying lessons at Schram's airport and at College Park Airport in Maryland and loved flying.

That Christmas season the mailman delivered a card addressed to me from one of the friends in Rocky Mount. It said, "How is the old married couple?" When I came home from work I saw that it had been opened and resealed. I knew my mother had opened it but I was mule-headed enough not to say anything until she admitted that she *had* opened it. She didn't say anything and I didn't say anything.

Jack came over on Christmas Eve and before we went out for the evening, he gave me a diamond engagement ring. It was in a box covered with red rose buds. The next morning my mother asked when we were planning on getting married and I finally told her about our trip to South Carolina. She asked me why I hadn't told her before. I said, "I knew you would try to stop me." She said that was right. Then I explained that we knew we wanted to get married but we didn't want to announce it because we were aware we couldn't live together until Jack had finished his time in the Service. I told her how important it was to us that WE knew we were married. She seemed to accept that and things went on as before.

It was only a matter of weeks, though, before she couldn't stand it. I'm sure she was afraid I would get pregnant and no one would believe I was married. (In those days the stigma of getting pregnant before you were married was one of the worst things that could happen to a girl.)

So one fine morning I picked up the local paper and saw, to my horror, the item that my mother had given to her friend–the local gossip columnist–about my "secret" elopement. All the details of our "cover story," etc., etc., etc. were there in black and white for everyone to see–including Jack's mother and family.

As you can imagine, this did not endear my mother to Jack.

Keeping Posted . . :

with Betty McDevitt

The week's Columnist's Friend came in plural form the past few days. For sheer newsiness we enter as our candidate for any kind of a contest the Banks Murray family, of Queen Anne's Drive.

First, they announce the marriage of their daughter, Kitty Florence, and then in the same breath, if they had time to take one, they tell us the whole menage is packing up in a few weeks to become Florida's gain.

That's only the headlines: You see, Kitty's marriage to Jennis (Jack) Morrell Strickland, jr., son of Mrs. Earl Byron Strickland, of Silver Spring, formerly of Rocky Mount, N. C., took place way back last September. The exchange of nuptial vows, it now can be told took place in Marion, S. C. The folks heard about the nice affair in the course of the Christmas holidays and, at the request of the youngsters witheld the info from Ye Olde Press and Ye Young Public until this week.

Here's how it was done: The Murrays, mother, dad, and their three year old daughter, Felicia, went out of town over Labor Day. Banks, jr., the only son, sunned himself at Virginia Beach, and they left Kitty in Chevy Chase with some friends. But not for long. Soon Kitty and Jack were en route South—and the rest we know.

we know.

Now, there's more to the story. Jack has enlisted in the Army Air duration his bride will retain her posi- duration hsi bride will retatn her posi- tion in the Department of Justice. After her parents leave for Florida, she will dwell with Mr. and Mrs. Laurence J. Clayton, of Philadelphia avenue. Both Jack and Kitty are alumni and graduates of Montgomery-Blair high school and formerly the groom was employed in Chevy Chase by a hardware firm. So there you have it.

As for the rest of the Murray family, it seems that cold and sinuses and asthma play a major role in the removal of the family to the sunny clime of Florida. And to prove they're in earnest in their quest for health, Mr. Murray, who has been on the advertising staff of a Washington newspaper, has accepted a similar position with the Tampa *Tribune*. Mrs. Murray and Felicia will spend a few months at Miami before establishing a home in Tampa.

The Murrays have been popular residents of Silver Spring for some years, having moved here from Washington. There are farewell parties on the horizon, the ones most clearly discernible now being planned by Mrs. E. T. Manning and Mrs. B. C. Patton.

In early May Jack was sent to Maxwell Field in Montgomery, Ala., for his pre-flight training.

Among the letters I found in the attic was this envelope with writing on the outside and a pressed red rose on the inside. I can only assume that the message of the Mission of the Southeast Air Corps Training Center was given to the fellows when they entered training. The fact that Jack copied (and, I'm sure, memorized) it indicates that he was very motivated by these words and tried to live up to them.

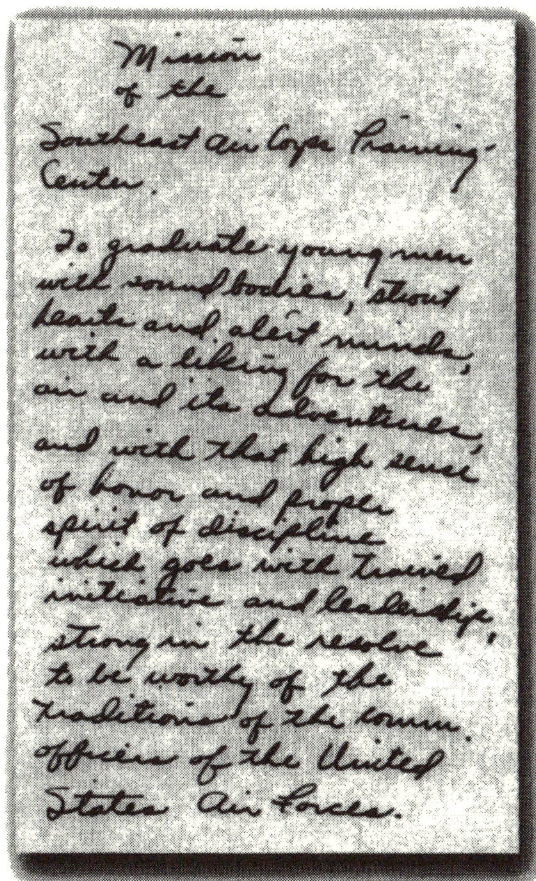

Mission
of the
Southeast Air Corps Training
Center.

To graduate young men
with sound bodies, stout
hearts and alert minds,
with a liking for the
air and its adventures,
and with that high sense
of honor and proper
spirit of discipline
which goes with trained
initiative and leadership,
strong in the resolve
to be worthy of the
traditions of the comm.
officers of the United
States Air Forces.

Enveope with writing, "Mission of the Southeast Air Corps Training Center"

A.C. Cadet Jack Strickland
Maxwell Field, Ala.

Cadets Ford Kelly and Jack Strickland, Montgomery, Ala.

[Editor's Note: Harvey Holland had graduated with Jack in June 1940. He entered the University of Maryland in September 1940. All male students were required to take ROTC for the first two years–after that it was optional. Members of the ROTC were allowed to continue their classes during the summer. Harp wrote this letter when Jack was in Montgomery, Ala.]

June 11, 1942

Dear Jack,

Gosh, it was good to see you even though it was for such a short time. When I first saw that tan head stick out of the car window I couldn't believe what my eyes saw, yet there you were. It really looked as if the training was doing you a lot of good–your face looked healthier and your posture straight.

I suppose you've started your primary or basic training. Boy, what I wouldn't give to be in your shoes!

I haven't started back to school yet but I shall in a few days. I am faced with the hardest semester of my four years at University and in this heat–wow! (carrying about 25 credits, if that means anything, the normal load is between 16–18 credits.) I just received my last semester grades and did better than I expected (1 A–rest B's) I'm really going to have to cut down on the social life this summer though. A close whiffle will probably solve the problem, however.

What do you do down there in your spare time for entertainment, that is if you have any spare time and I guess such a thing is becoming rarer and rarer. Are you near enough to Montgomery to get there very often? What kind of town is it–"Elucidate."

The Sunset concerts are starting this Sunday. Gosh, I'll never forget the time you turned fish down at Watergate. It may not have been so funny at the time but I thought I would die laughing. Best of all was when you got back in the water-filled canoe and all you could see was your body going through the water.

I'm still trying to get enough weight to pass the A.C. and the C.A.A. exam. Gosh, I hope I make them. I'll let you know as soon as I find out whether or not the final results are negative or positive. Knock on wood for me, will you?

I took Eileen up to the Lion's Carnival in Silver Spring the other evening. Saw lots of people I haven't seen for a long time. Eileen graduated from Jr. High today. Just to think she will be going to Blair next term. Gosh, am I getting that old?

I saw a short at the movies the other day about the aviation cadets. It outlined the training that was covered during the course. All the time I was thinking of you and placing you in different situations. Oh, you lucky dog, you. Well, I can still fly a cub until I reach that stage.

When do you think you'll next have a chance to get home? John was so sorry that he did not get another chance to see you. He is on his way out west by now, I suppose.

The other day it was so very warm here that I decided to go swimming. I went over to Chevy Chase pool and it wasn't open yet. Then, since it was Sunday, I decided Glen Echo would be too crowded to wiggle into so I decided to go out to Great Falls. Well the gas gauge, as usual, was as far down as it could go and I was coasting whenever it was possible and running the rest of the time on hot air. I got out to the entrance to Great Falls and the Army stopped me. Closed to the public. Hmmmm. Well, I coasted back down along the Potomac, parked the car along the road–decided to go exploring for a good place to swim. I guess I must not have been too optimistic as I left my suit (trunks) locked in the car. After hiking for what seemed like hours (Well, about 40 minutes) I found a little cove that appealed to me, but darned if I was going to walk all the way back to the car and get my trunks.

There were a couple of row boats tied up there, so I hung my clothes on a hickory limb and swam off one of the rowboats. Then I would climb out, sit in the back of the boat with my feet dangling in the water and get some tan. Well, everything was beautiful–just like my own private beach, until I heard voices coming down the little path which I had used some time before. I jumped over the far side of the boat I was in and very nonchalantly hung my arms and chin over the side of the boat (just as if I had trunks on.) There were four couples with a picnic lunch large enough to serve a banquet. The fellows spoke and they all looked at me as if they had designs on the boat I was hanging onto. But I just gave them that "not on your life" look. When they inquired, I told them that someone was going to use this boat in a short while. Of course "someone" never showed up, but I was effective.

I don't know how long it took them to decide that the opposite bank looked better for a picnic (it always does, thank gosh) and then the fellows decided that none of them could row a boat. Finally one of them volunteered, but it took them two trips to get everything across in the other rowboat (other than the one that I had a death grip on). I was in the water so long I think I absorbed 3 gallons of the Potomac–well the water level dropped about six inches when I got out.

I don't know how I got off on that, but it was a rather funny experience.

Are you still with any of the Silver Spring boys? Are you still in tents or have you been moved into barracks?

Did you know that I'm nineteen now? I'll have to register for the draft this month if I don't sign up with the Air Force.

The war in the Pacific looks considerably more encouraging now, doesn't it? That encounter at Midway was really something. Let's hope that things keep on in that trend.

Someday when all this is over you and I are going to take a trip together in a plane. Gosh, wouldn't it be fun to put pontoons on a ship and hop from lake to lake in the northern country or maybe down through Mexico or South America. It's a dream but it's something to look forward to.

If at any time, Jackson, you want someone to run an errand or to tell somebody something, or where to get off, up here, let me know and I will be more than glad to do so. Oh, yes - how about a snapshot or two of yourself in action. (you know, pick and shovel, peeling spuds, etc.) No kidding, I'd really like to have one.

Be sure and don't hesitate if Dad can help you in getting in or out of anything. Honestly, he really took a liking to you.

There's a lot of that sort of thing done so don't hesitate if and when the time comes.

If you haven't quit by this time, I'll say Goodbye for now. I really miss having you around. Please be more merciful in answering this letter than I was.

S'long

Harvey (alias "Harp")

[Editor's note: Harvey had two sisters: Eileen (nicknamed "Bonnie") who was younger than he and Lois, who was several years his senior. Their father was a Colonel in the Army Air Force.

In those days there was a stage built out on the Potomac River where free "Watergate" Sunset concerts were presented by the National Symphony Orchestra. We used to rent canoes and paddle down the river to listen to the music. Obviously Harvey is referring to one time when Jack's canoe began to slowly fill with water. Jack jumped overboard–then thought better of it and climbed back in and madly paddled back to shore as the boat gradually submerged.]

Chapter Five

Belle Mina

(Jack's letter to me from Maxwell Field, Montgomery, Ala. just prior to my "visit" for the graduation dance.)

July 26, 1942

Hello, there!

Strange–no mail from you today. Somehow today I was looking forward to a letter–but–guess there's little time left on weekends–to write, eh?

Miss "Frizzy" (*) here I come through with another typical act. STOP HERE AND GUESS WHAT IT'S GOING TO BE!

This is THE week now, and everyone has his hopes up–looking forward to a new town–better food–and what kind of climate conditions? I don't think there's going to be any trouble with grades now (Knock-knock.) 'Course there are wild, wild rumors floating around–Ga., S.C., Arizona–for me, I'll say it's going to be Georgia. (Wimpy is stationed at Savannah–"Hello" from he.) The furlough question is flitting all around. Seems possible–however I doubt it seriously–with a few abstract facts thrown in. I admit I'm not worried in the least either way. Is that an insult? Either way has its advantages and disadvantages for both of us. Sure, absolutely, I want to be with you–mainly because I love you–so don't think I'm suggesting that I would like it if I couldn't be with you and vice versa for two or three weeks–however I'll go into a detailed discussion about that Sunday.

The act I mentioned in the first part of this letter–well, it's a long, long story, of course. Two weeks ago I–Oh, guess I'll just have to tell you–must I? Anyway I went to the Jeff Davis, Whitley and Greystone hotels–it happened in the Greystone. The man said there would be plenty of time to make reservations a week before the dance–he was (he said) speaking from experience. Besides they were not supposed to take reservations more than a week in advance. You finish it!! The social committee here has taken over all three hotels and filled every room. There still is a chance here *that one or two of the cadets are going to have to let them go–one because his date isn't coming–the other is in the hospital–probably won't be out by Sat. night! Worse comes to worse–Sullivan's date is coming up from Orlando–single room–but that is the last resort. However I already have two alternatives but I'm waiting to see before I speak up. I think it would be best to go on over to Selma and get a room there. (45 miles) That would mean a rented car–which I hope to grab before the rush. That would also mean you would have little time for a nap and "fixing up" though–so, anyway–I'll guarantee you a room before you leave home. I'll either phone or send a telegram with address and who to ask for in Montgomery. It's rumored that we will be out by 12:00–however it will probably be the usual 16:30 (4:30)–If parading that afternoon–it would be 5:30 before I could see you. Either way I'll see you at the address I give you. If I can't meet the train or come in early, I'll call you there at 2 P.M. Saturday–and as often thereafter as possible until I get a line through. The phone here at the barracks is 9622–or the one I sent the first time. In case we were in formation–I would be notified immediately upon returning. Should you call–don't hang up until someone answers–the C.Q. must stay in the barracks (2 of them) at all times–and take all phone calls.*

Young Lady, may I suggest that brown dress you got in Rocky Mount among the ones you bring? No use bringing boots and trousers–but don't forget your "walking" shoes and a dress that will "walk" coolly, too. Should there be room (I should know better) you *will appreciate the radio. Be good and don't attract too much attention on the way down–and–should you get this in time, let me know your plans in conjunction with Pritchetts' sister–if any.*

Good luck, Miss.
I love you
Mr. J.M.S.

P.S. Probably more later–but not in time–see?

* I had written Jack that in preparation for the dance, I had gone to the beauty parlor. I had long, thick, black hair and the beauty operator who gave me the "permanent" left me under the machine for too long and my hair was completely "frizzled." I was so unhappy about it I almost didn't go to Montgomery. Later I took the scissors and cut all the permanent off.

Because the U.S. was so late in entering the war that had been raging in Europe, the military was having to play catch-up. The training was strenuous and grueling. Approximately one-half of the class washed out during pre-flight. I had gone down to Montgomery a couple of times when Jack could get weekend leave. Jack completed his course and I went to Maxwell for the ceremony. It was then I met two cadet wives, Margie Marshall and Dottie Hintenack, who were planning on following their husbands from base to base while they were in training. I was easily talked into joining them. The Army took a dim view of this behavior and a cadet's salary was $75 a month; however, for the rest of the tour we managed to find places to live and saw our husbands on most weekends.

When I made the decision to stay I sent a letter of resignation to the Department of Justice. They refused to accept it, thinking I might change my mind and return to D.C. After a month I knew that I was going to stay near Jack until he went overseas so on September 17 I sent another letter of resignation. They refused that one, too, and kept me on Leave Without Pay (or L.W.O.P.) for two and a half years.

Murray Marshall, Al Hintenack, and Jack were all sent to Decatur, Ala., for primary training. When we heard this and, knowing that housing anywhere near an army base was almost nonexistent, we gals took off and went to Decatur. We found a rental agency and were told that there was a big vacant house in Belle Mina, a small town near Decatur. A Dr. and Mrs. Graham owned it. Dr. Graham was a professor at the University of Alabama and the house was Mrs. Graham's family home. They weren't too interested in renting it out but the rental agent gave us their telephone number. Now Margie, who was from Indiana, and Dottie, who was from Baltimore, insisted that I be the one to talk with them. They believed that I had a "southern" accent that might carry more weight in Alabama than theirs would. I don't know if that was true but the upshot, after talking with them, was that they agreed to let the six of us rent the house at a nominal fee.

Our new residence turned out to be a huge ante-bellum home. Large entrance hall, sitting room, AND parlor with velvet upholstered chairs. Lots of bedrooms, adequately furnished. Having seen *Gone With the Wind*, we felt like we were living in Tara.

Frequently, on Saturday nights, the guys would bring their bachelor cadet friends home with them. Most of them were homesick and this was one way they could touch base. Among them was Joe Sulkin. Occasionally Joe would bring with him a girl that he had met in Decatur. I'm sorry to say we weren't always nice to his dates. He must have forgiven us because to this day we still correspond at least once a year. Joe graduated with Jack in Blytheville. Since the "wings" were awarded in alphabetical order, you will see Joe in the picture standing right in back of Jack the day they got their commissions.

The corn in the field in front of the house was grown for cattle feed. Although it was relatively tough, it furnished us with many meals. Being able to pick it and cook it immediately made it much more palatable.

There was a phenomenon that occurred in those years that I wish had continued after the war. Everyone in the U.S. realized we were all in the same boat and went out of his or her way to help others. This was especially true as far as the young men in uniform were concerned.

Belle Mina was tiny–one general store and post office combined.

The people there were exceptionally nice. By that time Americans had been issued ration books, as there was a scarcity of many commodities. None of us girls could cook very well (I was the worst of the lot) but we could make great fudge and fudge takes lots of sugar. These kind people would give us their sugar ration stamps.

We bought fresh milk, which we would put in a jar and take turns shaking until it turned into butter. Butter was rationed, too. Some of these good local women also taught us how to make cottage cheese out of what was left over.

One time they gave us a live chicken. We were looking forward to having a good dinner, for a change. The only problem was that no one knew how to kill it–or wanted to. Finally big, gentle Murray Marshall got tired of our discussion–or was hungry–and went out and wrung its neck. I don't remember who plucked it or cleaned it, but we cooked it. However, nobody enjoyed it very much.

The guys would bring us oranges, apples, cereal, and anything they could sneak home from the base in their duffel bags–also their dirty laundry that we would wash.

The Marshalls had an old car that we kept in Belle Mina. In order to drive to the base we had to cross an old dilapidated bridge. Almost every time we made the trip to see our husbands we managed to pick up a nail in a tire. We three females became expert at changing tires.

One weekend when our husbands hadn't been able to get leave we got the bright idea of driving to Evansville, Ind., to see Margie's mother. We were halfway there and it was late and dark when we heard the now familiar thump-thump of a tire.

We traipsed out of the car all set to go to work changing the flat. Just then a large truck stopped and the driver got out and insisted on changing it for us. I'm sure he had been traveling quite a while and was tired but he was being so gallant that we didn't have the heart to tell him just how capable we were of doing the job.

Margie's mother fed us sumptuously–the best meal any of us had had for months. The next day she sent us home with leftovers and a recipe for rolls. The recipe must have made enough rolls for three dozen people. We knew nothing about cutting down on the ingredients so we made it according to directions. I don't know what we did wrong but the dough didn't rise. We had used so much of our meager supply of flour, etc., that we weren't about to throw it out. We rolled it out very thin and made some peculiar tasting crackers and ate them for weeks.

Kitty at "Woodside"–Belle Mina, Ala.

Kitty beside morning glories at "Woodside"

Margie and Murray Marshall and Dot Hintenack at "Woodside"

Kitty and Jack at Decatur, Ala.

[Letter from Jack to Karl's mother and father]

Squadron 2
S.A.T.S.
Decatur, Ala.
Sept. 5, 1942

Dear Folks,

Surprise! No, this isn't an obituary or anything like that. Things have begun to be so exciting that maybe a letter wouldn't bore you so much as it would have during ground school.

Your birthday card and note caught me unawares. What with all this hustle and bustle of getting underway for war, I never expected anyone to remember something like a birthday. It came at a time when mail was pretty scarce and it gave me quite a lift.

Mom has probably told you all about Kitty's visit, which has turned into a pretty swell-stay! I'm certainly glad she did stay now. From all appearances she's enjoying it as much as I. We've rented a pretty good sized country home (two other couples are with us.) One couple is from Indiana, the other from Baltimore. The house, while old, is something that you read about. It's about as far off the road as your house-and the entrance reminds me of yours. There's a cotton patch on one side, a cornfield on the other. The house itself is hidden from view by cedars and maples. While it has water, lights and phone, the house is big-and going to be hard to heat this fall. However if the girls can manage to keep it clean-they certainly won't have any difficulty keeping their own small homes clean-IF and When.

Right now I'm waiting to be assigned my first actual solo ship. That is, the first one I take out-without supervision from anyone. This time I can more or less go anywhere I want-and practice what I please. I'm sitting on a glide marker under a wing, using my knee as a desk. Don't be surprised if this letter has plenty of Alabama red dust mixed in with it!

Speaking of red dust, this place has a very peculiar red loam.

When it's wet you can work it just like modeling clay without breaking it apart. Cotton is THE money crop. Everywhere you look is a large cotton field. Very little animal power is used on the farms. It's mostly tractor with wide adjustable rear wheels so that you can fix them to straddle any number of rows–which are needed at present. The wagons used for hauling cotton to and from the fields and gins are huge things about the size of these large transport trailers seen and "cussed" on most highways (before the "gas and rubber" incident.) Beef cattle seems to be about the only thing (besides cotton) that may be classified as farm income; there's quite a bit of corn raised but I guess that is for the cattle.

I'm including a small clipping that might interest Mr. Byron, although he's probably seen a similar article in Colliers *magazine.*

These Alabamans or "Bamas" are really fishing conscious and have quite a few well-stocked lakes and streams. We're situated about ten miles above Muscle Shoals on Wheeler Lake. So far I haven't had time to do any real fishing–but the ones I've seen in other people's hands keep my blood pressure well above normal.

Looks like I didn't have so much to say after all. Still worse, I doubt that you'll be able to make out what I have written. Every time something unusual happens I say–"Now I'll have something to write about."–by the next day, though, it's either forgotten or else appears in a more realistic light. Then you have to start all over again trying to get something interesting enough to interest someone else.

Guess I'd better put an end to this and practice a little flying. Then maybe I'll be able to interest you in looking the countryside over–from an angel's point of view. There'll be a little more noise–of course.

Mrs. Byron, in case I didn't mention it, would you mind telling "Miss Kitty" how to make those "Dog Biscuits" of Mr. Byron's?

Love,
Mr. J.M. "Ace" Strickland

I worked in the payroll division of the Department of Justice. My job consisted of typing stencils that were used for payroll checks. Not very interesting but the pay was good–$1,440 per year–and the people were fun to work with.

In June of 1942 J. Edgar Hoover, director of the F.B.I., announced the capture of eight men landed on the U.S. shores by German U-boats to spy and sabotage for the Reich. They were to be tried by a military court. The F.B.I. at that time was housed in the Department of Justice building.

Our office was on the first floor and all windows faced the courtyard. While these spies were on trial, they were taken through the courtyard twice a day. We were ordered to pull down all the window shades when this occurred. We complied, but I'm sure all of us managed to catch quick glimpses of them each time they came through.

That was the most exciting event that happened during my short tenure there.

The spies were convicted and executed.

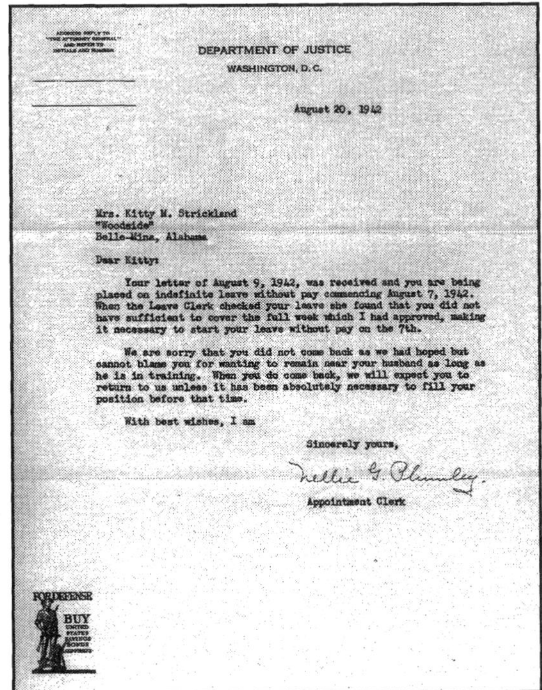

DEPARTMENT OF JUSTICE
WASHINGTON, D.C.

August 20, 1942

Mrs. Kitty M. Strickland
"Woodside"
Belle-Mina, Alabama

Dear Kitty:

Your letter of August 9, 1942, was received and you are being placed on indefinite leave without pay commencing August 7, 1942. When the Leave Clerk checked your leave she found that you did not have sufficient to cover the full week which I had approved, making it necessary to start your leave without pay on the 7th.

We are sorry that you did not come back as we had hoped but cannot blame you for wanting to remain near your husband as long as he is in training. When you do come back, we will expect you to return to us unless it has been absolutely necessary to fill your position before that time.

With best wishes, I am

Sincerely yours,

Nellie G. Plumley

Appointment Clerk

FOR DEFENSE BUY

[Letter from Jack's mom, Blanche, to me]

Sept. 11, 1942

My Dearest Kitty,

Since you have been so sweet about writing me, whether I answered or not, I will just make time for a few lines. Guess I've been waiting to find time to blab a lot about things that wouldn't mean much anyway.

I'm sorry you didn't get the dress in time but I was afraid of that when I mailed it. The mail isn't too dependable these days. Jack was already expecting you to wear your other "creation" anyway and he spoke very highly of it. Did you get the red carnations to wear with it? After all it was to please his eyes you were seeking and I'm sure he was well satisfied.

I can't find words to thank you and Jack for your gorgeous, precious invitation to visit you. You are both pure gold to even think of it. I am not saying that I can't accept it yet either but will have to let you know at the last minute. I would gladly sit on a nail keg all the way and it would be just like an air cushion. I have taken the transportation excuse for not visiting the Byrons this summer. I thought it really wasn't worth the money if I could do something else that I truly wanted to do.

I can tell by Jack's letters that he must be doing well with his work. He seems so wrapped up in every detail and writes such interesting letters about it. Sometimes I wonder how in the world I got to be his mother. Can you imagine me having a "genius" for a son? Yes, I practically "bust open" with pride when I even hear his name mentioned. Don't tell him, though, for I wouldn't want him to get a cocky-smarty attitude for anything in the world. I do have so many reasons for wanting him to come out tops–that is, my own selfish reasons that don't amount to a hill of beans. Really, though, it would be worth living a whole lifetime to me for him to keep climbing and doing the better things of life and have the outlook on life that he has. I think he has always had this attitude but for the past few years he has been able to show it more. With you there close by whenever he needs you is just what it takes to help him along. It really does not take a whole lot of big things to make him happy. Just the little things of life that he truly likes. You are many of the little things that he likes and loves. Just stick around, Honey Chile, and lavish him with such when you can and I think you will be cultivating one of the biggest and best men of our times. TWO people will be thinking so at least.

I will have to cut this short but will write again soon. I hope you are vice-versa-ing my letters for they are meant for both of you. Keep the old "Ace" flying and give him 1,000 kisses for me. Loads of love and the best of everything.

Mom

Read this first. This is the letter I wrote before I got your letter.

Aug. '42

Hi, Jackson,

How's the flying coming along? If you don't answer my last letter I may have to put you on my black list. Nothing could be worse than that, you know.

Have you heard that Uncle Sammy is calling out all Enlisted Reserve, including R.O.T.C., college students and Air Corp at the end of the semester? If I get my degree now, it will be only by the slimmest margin. I must admit that I have no more right to be in college than the fellows out there, fighting. But now that I'm this far to being through, I will certainly fight to finish. I will be glad to get into things, though, and I hope not too far behind you. I hope that someday we may be stationed together.

I have lately experienced a morale set back. The Army (bless them) has taken over National Park Seminary for a hospital in connection with Walter Reed hospital. Gosh, and I was really looking forward to seeing that gal this fall. I'll catch up with her some day. I must again warn you I may drop in on you sometime in the near future. If my five trunks start arriving, you will know I'm on my way.

The other night I did something I swore I'd never do–took a date to the Gayety. A whole gang of us were looking for something crazy to do, so we took in the midnight show. The show seemed to be slightly censored for that type of crowd and a swell time was had by all. Some loon in front of us (on the balcony) kept blowing up balloons all through the show, then he'd let them go and laugh his head off. I thought I'd split. (Fortunately due to overcrowded conditions, I remained in one piece.)

Dad is expecting to go overseas on some new organization of his. If he goes he will probably get his Brigadier General out of it, but I hope he doesn't go. That's all the latest flashes from these parts. I still have heard no word from John. Some Grizzly undoubtedly got him. Swell guy, too.

S'long
Harvey–alias "Harp"

[The Gayety was a burlesque theater in Washington, D.C.]

Hi, Jack,

How are you? Gosh, I was glad to hear from you and to find out that you were coming along so well. Believe me, my heart is down there, climbing into that cockpit with you every time, you lucky sucker.

Well, pal, I'm in there with you now, as I guess you know by this time if you received my (little) news flash. No kidding, I went down to that examining doctor about ten times. I used to go down there so often that we (the doctor and I) became regular friends. No matter how many were sitting there ahead of me, waiting to take the exam, when I came in, he would say, "Hi, take off your coat and shoes and make yourself at home." Then he would march me over to the scales and weigh me--then, "Sorry, come back in a few days, but while you're here help me examine some of these guys."

Then early one bright morning, I took my date home earlier than usual and reported down to the M.D.'s office for another tangle with the little weight that slides back and forth on a bar.

I climbed on the scales, and there was the usual silence as the doctor weighed me, disturbed only by the "clinkle" of the lead weights in my pockets. Then, as I stood there, the doctor's face turned ghastly white and he began to shake and tremble and he fell to the floor hysterically. With some help I revived the doctor and in two gasps of breath he told me I had passed my weight.

I must have been out for nigh on two or three minutes, for when they revived me, the doctor was already completing the examination papers and was affixing his signature. The tears were falling fast and the doctor began to tell me how much he was going to miss me. I agree, it was foolish, but I just couldn't help it--I began to bawl like a baby and we rushed into each other's arms. Oh well, all good things must come to an end.

I drove off with a stiff upper lip (both of us were in the front seat.) I turned to take a last look at the Dr.'s office-and there with his nose pressed against the window, and waving an eye chart with one hand, stood the doctor. Only my will power and my poor brakes (it was downhill) kept me from turning back.

Well, the early morning air helped me to forget the whole episode and I was soon back to normal, whistling at all the pretty secretaries as they hustled and bustled on their way to work.

Gosh, how did I get off on another one of these stories?

As it is now, I shall be deferred until I finish school. I, too, wish we could be going through together but I guess things aren't lined up that way. Be sure and tell me about the course, your flying, and your experiences, will ya, huh?

I shall continue taking the Advanced ROTC course. They really are making it quite a course now–a new tough obstacle course, frequent firing, battles, 20 mile "hikes," a required body building course and instruction every day. The last battle we had, I had the pleasure of going out in advance of the troops and planting and camouflaging a trench mortar and myself. Then when the "enemy" (senior class) came marching down the valley, I really let loose. I had the mortar set just right so that no one would get hit but they really got a bath with the sand, mud and limbs (tree) flying every which way. Some of the enemy (frat brothers) came along and they rested and we had a little chat before they went on to shoot my buddies–treacherous, wasn't it? Our side won, of course, but not before a lot of feuds were settled. You know–"I shot you first over by that tree." "Oh, no you didn't. I got you a mile off." I think it's good training, though, and may someday save my life. But then, when you get right down to it, I sometimes think how futile and useless it really is, spending so much time learning how to kill, when the time could be spent toward so many things useful to humanity– healing previously incurable diseases, a higher standard of living, a sounder form of labor organization and scrupulous application of machinery so that the working man might have more time for leisure and development of a higher type of society, both political and social, and more time to appreciate the finer things such as the beauty of nature, of love and friendships. But before we can have such things we must certainly smack into infinity the leaders who sponsor the abolition of them for their own personal gain. And, as we learned from the last war, that means the complete destruction of the structure supporting such power. And this means force against force and if that's what it's going to take I'm sure that you and I and fellows like us will be willing and even eager to learn to kill with such skill and proficiency that we will be assured of victory and the ultimate possession of those things so dear to us.

Hmmmmm–I did it again. From now on I shall control myself–but I do mean every word of it.

I was both surprised and pleased to hear that Kitty had decided to stay down there with you and that you all were taking a house with some other couples. (Sounds like a neat set up.)---

I am now sitting in on a lecture by the world's best lecturer–he holds me spell bound–"Corporation Finance"–sounds interesting, doesn't it? Well, back to the letter. Where did I leave off? Oh, yes–

So you love birds have feathered a nest for awhile. Sounds like a fine place. I'm glad that you and Kitty will have a chance to be together while you are in training, as must be frankly admitted will probably not be the case later. I would be most pleased to receive some snap shots of you all and your "southern mansion." Ya hear me?

About the CTP, it is but a dream now. Under new rulings (150 miles from the coast) Schram's and College Park Airports are closed down and that's that, I'm afraid.

Dad is down in that part of the country, picking out a site for a new Tactical School. I wish I could have gone with him and maybe dropped in on you all, but I must finish this little job in College Park by next summer.

Women around the University are a gross scarcity, in fact, a pretty girl is like a melody–or something (I don't get the connection.) I'm tired of this dating a different "chick" (de-icer, to you) every time, in fact I'm trying to find someone to fall in love with. I see some that look like they're just what the doctor ordered, but you can't just rush up and ask them for a date–I tried it, it's just not the right technique. Say, what's the right way to "woo" Rocky Mount style?

Well, Jack, I have enjoyed this little chat with you. You see, I do have quite a bit to say to you when I get the chance, and I could go on almost indefinitely–but your time piece is moving much too fast and I must get this in the mail and get back to my cell before those little men in white come by again.

S'long
Harp

Give Kitty my best regards.

Harvey Holland in ROTC uniform

Oct. 1, 1942

Hi, Jackson,

Just got your letter today and was really glad to hear from you, and that you're doing so well. Nice going, Buddy.

I'm sure you have no need to worry about those 20 hour checks since you've been getting along so fine up to now.

I don't feel quite as bad as I should about getting your two letters without an answer, as I did actually have a letter ready to mail but just couldn't get near a mail box. Just to prove it, I'm enclosing the letter. You see, I just finished my final exams (Seems strange this time of year) for the summer semester and have been through quite a session, you know, studying like mad day and night to do what I should have been doing all semester. Will I ever learn?

In the other letter I told you about the Autumn Carnival that was to come off at the University. Well, it came off and boy!!! what a weekend. I had a date for some time ahead for the weekend and just Thursday before the weekend it went flooey (the gal had to leave town–for a purely authentic reason.) So I knock myself out trying to get a date at the last minute. It was a widely advertised and published event and everyone and their <u>*cute*</u> *daughters had a date. Well, I called and called (unlimited line) and in the process I called Peg Fisher–well, she had a long standing date with "Franny" but she said she would try and break it, if I would wait awhile (half a day lost there and me with only one brown hair left on my head.) When I called back she was sorry but she had tried everything but no go. In the meantime I got Lois to look around down at the War Department section where she works and see if anyone would like to chance it with me. She called the middle of the next day and caught me between finals and said she had something cooking if I wanted to take a chance. (You see it wouldn't have made much difference that I hadn't seen or met the gal, if it wasn't such a big occasion) (Now back to the story–I bet you're a nervous wreck) so was I. You know the thing that shocked me most was that all this was so unlike me–me, getting a date at the last minute, imagine–no, don't.*

Let's see, oh yes,–I told Lois to go ahead and ask the damsel for me, and tell her I'd call her later and make myself known so she wouldn't have to call me "It" all weekend. Well, I breathed a sigh of relief and got out my best blue serge suit and shined up the seat and got ready for the big weekend. But the more I thought, the more worried I got–suppose this gal is "a dull thud" or a drizzle–just suppose she looks like most Maryland girls look–Oh, the horror of it all! and besides, suppose we didn't like each other at the outset–with the whole weekend to go–I felt sicker every minute–of course it was probably working the other way also–she was probably going through the same thing–poor girl–poor me. Then to top it off Peggy called and said that if I hadn't got a date, she would like too much to go with me. By this time nothing could faze me, I didn't even blink both eyes. What to do–should I cancel the blind date about whom I knew nothing and go with Peg who is a screwball and fun and so forth or should I keep the blind date, which was the right thing to do, and take a chance and let fate run wild. What to do–what to do???

Yes, this indeed was the crisis–the point at last at which the worm should turn–so I turned to Peg and said, "I'm sorry, woman, but I have another engagement." Well, it was done, now all I had to do was sit and worry–sit and worry, tick, tock, tick, tock. (dramatic effect)

I called the girl a little bit later and had a quick conversation with her,–you know, what time, what place, what to wear–click! Her name was Pat Maphis. Pat–hmmmm–Pat, now that was a good start right there–there's something about the name Pat that appeals–and her voice––sounded kinda nice–but I know how deceiving that can be sometimes, I couldn't let that fool me, not for a minute, but there was no turning back for H.H. Holland, Jr.

Well, Friday evening arrived but quickly and I was rushing around like mad, and I was late (another unusual event) and when I got to where she lived (way past Bethesda) I overshot and had to go around again. I finally found the right house, a beautiful home, put my shoes on and calmly ambled up to the front door. The first thing that met me was a honey colored

Cocker Spaniel–I thought for a minute and then convinced myself that that couldn't be her, so I rang the doorbell. A pause and I heard a feminine voice say, "I'll get it, Mother" off in the distance and then the pitter-patter of footsteps coming down the stairs–I looked around to see if someone was beating a drum but it was only my heart doing "The Rumba Jumps" and there in the doorway stood the most gorgeous, the most heavenly creature ever to walk in high heels–about 5′5″, little feet, shapely legs, a tan complexion, pearly white teeth, beautiful lips and beautiful eyes and blond hair

and now, going back up––

Well, I was flabbergasted to say the least. I knocked myself on the jaw to see if I was dreaming–I realized this was the real McCoy–or a direct descendant.

Then her lips moved and a heavenly voice said, "Hello, I'm Pat Maphis."

I moved my lips but nothing came out, then she asked me in –she opened the screen door and I fell in, under the hypnotic spell of her beauty and charm and under which I remained until we were on the way to the University. I later found out that I had met her Father, Mother and Brother. A swell bunch –I'll bet.

Gosh, Jack, I swore I wouldn't get off on another one of those stories and here I am in the process. However, with minute exceptions, the story happened as told and to bring it to a quick finish, everything turned out just swell!! She turned out to be a swell person, very pretty, very natural and sensible, and yet a heck of a lot of fun. She reminds me of a certain brunette you dated for quite awhile–let's see–what was her name? Oh, yes, Kitty. Say, wasn't the girl you married named Kitty? Well, by cracky, it must be the same girl. Must certainly agree with you that you really hit the Jackpot, I want to let you young folks know that my blessings are upon you and I wish you all the luck and happiness in the world.

Signed
Father Harp

Oh, yes, you speak about your letters being boring. I believe them to be just the opposite. I read them over and over and really enjoy hearing about your flying and how things are coming along with the Strickland family.

For awhile up here we could almost go skating as some mornings it was down to a few degrees above freezing and I'm still wearing a summer uniform. Brrrrrr.

I'm out now for about five days vacation before I go back for the fall semester.

Dad expects to go on a flight around the country for some sort of inspection and I may go with him, if I can get back in time for school. He was glad to hear that you were getting along so well. And remember, as I told you before, if at any time you get into some difficulty or trouble where you could use a little outside help or influence, be sure and send the word. Ya hear, now?

Did you say you were about to go into Basic? Where will that be, or is it a military secret? Be sho and let me know!

I'm sure you all know that Nell and Dick got married a short time ago. I saw them the other day–they really make a cute couple. Dick's such a good-looking fellow and Nell's such a cute little gal. I hope you two realize what you started around here. I'm beginning to feel like an old bachelor. Don't be too surprised if I drop in on you and introduce some little chick as my wife, one of these days–well, one of these years. Very frankly, if I get married, it will be within the next year and a half or not until the war is over.

Mother said to tell you and Kitty "Hi" and that she hopes everything is coming along "Hunky-dory" (my Mom's words) with you all. She is really doing fine with her work as she's received two or three raises since she's been there.

Eileen is not directly in any war work (the family slackard) but it seems Blair, setting the pace for the nations' high schools, has turned all out for Victory. They have organized the girls as well as the boys into companies and are teaching them to drill, and all the subjects are built around or upon a wartime basis. Incidentally, I happened to see Mr. Knight standing out on the field the other day as I went by and he had on that same gray, droopy suit that he was wearing when I first started Blair. If I ever get rich enough, I think I'll send him a new suit. Bless him. He's really the heart of that school, isn't he?

(Editor's note; Owen Knight was our high school principal. We all were very fond of him.)

I just received a letter from Laura. She is still down in "Te - yax-sis," darn it, and she's going to some junior college 200 miles from Houston. She really gave me a bawling out for just sitting up here and letting the Army take over National Park Seminary. She writes a cute letter–sometimes rather encouraging, if you know what I mean–there may be a spark there somewhere, but what can a fellow do if he's in Washington and a gal's in Texas? Something's got to be done.

Just in case you didn't happen to see the headlines a couple of weeks ago, the weekend of the Autumn Carnival, M.U. won its first game with flying colors, 34 to 0. WOW! We were slaphappy. This new T formation really clicks and Shawnessy is really a top coach. Yesterday we won our second game 14 to 0 against some real stiff competition, a service team of professionals. Boy, now we're rolling.

This gal, Pat, that I had the date with at the Autumn Carnival likes to horseback ride. Soooo–I see where I do quite a bit of riding this Fall, heh, heh. I got the old boots out the other day, massaged them with Neatsfoot oil (courtesy of J. M. Strickland) and shined them up good, now I'm raring to get out and break my neck again. Gosh, remember the rides we used to have on Pal and Bill? Those little horses could really travel. That's probably why you were able to solo as early as you did.

How do you all like that piece, "Praise the Lord and Pass the Ammunition?" Right tricky, don't you think? Somewhat of the type of "Amen" but I think the lyrics are better.

Did I tell you that Mom and Dad have been doing quite a lot of entertaining here. We've had all the big generals out who are up here in Washington and quite a few senators and congressmen, one of which was Sen. Tom Connally of Texas with whom I went out of my way to make friends. He is a very fine old gentleman.

I'm afraid, Jackson, I've written a lot and said practically nothing. However I shall send it on its way hoping that it will catch you before you change stations. Be sure and let me know what's cooking.

S'Long for now–Harvey

Chapter Six

Jonesboro, Arkansas

When the cadets finished one phase of training they were not told until the last minute where they were being sent next. A few days before the course was completed we found out that they were being transferred to Walnut Ridge, Ark. for Basic school. We girls quickly packed up and drove to Jonesboro, Ark., a town near Walnut Ridge. In a section of town just opposite Jonesboro State College our method paid off. We set out knocking on doors and asking if anyone had rooms to rent. We knocked on one door and a nice elderly (at our ages anyone over 30 was "old") woman answered. Her name was Mrs. Whitsett. She was a widow and her grown children had all moved away. Not only was she lonely but I think she wanted to do her part and help the war effort. She decided to let Margie and me become her first tenants.

Mrs. Whitsett was a love. Knowing we were operating on a very low budget, she would give us homemade jams, jellies and cookies. She was also glad to let Jack's mother, Blanche, come to visit us for 10 days in early November. I think she thrived on our company, as she missed having her own children around. Jack and I had a wonderful time with Blanche and were both very sorry to see her go.

Our mail was sent to the General Post Office at the State College. Margie and I would walk over there every day to collect it. Between Mrs. Whitsett's house and the college was a magnificent hickory nut tree. If Margie and I could beat the squirrels to the nuts that fell off the tree, we would gather up as many as we could carry. We would sit on our front steps and crack and eat them. Cracking hickory nuts was hard work but they were a good supplement to our limited diet.

The guys only had Saturday nights away from the base. On one of those nights Jack and I were sleeping when I awoke, sobbing uncontrollably. I had had a vivid dream that I was dressed in black and attending a funeral. I looked into the coffin and saw the body was Jack's. Going back to sleep was impossible. I could not shake the dream off. We stayed up the rest of the night, talking. I did a lot of thinking and came to the conclusion that I wanted to get pregnant. He argued that he might not survive the war and did not want to leave me with a child to raise by myself. I was adamant that if anything happened to him, I could not bear it unless I had his child. We had always planned on having a big family someday when the war was over but with the ever-present danger now facing us, the plans were changed. I conceived our first child in Jonesboro.

Without being aware of it as it happened, we now realized we had left our childhood behind us. We had been forced to face the fact that many of the cadets we knew had been killed in training and some of our friends from home were already overseas fighting, getting wounded and some dying. We had no idea what the future might hold for us.

A large majority of the young men who entered pilot training did not make it through to graduation. I had worried that Jack would have difficulty with the complicated math lessons that he was taking. It was essential that he master them in order to get his "wings." I should have known by then that he could do anything he set his mind to. He passed all the tests with (pardon the expression) flying colors.

Our next post was to be in Blytheville, Ark. Unfortunately for me, Murray Marshall was being sent to Smyrna, Tenn., instead of Blytheville. Margie and I, who had become great friends, had to part company.

[Murray became a B-17 pilot and was stationed in England. He was killed January 5, 1944.]

Army Air Forces Basic Flying School
Walnut Ridge, Arkansas

Nov. 21, 1942

My Dear Miss,

Here it is Saturday night again only this time I'm afraid we're both going to be alone. For some unearthly reason we've been notified that there will be no open port either tonight or tomorrow. Seems as if we're behind our flying schedule and will have to use tomorrow to try and catch up. No need to guess what the outcome will be–either everything will be grounded because of weather or else each cadet will probably get about an hour's flying time.

I'm what is known as damn glad I had someone stand in for my link training last Wednesday–or else I'd not even been able to see you then!

There was a general mix-up about going into town last night. My idea–but somehow I wasn't told that they'd decided to go into town. There are quite a few conflicting reports so far–but it looks, though, that they were only going as far as Walnut Ridge anyhow, so maybe it's just as well I didn't go.

Sorta lonesome without Marge, isn't it?–especially in this kind of weather. I noticed on a radio here–that the tower and planes can be received on the SHORT WAVE band of a radio–with the needle resting on (or about) 12:50 of the highest numbered band of numerals. Maybe you can pick the tower up during the daytime. Listen for the call DB 91 to 307, go ahead! or 307 to DB 91, go ahead!

On my solo flights I'll see if I can't come over sometime and say a thing or two–if you should ever pick such up, open the back door and stand there until I waggle my wings–otherwise stand out back or out front.

I haven't heard much–or any news from home except two copies of the Evening Telegram and one Silver Spring Post. Not much doing except there was a notice of a Mr. ––Dickens, son of Mrs. Anna Dickens, enlisting in the Air Corps–stationed in

Florida. He is the well known "Skinny" Dickens with whom I helped lug gasoline–way back when. We were both small enough to ride side by side in an open cockpit ship. The well known "Flying Jenny." Funny that he should turn back to flying after getting a good start as a wholesale salesman. Sorta funny, too, that we both end up back here in the air.

Thursday night we flew. Quite an experience–very monotonous though–and very dangerous because of that reason. I dozed off once–I hope never again!!

Came in at 1:15 A.M. and felt very much like writing you - however, we've got to keep in the very best possible shape to stay in the game–and every little thing helps–or retards. I have a lot to tell you–as usual–about my instructor–and general current events here. Guess they can wait, though.

Well, guess I'd better sign off. It's hard to realize that there's nothing here–and you–over there yet–so far over there. Something like a mirage–in the middle of a desert. The image in plain view–the real thing is so far away.

Maybe it would be best if I tried to sleep–and dream–then I'd be there in spirit anyhow–or maybe we'd be in dear ole South America–or Australia–or what do you say–I'll meet you there.

So long

P.S. I love you!!!

Army Air Forces Basic Flying School
Walnut Ridge, Arkansas

Thursday morning
(Not so bright and early)

My Dear Miss,

Here it is three days since I've seen you–and all we've done those three days is sleep and eat. So long as we have to be away from each other–maybe it's a good thing that there have been no furloughs or leaves that might have made me miss you even more than I do–if such is possible. It's harder to leave you each time I see YOU!

Now that the time for moving is closing in, I've sorta wondered–when we'd be able to get settled at the post–and find out about open posts! Since it might be a week or even two weeks I have a few things I'd like for you to do for me–please. Those cards, you know–and don't put it off for another day! I have most of the addresses written down on a piece of paper in the card box. To the ones that we've met or known personally, sign both your name and mine–To the ones you aren't so sure of–just sign mine–or Jack, except for Uncle Otha's, then how about Mr. and Mrs. J. M. Strickland (Jack) or some such.

So far I've written home–and surprise of surprises–to Mr. and Mrs. Banks Allen Murray! That was just in case you didn't have time. I'm afraid I made a mistake in mentioning nylon hose to your mother–because there are none here–yet!

Seeing as how it's time to check my boots and blankets at the Cadet Supply–I'd better start moving now–so, so long and should you be up–and at the Blytheville Station about 9 A.M. Friday–perchance I might be able to shake your hand–no promise, though.

All my love from me to you,
Mr. J.M.S.

P.S. Send film to be developed.

Chapter Seven

Blytheville

In December, without waiting to attend the dance that was held at the close of each training period, I made a beeline for Blytheville. That way I had a better chance at locating any housing that was available.

(Incidentally, Jack did attend the dance. He had had one outstanding, gray-haired instructor whom he liked and admired very much. This man arrived at the dance with an attractive young woman. Jack approached him and asked if he could dance with his daughter. You guessed it –the instructor said, "This is my WIFE." It was lucky that Jack was leaving the next day,)

At Blytheville I followed our previous routine and knocked on doors. I came to a lovely old brick house and when I knocked at the door an extremely attractive young woman opened it. She said her name was Anne Hamilton and she was there visiting her parents. After finding out what my situation was she told me that she and her husband led an active social life and she had been looking for a live-in baby sitter for her two boys, George, 4, and

David, 2. She lived nearby and had a woman who cleaned and cooked. When I told her about my beloved baby sister and my feeling for children, she offered me a room, rent free, in exchange for my sitting with her boys. It seemed too good to be true. I was afraid she would change her mind when I told her my husband was only allowed one night a week off of base so I would have to have my Saturday nights free. She readily agreed to that and I moved in with them that day.

Anne's husband, George was a violinist and orchestra leader. He, along with Glen Miller, had played in Paul Whiteman's band in New York. George left Whiteman and formed his own band. He was getting quite a good reputation when the war came along. A lot of good musicians had been called into the service and the big bands had to break up, George's among them.

They moved to Anne's hometown, Blytheville. Anne was happy to be home but George missed the lights and excitement of the big cities he was used to. He was like a fish out of water. His orchestra had been called, "George Hamilton's Music Box Orchestra." He showed me the very large music box that was played as a lead in to all his performances.

One of the highlights of my life was when Glen Miller came to Blytheville. He was a Major in the Army with the Special Services Division. George got in touch with him and invited him to dinner at the house. Glen accepted. I wonder if you can imagine the thrill of being 18 years old in 1942 and knowing you were going to have dinner with Glen Miller. The evening came and there were just the four of us. Glen was a sweet, unassuming man and we had a great time. With much effort, I was cool, calm and collected until the evening ended and he was leaving. I couldn't stand it another minute and, like the star-struck teenager I was, asked him for his autograph. I still have and treasure it.

Shortly after that Major Glen Miller went overseas with a 45-man band of GIs where he performed for the troops. On December 15, 1944, he was on his way from England to

France when his plane disappeared. No trace of it was ever found.

Christmas was fast approaching and for months I had been collecting, little by little, things to give to Jack. I remember one of them was a towel that I had embroidered with his initials. I shudder now when I think of how that must have gone over in the barracks. I was getting enthused and had bought a little table-top tree. I decorated it with things I had made. It was touch and go whether Jack could get away for Christmas Eve. It happened that he was not granted leave. That was probably the only time Jack went AWOL. He sneaked out of camp and showed up at the Hamiltons around 11 p.m. Anne gave us a bottle of wine and then left us alone. I gave Jack his presents and as he opened them he became quiet and unhappy. I didn't know what had gone wrong. I went to the kitchen to get something and saw Anne. She asked me how it was going and I said it was terrible. I told her what was happening. She asked me if Jack had brought me anything. I said, "No, but I hadn't expected anything." I knew he had neither the time nor money to get me a present. Anne then took me into her bedroom and gave me a brand-new box of expensive perfume that she had. She told me to show it to Jack and tell him that I knew he couldn't get me anything and so I had bought this for myself to be his gift to me. I did as she said and Jack's face lit up like our little Xmas tree. The rest of the evening was wonderful. That was a lesson that has stood me in good stead ever since. It's great to give people things but you have to let them be the giver now and again or it defeats the purpose. That Anne was a smart cookie.

I hadn't been in Blytheville very long when I found out I was pregnant. I was overjoyed. One day Anne asked me to help push her car out of the driveway. I'm ashamed to remember that I refused. Not knowing a lot about pregnancies I was afraid I would injure my baby. No amount of talking on her part would convince me that it would be O.K.

Anne had a 14-year-old son by her first marriage and she asked me to chaperone his birthday party. She and George were going out. She had only one request–I was to see that NO KISSING went on. Things went well for awhile and someone asked if they could play "Five Minute Date." When asked how it was played I was told, "A boy chooses a girl and they both go outside for five minutes."

I said, "NO." Apparently these 14-year-olds were not intimidated by an 18-year-old. I spent the rest of the evening going outside and bringing back the couples who kept sneaking out. It was a long evening!! I was glad when it was over.

At long last on February 16, 1943, the student class of "43-B" graduated. They got their silver wings and a commission. LIEUTENANT Strickland sounded *so good.*

Jack wanted to be sent directly overseas but instead got orders to report to Selman Field in Monroe, LA. Selman was a training school for navigators. There Jack was to pilot the planes used in training.

Several years later I heard that the Hamiltons had divorced. George had gone back to New York and Anne had custody of the boys. I was saddened as I remembered how much George loved his sons. He used to say, "The most important things in my life are my boys and my 'fiddle.' "

Years later the 4-year-old George for whom I babysat grew up to be a very successful movie star.

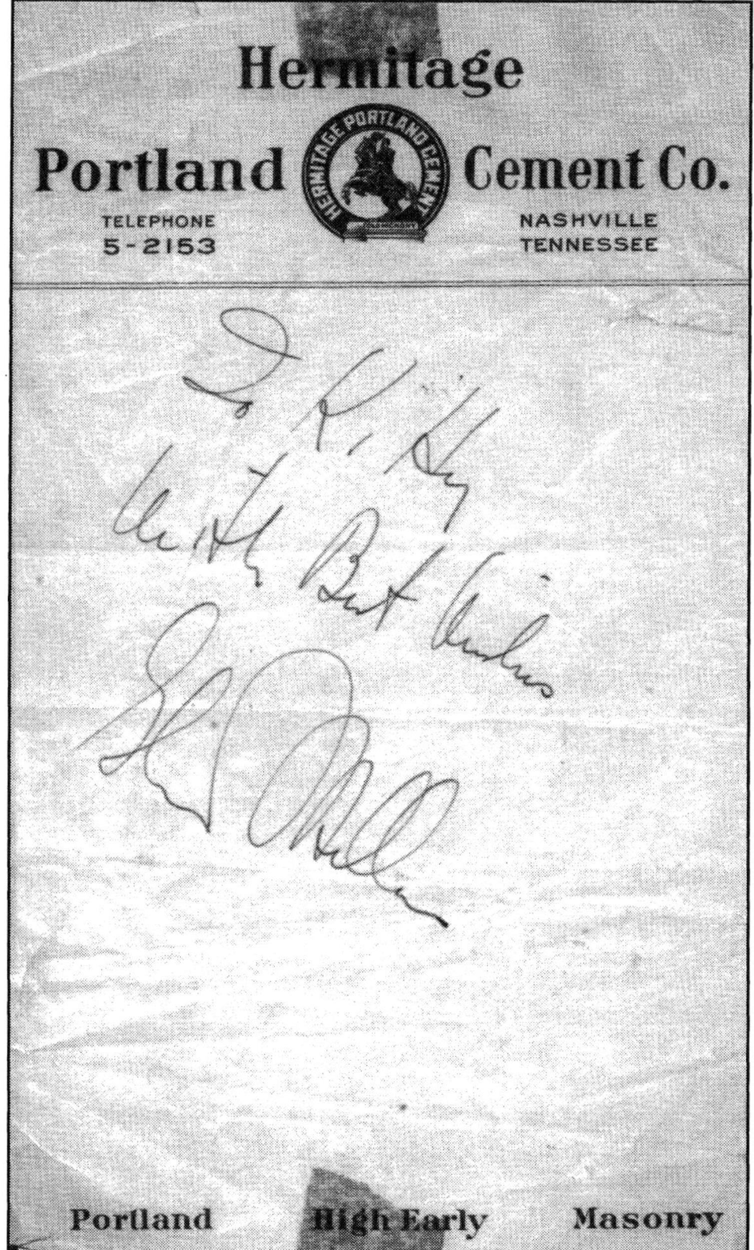

Hermitage

Portland Cement Co.

HERMITAGE PORTLAND CEMENT

TELEPHONE
5-2153

NASHVILLE
TENNESSEE

Portland High Early Masonry

THE SOUTHEAST

ARMY AIR FORCES TRAINING CENTER

ANNOUNCES THE GRADUATION

OF CLASS 43-B

BLYTHEVILLE ARMY AIR FIELD

ON TUESDAY, FEBRUARY SIXTEENTH

NINETEEN HUNDRED FORTY-THREE

BLYTHEVILLE, ARKANSAS

Jack and Joe Sulkin receiving their "wings"

Feb. 8, 1943

Dear Kitty,

How are you?

Gee, I'm sorry about being so darned dilatory in answering your letters. I have excuses but don't suppose they hold water, so I won't even try them out.

Are you still "Unca Sam's" star Army wife? Atta girl! Gosh I'm really glad to hear that Jack is doing so well but then, with the inspiration that guy has, how could anyone go wrong? I know you're proud of him and so am I even though I'm that way about answering letters.

I have lost Jack's last letter so I will have to call your mother to find out where you are staying. As I remember, it seemed to me to be a pretty neat set up–I mean handy and all that sort of thing. It seems to me that you have been quite lucky in finding a place to stay in your gallivanting around the country. Here I am, stuck here, and the farthest I ever get is College Park. Of course it's a great place but after 52 weeks a year of it I could almost go down to George Washington U. just for the change.

Speaking of college, I have really been working hard this semester. I have been carrying about 7 credits over my normal load and they have clamped down on the military so that I do about 4 times as much work. Besides my regular Army classes and drill each week, I have Freshman and Sophomore classes to instruct -good practice but a headache. In spite of this I managed to get through the semester (I just finished my finals yesterday) and I have piled up enough credits now so that with what I get next semester I will have enough to graduate. It would be rather unorthodox and so far the faculty has said "Thumbs Down" but I still think they'll break down. In case you didn't gather as much I'm a "SENIOR" now. Ahh, yes. I'm to be addressed with "Sir" now. Boy, I'd hate to miss getting that sheep skin by a few months after working all these years.

Why aren't I in the Army by this time, you say? It's like this. It seems I made a good move when I signed the Advanced ROTC contract because that defers me (only until June and I'm not supposed to graduate until the end of the following semester.) whereas the rest of the Enlisted Reserve has been called. A large number of them have already left and the rest are awaiting orders. It has really cut down the classes. I'm in a couple that have only 4 or 5 students in them. The latest I've heard is that Maryland is one of the Universities to handle part of the Government's new Military Specialists training program so I guess the school will operate for the duration.

Oh well, the co-eds are still there. Of course that's no sign that any men will still be around.

Everyone and their uncle are getting married around here and if they've been married once, they're getting married again. Half of my friends out at school are married and the rest have that certain sparkle in their eyes so I know it won't be long before it will be all. Gosh after thinking of all the kids getting married, I've almost made up my mind–Yes. sir, I'm going to demand a 25 cents increase in my allowance so that I can get married. What would my children think if they found out that out of the whole crowd I was the only bachelor? What would they think anyway? Hmmm. I'll stay a bachelor in spite of the increase in allowance until I'm sure I'm walking around with the right dream.

Lt. Buck was in town lately. He was on his way overseas. You remember - the fellow who took you for that Cub ride that bright sunny day that you cut school and someone almost wrecked my car for me.

I haven't been over to our old Alma Mater since before you left, I guess. I plan to go to the next dance to see just how much the school has come down since the class of '40 has left (Also, the class of '41–pardon me!) You know Eileen is in her first year over there. (hmm–can I be that old?) She tells me that Mr. Knight is still wearing that old gray, baggy suit. I suggested that start a "get a new suit for Mr. Knight" fund. But I guess that as soon as he got wind of it he would "see no reason–"

We have been having some swell dances at school lately. The other weekend we had a "Snow Ball." The gym was decorated with icicles all over everything (well, I thought it was decorations in spite of the oil shortage) snow scenes, etc. and everyone wore ski suits and skating skirts (whistle) Mine didn't fit so well (ski-suit) so I just wore my skies. It really wasn't so bad until I started "jitter bugging"–wow–it took them 2 hours to untangle me from my partner, or vice versa–mostly nice versa, to be frank.

I saw Miss Leah B. at one of the dances lately. She wanted to know how you were and how Jack was getting along. I told her that you were fine and that Jack was fine and that I was fine, and didn't she think the orchestra was fine and then I couldn't think of anything else to say–a most amazing position–so, I took her in my arms and started to dance, with the hope that the band would start playing soon. Darn it, it was just my luck for this to be the long intermission. But did that stop me? No, sir. Well, anyway, the band started playing again in about 40 minutes, and then we had a tempo to dance to. It wasn't long before someone cut in and as I left I could hear her muttering something that sounded like "Thank God---thank God I'm engaged to a sane man---thank God, I'll gladly wait for the duration" and then one "Thank God."

O.K. then I'll get serious. You know I think that too much studying does make me punchy. For the last semester I studied on an average of two or three nights a week all night through to classes the next morning and I'm the same old skeleton. Barnum and Bailey have been after me every minute since last year when their thin man died–I'm holding out for more pay. I'll have to be careful about getting too much rest now between semesters–I have to think about my career, you know. Ahh, I can see me now, "Step right up, you all. The chanct of a lifetime–just one thin dime to see the living skeleton, you won't believe it when you see it, but it's true–he is alive."

I was over to see your family some time ago. They seemed fine and you're going to have to fight the men away from that young sister in a few years. She is really getting cute.

Guess what!! Our boy, John, is now in the Army. He's in a radio school for the Signal Corps in Kentucky. I don't know whether you knew, but John has a real talent for writing and has always been interested in dramatics. That's what he's been studying at the University of Michigan (before he entered the

Army) and he has done some really fine work. He has written many short stories and many poems. I'm going to copy a short piece of work he sent me (He sends me all his work–"Human Guinea Pig Holland"–and I knock it.) He has done several better but the one I will send is my favorite poem, the more I read it, the better I like it.

Kitty, I'm going to include his address and I wish you would get Jack to write him. I'm sure Jack doesn't realize it and I promised not to say anything about it, but John was really hurt when Jack never answered his letters or wrote him, not even about you and him getting married. John thought of him as one of his best friends. Not that it is directly any of my business but it is for the sake of the close bond that once existed between Jack, John and myself and I feel sure does still exist. The only reason why I'm pouring all this out to you is that I swore not to say anything to Jack about it. Will you tell Jack about it for me? Thanks, Pal.

Gosh, I've written quite a lot and said practically nothing. A little booklet on how to read and interpret this mess will follow in the mail. Tell Jackson "Hi," for me and that I am in the process of writing him.

Love,
Harvey (alias Harp)

P.S. Tell that husband of yours to stop flying so well or he's going to get that Strickland name mixed up with some of the Lindbergh, Rickenbacker, Doolittle crowd.

Ode to a Lovely Lady
by
John Cook

I have known beauty.

I have known the beauty of glistening black railroad ties, seen through sheeted mist, by the light of an overhead lamp.

I have known beauty of meeting old friends after many years. The first shouted words of greeting, the good grip of hand on hand, the coarse oaths hurled delightedly at each other.

I have known the beauty of a Chopin waltz, and the Beethoven Pastoral.

I have known the beauty of the last rustle whisper moment before the curtain went up on a new play. The dimming house lights, the glowing curtain base, the tense expectancy of the audience.

I have known the beauty of a moonlight night on a great river, gloating silently on the oil black depths, the trees etched eloquently against the sky. A postcard beauty almost trite in its perfection.

I have known the beauty of solitude and memory. The beauty of a warm slow, darkening evening, misty soft rain, of night and stars and the silence of the sea.

I have known the beauty of flaming October, pungent leaf smoke, the thud of toe on leather, the clean hard shock of a good tackle.

I have known the stupendous beauty of a rainbow - - - - and a cloud.

I have known the beauty of darkness and deep waters, yellow rippled by mysterious light.

I have known the beauty of forests in the sun, the rustling scurry of unseen creatures among dry leaves, two sunbeams playing tag on a strand of cobweb.

I have known the beauty of crunched snow, the bracing sting of wind past speeding sleds and frosted faces.

I have looked into your eyes - - - - - - - - - - - -

I have known beauty.

Well, what do you think, Kitty? Don't say now–put it aside and read it again later. I have found that every time I read it I find something new, previously hidden detail and I grow fonder of it.

Did I tell you that Dad is now commanding the AAF Intelligence School in Harrisburg, Pa.?

That's all for now, I guess, before I start digressing again. Speaking of digressing–did you ever go off on a tangent? The Capital Transit Co. has monopolized the bus and streetcar business, but they haven't been able to control the tangents here. Believe me, in these times of gas rationing, no pleasure driving and crowded buses and streetcars, it comes in mighty handy to be able to go off on a tangent. Why don't you and Jack try it? There's really nothing quite like it. In fact, why don't you and Jack get off on the next tangent for Washington? It would be swell to see you all. I hope Mr.–er–Lt. and Mrs. Strickland will be able to get home after the completion of the course. Having lost Jack's letter I'll have to find that out from your mother. It must be pretty darned soon, isn't it?

Do you realize what time it is? It's three thirty A.M. I have gotten so used to staying up studying late during the semester that I can't seem to get out of the habit. I'd better close, anyway.

S'long again

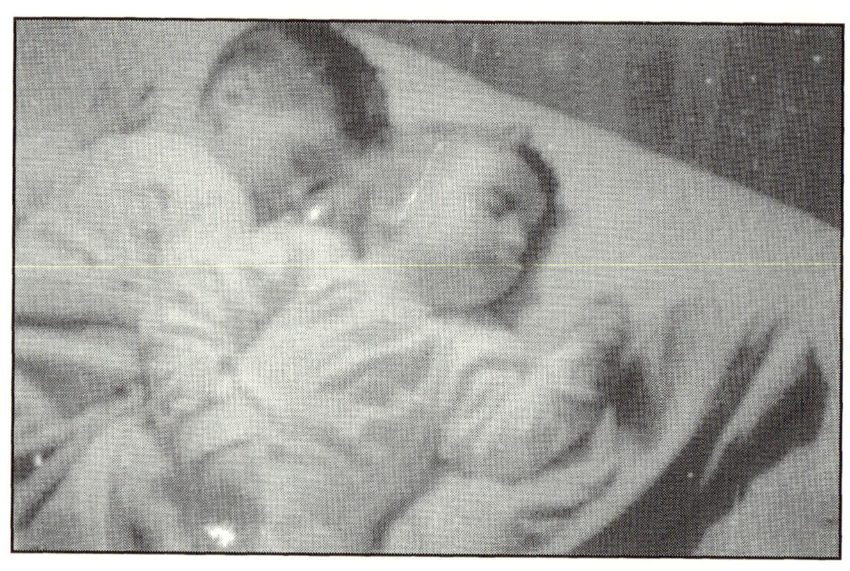

Snapshot taken by Jack of George Hamilton, Jr., age 4, and David Hamilton, age 2

Chapter Eight

Hedy

After the graduation ceremony the new Lieutenants began to receive orders for a 10-day leave before having to report to their new bases. The orders were coming in batches. Jack had not received his by evening but we packed up our belongings and went to the train station where we bought tickets to D.C. on the midnight train. There we waited. Jack would call the base every half-hour to see if his orders had arrived. At one point he left me to guard our luggage (plus two fishing rods) while he made yet another phone call. By this time the station was quite deserted and it was very dark. I felt a little nervous being alone in such an isolated situation. I suddenly saw a man approaching me from the other direction of the station. As he neared he had a grin on his face and he said, "Hi, there. Are you going fishing?" I didn't answer him and he persisted "I said, are you going fishing?"

I was pretty scared at this point, so I called, "Jack." The man said something else to me and I called, "JACK" in a louder voice. This time Jack heard me and came back quickly.

The man said, "Is this your wife?"

Jack said, "Yes." Then the man said, "I was just asking if she was going fishing." Turned out he was an avid fisherman and he and Jack stood there for half an hour discussing fishing. I felt like a perfect fool–well, not exactly, no one is PERFECT.

Incidentally Jack's orders had come through and we caught the midnight train to D.C.

Ten days later when we arrived in Monroe, LA, the housing angels seemed to have deserted us. There was absolutely no place to rent. It was so bad that when a cadet washed out, before he could tell his wife, someone had already called her to see if they could rent their apartment or room.

It was fortunate that Jack's commission came with a big raise in income. We needed it as we were forced to stay in a hotel. Another young Lieutenant and wife, Lou and Jane Agnew, were in the same situation and the same hotel.

We tried everything we could think of to get housing. We put ads in the paper, listing all the things that would make us desirable tenants–no kids, no pets, quiet, conscientious, etc., etc. We didn't get the first bite. The Agnews were not having any luck, either. We were getting desperate. Even with the increase in salary we couldn't afford hotel living for very long. So, for the hell of it, we put yet another ad in the paper. This one read, "Two pilots and wives seeking large house. Love loud parties. Have six wild children. Must have spacious yard for our 4 dogs. Prefer a place on the water with pier to dock boat."

Lo and behold, we got an answer. A couple called and said their parents' house was vacant. Like our first two landlords, they had not planned on renting it out. However they said they got such a kick out of our ridiculous ad that they were willing to reconsider. We met them and they took us to see the house. At this point we would have settled for anything. The house was outside of town and was ideal. It was beautiful, had a huge yard (about two

Jane Agnew and Irish Setter

acres) and was completely furnished. It really could have fit the requirements we had listed. No pier, though, but they said it would be O.K. to have animals.

The Agnews and the Stricklands quickly moved in.

The first thing the Agnews did was to get a dog. She was a beautiful red Irish Setter. She was very smart but it soon became apparent to us that she had been mistreated. It was one of the most intimidated dogs I've ever encountered.

Instead of also getting a dog, Jack opted to buy a baby goat. Being a "city gal," I was leery of having a goat for a pet. Jack assured me that female goats didn't smell bad, were extremely smart and also ate grass, which would save us from having to mow so often. He brought the goat home and I fell in love with her. She was darling and had beautiful long eyelashes. We named her Hedy after the movie star, Hedy Lamar.

I found that goats make wonderful pets. Hedy was my constant companion through the day but when Jack came home in the evenings she would desert me and follow him around and lie at his feet when he sat down. To keep from making a liar out of himself, Jack would frequently take her out in the yard and give her a bath in a big tin washtub so she really didn't smell. We had a leash for her and I would take her with me when I walked down the road to the post office. It didn't take long for her to learn the routine and from then on the leash would go slack and Hedy would walk docilely beside me.

It was fun to watch the Agnew's Irish Setter and Hedy play together. The dog would chase the goat and she would run, occasionally jumping up on the hood of a car or some other higher ground. Then she would hop down and let the dog chase her some more. When she tired of the game she would stop abruptly, turn and face the setter who would also stop. For about a minute they would stare at each other, then Hedy would stomp her front hoofs and the dog would turn tail and run.

Since Hedy was so tame we let her run loose outside. Although we had a large yard there were still neighbors on either side of us. One of the neighbors was an avid gardener and had a row of flowers that were called "four o'clocks" because they bloomed in the afternoon. The blossoms grew on a long stem–sort of like a hollyhock. Evidently they tasted great to goats. One day I watched as she reared up on her hind legs, pushed down the stem of a "four o'clock" with her chest and proceeded to eat the lovely flowers which were now within her reach. After that we kept a much closer eye on her. By the way, she never ate one bite of grass.

Eventually she grew bigger and we recognized the fact that being a house pet was not the ideal situation for a goat. Jack gave her to some nearby farmers who raised goats for milking.

Jack bathing Hedy

CHAPTER NINE

Jennis

Sometimes Jack would buzz (fly low over) our house. I would hear the plane and rush outside to wave at him. He would dip the plane's wings, then leave. One morning bright and early I was sitting in the kitchen, in my nightgown, drinking coffee when I heard a plane. I rushed outside to wave. The plane's wings dipped and it left. I came back into the house and soon heard the plane again. Same procedure–went out, waved and came back in. This went on for half a dozen times or more, which was very unusual. That night when Jack came home he told me he had been leading a practice mission that morning and I had waved to every pilot in it. They were flying so low that I was clearly visible. He asked me to please get dressed next time before I came out to wave.

This house, though very nice, was quite a distance from the air base. That meant long commutes for Lou and Jack. Jack disliked having to fly student navigators around. They often got airsick and threw up in the plane. A lot of them had washed out of pilot training and weren't too gung-ho about becoming navigators. Jack was hoping he would soon get orders to go overseas and help win the war. He was under tremendous pressure.

Meanwhile, as my pregnancy advanced, my emotions became unpredictable. I began feeling sorry for myself, as I was not getting the attention to which I thought I was entitled. We both needed strong emotional support but we weren't capable of giving it to each other. We were unhappy. I decided the best thing for me to do was to leave Jack and go back to Silver Spring. When I told him, I was hoping he would tell me not to go. He didn't, though. He said, "O.K." and bought me bus and train tickets home. The day I was to leave I had packed a trunk. Jack came, saw it and started emptying it. I thought for a moment that this was his way of asking me to stay but as I watched, he repacked it much better than I had done. He put it and me into the car and drove me to catch my bus. I boarded the bus and as it pulled out of the station I was heartbroken.

The bus made many scheduled stops along the way. After several hours of riding we stopped at a station. The bus driver went inside. He came out and approached me and asked if I were Kitty Strickland. When I said, "Yes," he handed me a telegram. It read, "Come back. Have found us an apartment across from the base. Love, Jack." I got off that bus and caught the next one back to Monroe where Jack was waiting.

The apartment he had found was right across the road from the base. It was small–a tiny living room, kitchen and bedroom–but had a huge screened-in porch. We were right on the bayou which was breathtaking. The water was black and the many trees that grew in it were dripping with Spanish moss. There was a big pecan tree in the yard. I thought the whole thing was beautiful.

I wasn't too thrilled when Jack told me that five of the seven poisonous snakes in the U.S. could be found in Louisiana. Fortunately I never saw any of them. I did see lots of scorpions, though. I lost my fear of them when Jack explained they were not dangerous to humans. I liked to watch them. A scorpion would grasp a small bug with its front claws. While holding it, it would lift its tail up over its back and inject a small amount of venom into the bug, thus paralyzing it until the scorpion could eat it. Sounds gruesome but I was learning from Jack to be a Nature appreciator.

I remember once there was a big, shiny spider on our porch. I named him "George" and spent many an hour sitting on that screen porch, watching him spin an absolutely gorgeous web in one corner.

When my mother came to visit us, one of the first things she did was to get a broom and knock down the web. Mothers are like that. I was sad, knowing all the work that "George" had gone to in order to create it. His work wasn't wasted, though, because its beauty still lives in my memory.

Another lovely memory was the sight that greeted us when we awakened one winter morning and looked outside. We saw that ice had covered every blade of grass, every Cypress tree and every strand of long gray Spanish moss that hung from the trees. It looked like the whole scene was made of glass and was reflected in the black water of the bayou.

This was the first time since we had married that we were living alone. Jack was to discover that any meals I had made prior to this had been with a great deal of help from the wives with whom we shared lodgings. He did not know that the fudge and cookies, that he loved and I often made, were just about the only things I knew how to cook. I remember the first dinner I made for him. We were having calves' liver and baked potatoes. I started cooking both of them at the same time. (For you non-chefs–calves' liver takes 5 minutes to cook and baked potatoes take about an hour.)

But I kept trying. Once Jack mentioned he loved calves' tongue. With red ration stamps in hand, I hied me to the butcher shop and bought a large calves' tongue. I found cooking directions somewhere and simmered it until it was tender. I was looking forward to surprising him. I surely succeeded. I served it and Jack took one look and started turning slightly green. He said, "I think there's something else you're supposed to do to it–like skinning it and cutting it in slices." I had put the whole thing on a platter and served it warm. It was not a pretty sight.

Jack kept body and soul together by eating at the base fairly often. He was required to buy 30 meal tickets a month. I was getting pretty tired of eating my own cooking, too. Often we were invited to have dinner with friends. Whatever they served tasted heavenly to me. I found myself eating and enjoying things that I had refused to eat all my life. The friends' wives would give me recipes and I began to learn how to cook.

As my culinary skills improved Jack ate at home more often. The base meal tickets could not be carried over from one month to another. When Jack ended up with tickets left over at the end of the month, he would go to the orphanage that was nearby and take as many kids as he had tickets for and treat them to dinner at the army mess hall. They loved it. He also would fill bags with the pecans that fell off our tree and drop them by the orphanage.

In Louisiana, Jack often went fishing. His favorite prey was the small mouth bass. I was made aware that small mouth bass are bigger than large mouth bass. Once he caught a big one of which he was excessively proud. He took it to a taxidermist and had it mounted on a wooden plaque. This he hung on our bedroom wall. I stood it as long as I could. Finally I told him that I refused to wake up one more morning with that glass fish eye staring at me. He moved it into the living room.

The only time I had flown with Jack was in Maryland at the College Park Airport where he had learned to fly. He used to take me up in a little two-seater monoplane called a Piper Cub. The struts between the wing and the fuselage would vibrate in the wind, giving one the feeling they might break away at any moment. Nevertheless, it was the most wonderful sensation to feel the freedom and the unity with the heavens that birds must experience.

I had wanted very much to have him take me up in an Army plane. It was up to the Commanding Officer of the base whether to permit this or not. No C.O. had ever authorized it.

One day Jack came home and excitedly told me that the C.O. had been transferred and his replacement wasn't arriving until that evening, so there was no one there to say "NO." "If we hurry, we can get by with it," he said. I was all for it. I got my 8 ½ mo. pregnant body dressed and we headed for the field where the ground crew was waiting for us.

Army planes, unlike commercial planes, had no frills. It took three guys to get me up onto the wing but I managed to crawl into the plane and we were off. I loved it! We flew through clouds (which was a first for me) and I was surprised to find that those white, fluffy, cottony things were just like mist when you were in the middle of them. We flew over our house and various places that I knew. It was exhilarating. When we came back and landed, we were greeted by some happy faces and some not so happy faces. Seems the ground crew took bets among themselves on whether I would have had the baby by the time we got back.

There were never any repercussions from that particular flight so I assume the new Commanding Officer never heard about it.

All this time Jack insisted I keep up with target practice. He would often have three-day proficiency runs and I would be alone. We kept a revolver in a magazine rack by the bed. I would mentally rehearse how I would behave if an intruder ever did come in when I was by myself. Much later I had the occasion to find out. More about that later.

We had a number of friends while at Monroe. One of our favorites was Joe Sulkin. He had been all through training with Jack and now was also stationed there. He was still a bachelor. He met and started dating a local girl, Marilyn Nelson. She was a college student who had been born and raised in Monroe. Joe would often bring her out to visit us. She and I formed a friendship that has lasted over the years. In fact, although she now lives in San Francisco and I in Maryland, we keep in touch via E-mail. Actually, she is the one who suggested I put my memories down on paper and is a constant source of encouragement to me.

We were unprepared for the weather in Louisiana in the summertime. I was getting bigger and bigger and often it was 104 degrees in the shade.

Jack's mother had been writing me the most encouraging and sympathetic letters. I asked her to come down to be with us for the big event. She answered that she wouldn't be able to do that but continued to lend me morale support in her frequent letters. My mother said she would come down and bring my baby sister who was now four years old. I had missed Felicia and really looked forward to their visit.

The baby was due August 26th. Mother arrived a week ahead of time. I went into town to meet them. The train tracks ran across the main street and the station was way off the road. In order to get to the station I had to walk the length of the train, which was filled with soldiers. As I walked past the first car the soldiers leaned out of the windows and started singing, "Oh you beautiful doll–YOU GREAT BIG BEAUTIFUL DOLL." As I walked past each car its occupants would pick up the refrain and serenade me. I was mortified.

My due date came and went with no sign of a birth pain. I kept getting even bigger and bigger.

One day I took Felicia into town with me. As we queued up for the bus to go back home there were dozens of soldiers also waiting. Felicia looked at them and then at me. In a loud voice she said a phrase to me that my mother had often said to her, "Hold your stomach in!" The soldiers thought it was hilarious.

As the days went past I made numerous trips to see the base's doctor. Each time I would come home, Felicia would ask me eagerly, "Did you get the baby?"

I would say, "No. I didn't see any that I liked."

One day after this exchange Felicia said. "Kitty, if I were you, I'd just take *any* baby." She thought a minute and added, "Just don't get a German or a Jap."

Many of our military friends were having babies. I was apprehensive about what birth felt like, so I would query them about their experiences. Although each had a different story, the consensus was that it was painful but the doctors gave shots that dulled the pain and it wasn't too bad. This information was reassuring.

So the days went on. On the night of September 15 Jack and Felicia had gone to sleep. Because I had felt a few twitches in my side that day Mother and I decided to stay up a little longer. We were playing gin rummy when I suddenly got an awful pain in my stomach. I lay down on the floor and tried not to scream. Mother awakened Jack and got me to the bed. Then another pain hit. Worse than the first. I grabbed the headboard and held on for dear life. My mother meanwhile got a wash rag and was washing my feet. (I had been barefoot all day and my feet were very dirty.) I had another pain and couldn't help screaming. Mother said, "Hush. This is nothing compared to what it's *going* to be." While this was going on my husband was calling the doctor, whose name, if I remember correctly, was Captain Meenge. I heard Jack saying, "This is–uh–Lt. Strickland. (pause)–My wife is–uh–expecting a baby (pause) and we think–uh–it might be tonight." I had always loved Jack's southern drawl but this was one time I prayed he would talk faster.

The doctor told him that he had checked the X-rays that had been taken that day. He said the baby hadn't "dropped" yet and was not in a good position. He thought he might have to help turn it around. In any event it would be a long labor. He then suggested that Jack take me to the hospital where they could get me comfortable and he, the doctor, would come down and see me in the morning.

Jack called an ambulance and we went to Saint Francis Catholic Hospital in Monroe at one a.m. The sweetest, most gentle Franciscan monks and nuns ran this hospital. I remember how quiet it was at that hour. All the patients were asleep. I didn't want to cause a disturbance but I was hurting so much and I wanted some of those "shots" my friends had told me about. I couldn't help it–I shouted, "Jesus, give me something. God have mercy. Jesus DO something." The nuns (who were nurses) tried to calm me down and assured me that I would get something soon. I kept yelling. When they started to "prep" me they saw the baby's head being presented. They immediately stopped their ministrations and called for a gurney. I gave birth to Jennis M. Strickland III at 1:20 a.m. on September 16, 1943, as I crawled onto the gurney–1 hour and 20 minutes of labor.

Before we had left the apartment, my mother had told Jack to give her a call when we got settled in the hospital and found out when they thought the baby would arrive. She wanted to know whether to stay up or go to sleep. When he called her at 1:25 and told her that the baby was here, she didn't believe him. Captain Meenge showed up at 8:30 a.m. and I introduced him to my beautiful, perfect, 7½ hour-old baby boy. I don't know if I had believed in miracles before that night, but now I KNEW I had just been privileged to participate in one.

The next day was a Friday. I was in a six-bed ward. When lunch was brought in, the five other women were served chicken. I got fish. I asked the nun why. She said, "Aren't you Catholic?" I told her I wasn't and she said, "I'm sorry, but you called on The Lord so much last night when you were brought in that we thought surely you were Catholic."

Jack was beaming when he came in to see us. He said, "You did a good job." He kissed me and picked up his son and put him at the foot of my bed, where he proceeded to take pictures of him. I still have the pictures of my feet under the covers and 1-day-old Jennis lying beside them. My face was in none of the pictures.

One month later, to the day, Blanche, Jack's mother, gave birth to Patrick Byron. Again, she had not said a word about her pregnancy, but that was why she couldn't come and be with us for the birth of her first grandchild.

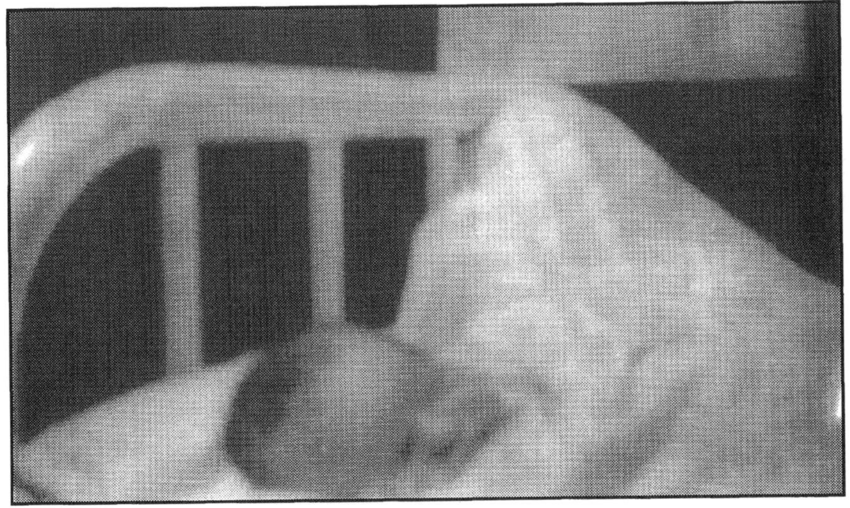

Baby Jennis and Kitty's feet

ARRIVAL REPORT

Commanding Officer:

Lt. and Mrs. Jennis M. Strickland

Destination:

Monroe, Louisiana

ATA:

1:20 A. M. September 16, 1943

Cargo:

Boy

Call Letters:

Jennis Morrell

Tonnage:

7 Lbs. 7¼ Oz.

[Jack kept a journal of his observations of wild life. These are a few excerpts that he wrote while in Monroe, La.]

Reactions of birds to airplanes

Hawks

Most of the smaller hawks show no fear what ever of airplanes–merely keeping out of the way, usually without flapping wings. Have yet to catch hawk unawares while flying. When chased by plane they depend on acrobatic maneuvers to elude plane – diving up to 120 mph then either doing vertical climb and towering while heavy, less maneuverable plane shoots beneath. Have seen many hawks do "immelmans" to elude plane. Hawks allow planes to approach very closely.

Buzzards (Turkey and Virginia)

Buzzards never seem to look about them in flight, seemingly concentrating on earth's surface. Very easy to catch them unawares whereas with hawks, which never make flying hazardous, they present a contrast. On low flights a pilot must be alert at all times to "dodge" them. When they finally notice a close flying plane they flop awkwardly from side to side while diving. Most buzzards in this section (Mississippi Basin) seldom are found above 1,000 ft. although I've seen a few up to 3,000 ft.

Geese

Geese flying in formation refuse to be separated by planes. They show signs of noticing plane though it may be 2 or 3 miles away. The formation will turn away from planes almost as soon as you notice them. When dived upon or otherwise hard pressed the formation draws into tighter and tighter formation meanwhile gaining or losing altitude according to position of pursuing plane. Formation will finally be so low to treetops as to be too dangerous for plane to bank in order to keep up with them. When diving or climbing they continually turn away from plane until they are in a circle so tight that plane cannot stay with them–"overshooting."

Wild Turkey

The bird called the Water Turkey in the south is very similar to the Chinese Cormorant except that it has unusual powers of flight. Between bodies of water or rivers they seem to prefer to fly almost exactly 3,500 ft. with few variations. Seem to be aware of planes approaching although altering course but little. They invariably depend upon diving to elude a plane. Have yet to catch one in a dive though well over 150 mph. The Water Turkey seems to adjust diving speed by merely drawing in wing area closer to body. They fly much faster than geese do while "cruising along" though they glide more than fly. I cannot say they dive at rates above 150 mph simply because at 3,500 ft. you have to pull out long before you make any noticeable gain on them.

Smaller Birds

Many small birds are passed in flying. They apparently make no alterations in regard to eluding the plane. As a rule they are so small as to be unrecognizable–or direction of flight. The plane either hits them or, due to last second change in their flight, misses them by inches.

Owls

So far I've known of no instances in which owls have been hit, however it isn't unusual to pass barn or barred owls at night when coming in for landings with lights on. Since the slower marsh hawks or buzzards spend quite a bit of the day hunting about 3 to 5 ft. over the field and runways I imagine the owls do the same at night since there must be a pretty reliable or "easy" source of food there. The hawks usually get off to one side of the runways to let the plane pass, the owls usually "pull up" over the plane the same as they do with automobiles along the highways.

Jack in Louisiana

Jack on bayou

Bayou, Monroe, La.

Bayou

Chapter Ten

A Visit Home

In those days new mothers were kept in the hospital for 10 days. They let us sit up on the side of the bed the third day after giving birth. By the time we came home we were weak as kittens from all that bed rest. In spite of that, we enjoyed the coddling we received very much.

By the time I got out of the hospital my mother, who had come to Monroe so long before Jennis' birth, had to go back home. Shortly thereafter my father was told that his job had been abolished. He had been a top salesman for the automobile classified section of the *Washington Times* and *Herald* newspaper. All of the car manufacturers were now making tanks, etc. for the military. There were no cars to sell–no advertising–no job.

My brother was in Lubbock, Tex., in Glider School. He had married a girl from California. He told our folks that when the war was over, he planned on living in California, a place he described in glowing terms. I had told Mother and Dad that Jack and I had no intention of settling in Silver Spring, either. Lots of their friends were either in the service or had moved away. They were lonely, dissatisfied and frustrated. Much to my amazement they sold their house in Silver Spring and moved to San Fernando Valley, CA, where they bought a house.

While all this was going on I was busy taking care of my husband and baby. I tried to keep the baby dry at all times, which was an exercise in futility, as all mothers of little boys soon learn. We didn't have a washing machine or dryer, so now in addition to Jack's and my clothes, I was hanging as many as 20 diapers a day on the clothesline. (Disposable diapers had never been heard of.)

I felt sorry for the doctors at the base. I'm sure when they joined the service they had not planned on taking care of new and dumb teenage mothers. I remember calling the doctor one day in a panic. I told him that my baby was bleeding internally. He asked me what made me think that. I told him that when I changed the diaper, the BM was bright red. In a disgusted voice he asked me what I had fed him. Naively, I answered, "Strained beets." Another time I called him, I told him my baby had "cradlecap" (a flaking of the skin on the scalp). I asked him what percent gentian violet (a purple bactericide and fungicide) should I use. He said, "Why do you want to use gentian violet?" I answered that ever since Jack had joined the army that was the only thing the doctors had prescribed for any ailment. (There was a saying in cadet school that anyone using any other medication was impersonating an officer.)

In spite of my ignorance, little Jennis thrived. He was healthy, had a good disposition and was very advanced for his age. I doted on him. Jack thought he was pretty wonderful, too, and proudly called him, "The Boy."

Around this time Jack bought two AKA registered Beagle puppies. He named them "Havoc" and "Lightning" after the fighter planes that he loved. He flew them to Rocky Mount and asked Uncle Richard to keep them for the "duration."

When Jennis III was three months old I took him to

visit my family in Maryland for a week. I wanted to show off my pride and joy to family and friends. The flight up presented no problem. Coming back, however, was another story. At that time military personnel had first priority on all means of transportation. We got "bumped" off the plane in Montgomery, Ala. I managed to get a train ticket but had a 2- or 3-hour layover. Having a lot of time to kill, I looked up the number in the phone book and called Mrs. Graham, the lady who had rented us the house in Belle Mina. I thought she would be interested in knowing that all three couples who rented the house now had babies. She was glad to hear my news and invited me over to her house. I told her my situation. I was afraid to leave the station. I only had two bottles of formula left for the baby and had to make sure I got the train to Monroe before they ran out. We said "goodbye." An hour later a man entered the station and came over to me. It was her husband, Dr. Graham. He gave me a box that contained fried chicken, fruit, cake, and a can of Carnation milk. I can't tell you how much their kindness meant to me.

I caught the train but somewhere along the way I got bumped off that and ended up in a bus station. I had run out of formula. I asked the woman in the cafeteria if I could use the kitchen to make some more. She said, "No, it is against the health regulations." I pleaded with her. She was unyielding. Finally she took pity on me and said *she* would make it. I gave the Carnation milk to her with instructions on how to mix it. I doubt if she boiled the water and I suspected she didn't measure it, either, but she came back with three bottles of milk that lasted my son until we got back to Monroe.

Chapter Eleven

California

For months things were busy and uneventful. We bought an old Buick that wasn't in the greatest of shape, but it ran. It certainly made shopping, etc., a lot easier for us.

In March of 1944 Jack got orders to report to Smyrna Army Air Field in Tennessee "without delay." He had no idea what this duty would entail. It was obvious that Jennis III and I could not go with him. So he was forced to leave me in Monroe and report to Smyrna.

When he left, I packed up our belongings, put lots of things in storage, put the rest and the baby in the car. I bid a sad farewell to Mr. Parker, our landlord, and started out for San Fernando Valley to stay with my parents until we found out what was happening next. The baby was 6 months old when we left Louisiana.

I didn't tell my parents of my plans. I knew they would worry and I was quite confident I could make the trip with no problem. We had tire rationing, food rationing, and gas rationing at the time. We had amassed some stamps, though, and I figured we had enough to make it there.

Texas was a lot bigger than I had thought. One could ride for miles and miles and not see another car or a town. I would stop along the way and feed Jennis III, then continue driving. At one point I came across a filling station. Just as I pulled into it one of my tires blew out with a loud bang. If that had happened before or after that station we might have been killed–or at least been in an awful spot. The service station people were wonderful and either sold me another tire or repaired that one, I'm not sure which. We were soon on our way again.

It was taking longer to drive through Texas than I had planned. As I drove along I saw a sign saying, "Sweetwater –100 miles." Later another sign, "Sweetwater–50 miles." Then, "Sweetwater–25 miles." I was thinking how nice it would be to get to a town. I drove past a few houses and a store and not much else and was on the open road again. Fifteen minutes later I realized I had just driven through Sweetwater. I'm sure it's a much bigger town now but I've never been back to see it.

One time I had stopped beside the road to feed the baby. A car, pulling a trailer, came up in back of me and stopped. There was a young couple (older than I) driving it. They asked if I needed help. I told them, "No, thanks." Bless their hearts, when they heard where I had come from and where I was headed, they insisted on waiting for me and following me for miles all the way to the next town where I planned on spending the night. They saw us safely ensconced in a motel and waved, smiled and went on their way.

We had been traveling three days when we reached El Paso. This journey had not been the snap I thought it would be. The car was acting up and I had lost my enthusiasm for traveling on with a baby. I put the car in a storage place, figuring we would take a train to California. There I could leave the baby with my parents and come back and get the car and finish the trip. Before we left El Paso I carried little Jennis across the border to Juarez. I wanted to be able to tell people that we had been to Mexico.

I bought a few silver trinkets and then went to the train station and was lucky enough to get tickets to L.A.

My parents were horrified at what I had done but were overjoyed to see us. My father would not hear of me going back for the car. He took a train to El Paso and drove it back, himself.

California was gorgeous. Even the empty lots were covered with bright orange and red poppies. All the lawns were bright green. I was to learn there was a low maintenance ground cover called "diconda" that was used there extensively. My folks' house was so pretty. They had planted carnations and other flowers in the yard and even had an asparagus bed. It appeared to be ideal but I had never seen them so bored. They sat in this lovely house, in this lovely state and had nothing to do.

They drove me to see all the neighboring towns. The whole place was incredibly beautiful but something was wrong. I didn't like California and tried to figure out why. It finally occurred to me that everything there was man-made and new looking. I missed the big old trees, old houses, lots where kids could play baseball, the feeling of continuity that I was used to.

Jack and I wrote letters back and forth and talked on the phone frequently but I missed him very much.

These are some of the letters he wrote me from Smyrna, Tenn.

April 1, 1944
AAFIS Smyrna, Tenn.
(Student Officer Gen. Del.)
in case you write
before I find my address here.

Dear Miss,

Well, here we are–and you know more than I do, still! Sorta lonesome around here at this post - full of men. (women, too, but –oh well, still it's lonesome.) Yes, I miss you - quite a bit, too. Everything else –down there–I miss the Baby, the apartment, the Parkers, the bayou, the Cypress trees, moss and nice low flat swampy land.

However, as of tonight, I refuse to be lonesome–anyway–to think about it.

Should I start with this–hole–?

Hilly country, town smaller than Walnut Ridge (Nashville 18 miles) B-24s overhead that ROAR instead of singing, post spread over hell and creation–Flight Line about one and a half miles from BOQ and we're to be titled, "Student Officers"–a name which, as used at Selman, stinks! Stinks mainly because of the dirty reputation they've carved for themselves down there, due to bellyaching and knuckle-headedness.

Look at me now! The only officer on the post from Selman Field! That "without delay" business I must have taken too seriously–layover in Memphis from 1230 to 2300–so I took a plane! Arrived at Nashville–Bus's on strike! Evidently Greyhounds were still running but way behind schedule. Finally one comes over the hill, I wave, he stops immediately–still a forth of a mile down the road broke down! So I hitch-hike–more or less (No thumbing–just a pleading look.) Finally the road off the highway to the post arrives–I get out–and walk and walk –and walk–and still I walk. Smyrna arrives–all three blocks, two groceries (one nice one) and a barbershop. Smyrna retreats into the background. I walk, I walk–meeting plenty of the cleanest bunch of enlisted men I've ever seen–while officers drove past going to the Field. I walk–get a ride the last mile–civil-

ian! Get out to the post–I walk, I walk, I walk all the way across I walk (spread much larger than Selman.) Sign in at Hdqt's–only Selman name on the list! They suggested I WALK back across the post to flight line to get assignment to Sqdn.–oh, no–I phoned–no one there–so eat–walk halfway across to the PX–back again and here I be. See why Student Officers get so much of a bad rep. for bellyaching?

No idea as to set up yet. One group of new officers stayed one and a half days the first of the week (Maybe we're replacing them.) Some stay only six weeks–some indefinitely as instructors. From where I sit, good! I'll check out night–day–instrument and formation–yep, glad to, however, I won't like it. (I don't think so, anyway) so at last–awakening from at least nine months of being a stupor-man. Watch the prop wash now –all cylinders cleared, mags checked, raring to go–so now for destination and route. Unless they have already chosen our destinies–AAAFIS (After Army Air Forces Instructors School) then there's going to be some fast and furious digging going on for ATC, Long Beach, Calif. Starting early in the coming week; timed–Please!–I hope to come off the day I get out of here–please –I hope. Pardon the prisoner's outlook but–more than ever I want to be alone–or almost so, no matter if it's a huge ship–or just a tiny one–the fewer men on board–the better it's going to be–and 10 men are 8 and a half too many!

So saying–with "I" as the subject of every sentence–wait-out:

Until further information is gathered,
Keep me informed as to: You, the Boy, the car, etc.

For luck, keep mum on the ATC and plans.

I love you,
Jack

[Editor's note: This letter was sent to Monroe. As I had already left Louisiana, it had to be forwarded to California.]

Smynra Army Air Field, Tennessee

April 5, 1944
AAFIS (4-E)
Student Off. Det.
Box 422
Smyrna, Tenn.

My Dear Young Lady,

Here it is five days later and still not too much going on. Things are a little more near normal–though I'll never get used to missing you. Seems as if we almost took a vacation between cadet days and now. Things are much more lax than they were as cadets, however we're in individual barracks rooms. Ground school, links, PT and flying–all on schedule.

So far there is no indication as to where we go from here–except that being assigned as instructors is a pretty remote possibility. From all appearances we will be especially trained for a specific duty or mission–what ever it's going to be. Maybe a special group for Tokyo even–however, that's a wild rumor. Since we are a special group–it won't be so bad if I go over with it. Still trying for ATC though. Put in a request to Col. Holland this morning to see if he will have the time and be in a position to help me.

The course here is to be finished April 9th if everything is according to schedule. In that time we have to master a complete course that ordinarily consists of 9 or 10 weeks training. Apparently we'll be able to get through easily enough–unless things begin rushing along much faster than they are now. However we will have to get 15 hours of link, which smells sweetly of night fighters! (a guess, again) Ordinarily 15 hours would stretch over 6 to 8 months.

Training has started. We're not only taking a course in Navigation (drift meters, stars and all) but also are learning to operate two different types of bombsights. Sounds rough–yet it is actually interesting.

The food is good–service terrible, however the BOQ faces*

the club where most of us spend our time writing. Low ceilings, overstuffed chairs, and a large fireplace help a lot in making us comfortable.

Maybe you are through packing by this time and ready to shove. Be a good girl and in the meantime inform all old acquaintances that things don't look too bad–so far we haven't been told to keep quiet about our training, however maybe that's because we won't be a special assignment after all. We've even been assigned a class number 44.4 W Special–whatever that might mean.

The rumors as to what when and where would fill a book–still they keep a good fast conversation running. We may even be taking a cut down preliminary course to B-29s. The persons selected for the training have nothing that would indicate why they were selected–except that possibly the very large majority or entire group are almost total abstainers and pretty well settled down in other ways–which goes to prove–what?

Keep me posted as to all personal current events from Washington to California. When further information is available - Strickland will furnish it.

Lots of love to you and #3
Jack

P.S. We wuz shanghaied and should be spoken of as "That Shanghaied Bunch."

[Editor's note: BOQ stands for Bachelor Officers' Quarters.]

Smyrna Army Air Field, Tennessee

April 11, 1944
AAFIS (4E)
Student Off. Det.
Box 422
Smyrna, Tenn.

Dear You,

What's wrong, first you keep me posted pretty closely on the whys and wherefores of what's going on–then no news for a week. Don't you think I'm interested or is this business of moving proving more difficult than you expected? Come on, Miss, give!

You wouldn't be trying to kid me about the Boy cutting teeth, would you? Three teeth all at once–just like that! Good thing I got these good shoes out of the way in time.

What happened with the car? Just about the time you passed Fort Worth it struck me that you were going to have trouble with the tires. Especially so when I thought of the changes in temperature you had ahead of you. Bang!! Don't tell me. The spare seemed to have a slight leak and I'd never gotten around to having it looked at–in fact I had let some of the air out to relieve any excess pressure. Such a comfortable car, too! Now I realize that more than likely I wouldn't be able to use it for quite some time and just about now is probably about the last days they will bring such high prices.

The folks at home are keeping me pretty well informed with general information. So far the weather in Washington has been cold–a heavy snow last week–slush the next day. Here in this–place–we've had a front pass over every day–sunny mornings–rainy, foggy middies, nice clear sunsets and nights. This morning (and all day) we've been waltzing to the tune of extra undershirts, short coats and gloves! Yesterday I sweated until my beard was twice as heavy as usual by suppertime.

Speaking of supper–no reflections now–but I think I'm beginning to put on a little (very little) weight. Slushy meals–regularity will do that apparently.

Looks as if we've hit some sort of Jackpot in this Smyrna deal. I've developed even more misgivings on how this 24 is going to satisfy us. Talk about a barge–this is it. Still there are some very encouraging rumors–and statements floating around. There are quite a few Majors in our group (44.4W Special) that weren't shanghaied! They volunteered. One of the Majors is from Maxwell Field Hdqtrs. He says–quote "This is to be one of the best deals in the war–we're darn lucky to be in it." She's still one hellofa handful–and talk about technicalities! We're learning her from paint to type of powder in the ammunition. There's a General's son on this deal that was assigned at his father's request. So what, so when, so where and into what do we go from here? I still think this is training for a newer type ship–BUT WHAT???

The 24 is full of about everything imaginable. The hydraulic and electrical system is so big and elaborate that it would easily outfit a good size house with plumbing and wiring. Row on row of pipes, relief valves, strainers, accumulators, pumps, star valves, to say nothing of alternate methods of getting them to operate whenever trouble develops–this we gotta know from stem to stern.

Emergency procedures–you bet–landing with 1, 2 - 3 engines out–sometimes both on one side. That means that just as you get close to the ground for an emergency landing - you've got to go around again–working like––to get flaps and undercarriage up–barely keeping speed enough to stay in the air. To hold her on two engines takes more than muscles–will power comes in, too.

Last week I dropped a line to Col. Holland and as yet haven't received an answer. Looks like the mail is tied up somewhere. Should this deal out of here be in planes that don't fly (this doesn't) then anything will do. 38's - 20's - 25's. I'll even gladly take the B-26. Sitting here, hands tied - no way of completing plans–gets you down. There's bound to be a fork in the road–but for once it's impossible to see that far ahead and decide–which.

So far there's been no news from down Monroe way–guess I'll have to lead off though if I expect to get any.

Did you send the radio, etc.? If so–good–if not, good. Those whetstones would come in mighty handy in case we have to pack up. How about letting me know if they're packed away–so I'll know whether to get others. Do you remember the moccasin-toed rubber soled shoes I had–big thick red rubber soles–could use them in this mud–it matches. They're probably stored, too so don't worry about it if they are.

I have a small picture of you (in the plastic envelope.) How about another, though and that case that Mr. Murray gave me–whatcha trying to do, pull a fast one? Tell everyone something like Hello for me–and tell me more.

1-X and 8

Be seeing you
Love,
Jack

Smyrna Army Air Field, Tennessee

April 17, 1944

Dear Lady,

Looks like things get sorta tangled occasionally. I'm sorry I couldn't understand you this morning. The connection was bad, evidently. On top of that, I'd run over from the mess hall and maybe my ears were pounding a little.

From what you say, looks like California is a right nice place, at that. The new modern homes must be something like the newer towns of Texas–up to date, eager and alive. Tell the local Chamber of Commerce to improve on those phone connections, though. The weather down that way is quite an interesting arrangement. The meteorology class here is darn good–one instructor in particular knows his business. Now that we've polished up on weather in general, we're branching out into worldwide weather conditions–why what happens, when and where. Darned interesting, too.

There's a pretty good creek two blocks from the BOQ; for once I don't have any rods along–darn-it!! The little emergency pocket kit I made up last summer is going to work over time, though– if I can find a suitable pole. Possibly I'll write Mr. Parker to send me the fly rod. That's not a cheap one and I hope the extra tip is still lying around. Now if you'll bring the paddle on up I've got a nice little job all picked out for you. No moss or Cyprus trees around but you can help catch fish to make up for that.

Lately there's been a slight change hereabouts. Things have straightened out considerably in regards to what I intend doing from here on–and after the war. The Army holds you back too much, almost takes every bit of initiative away. This business of having to wait for an outcome before you're able to plan anything, is hell. Maybe there'll be a chance to get a lighter ship–unless it turns out we're headed ATC way, anyway. Small chance, though. There have been too many eliminated from the group already–we're below the desired number. More than likely there will still be a chance to refuse the B-24 for combat–I'm counting on it anyway.

Saturday night I called Mom and everything is O.K. at home. Doris' birthday was Saturday and I forgot–as usual. Since she and Harold were up at the Clark's at a party I went on and called–don't hit me!! Harold's voice has changed again and believe it or not, I've never heard anyone with his tone and enunciation, you could listen for hours. Besides that he's over his shyness–sounds more like a man. What's more he is a man, now and is heavier than me by almost ten pounds. Mom says his chest has filled out until it almost takes him away from the slender side. Some guy, I bet!! She wrote me Saturday and bragged again–not on we-uns–but on you. What have you been up to, young Lady, sending candy or something? Maybe you deserve a little bragging about, though–still sticking by after these years with me. Some times I wish you had been able to come here, no go, though–it would have been pretty bad, what with the boy to look after, stuck way out here and probably no chance I could see you even once a week. Now, should I get out that way, things would certainly be O.K. again. Now that the time has come for me to do something–well, I'd feel much better all around to go ahead, then get back in a year or so and start things off on a good foundation.

There's a hellofa lot to be thankful for and it's all worth fighting for. Yep, should it be that way, it's worth dying for just to keep it the same for the boy and on down the line. Just to make sure I'm getting my money's worth, it would be better if there were another somewhat like him–or don't you think so?

Every rock, tree, swamp and mountain should be kept American, no matter what the price. That's the only way it can be and I'm mighty glad there are plenty others who feel the same.

By the way, Miss, be sure to keep me posted on what's happening to the car and when. That's quite a distance for Mr. Murray to be traveling just to do us a favor. Just what's missing on it now? Possibly a deal could be made with the person with whom the car is stored. Those prices you quoted sound a little high to me- no matter what section of the country you're in; not knowing definitely about such things, I can't be sure.

That Jack Daniels deal I spoke of was pretty raw all around. Jack Daniels #7 is a straight whiskey sold (so far) south of Vir-

ginia and Kentucky only. The distillery license number is US#1, so it's the oldest licensed distillery in the country. The whiskey itself used to be just as pure and smooth as honey. The boys here had been bragging about Canadian Club and other such, which ordinarily don't throw a glimmer on Jack Daniels. Well, anyway to prove my point, I decided to get some and prove it first hand. Just about the time we were going to give up on any kind of whiskey, we found a dealer–with whom you could name your brand–he had it. He had it, all right–this stuff we got tastes like a mixture of hard vinegar, tabasco and anti-freeze!! So-o-o I wrote the distillery the facts, offering to send the full quart to them for analyzing and the name of the dealer if it had been tampered with. Maybe they'll either send me the real stuff or tell me where I can get one quart more to keep for the celebration due in two or three years.

What do you hear from the Parkers, etc.? You know, that isn't such bad country and climate down that way. Nothing but the politics really smells. Maybe if we could live there for say 10 years, learn to harmonize on guitars or something, then maybe we'd be the first governor and governess to win the election together. Start practicing any way and we'll see how things shape up. If things worked out, we could buy a motorboat that would go 30 miles per hour and beat James K. Long at the same time. You wouldn't have to paddle then, so we'd both be improving ourselves.

Maybe I'll be able to give you a ring the latter part of the week–especially if you could shift the call to the corner drug store before you accepted it. Could be the entire system, though, and we'd lose out there, too.

Well, anyway–be seeing you. Give everybody my hello and tell them I said Love. Switch that sentence after that with one third love on the left and two-thirds on the right. You be my right hand gal and let J.M.S., Jr. take care of the rest. Get that taken care of, then let me hear from Mr. Murray, Mrs., little, by and in-laws.

P.S. I love you
Jack

[Editor's note: While we were in Louisiana a campaign for governor took place. Coming from D.C. we were naturally interested in politics and listened to the campaign on the radio.

To our amazement, one candidate would get on the air and make the most outlandish promises I'd ever heard. He would say, "Elect me and I'll see that roads are built through every bayou right up to your door." and so on, and so on.

The other candidate, Jimmy Davis, would come on the radio and say, "I ain't gonna make y'all no promises. You know and I know the best man's gonna win. I'm just gonna sing you a little song I wrote." Then he'd tune up his guitar and sing, "You are my sunshine, my only, only sunshine, etc." I never heard him discuss anything political. He won the election!!

Both were very astute, intelligent men, but, as we all know, politicians gear their rhetoric to garner as many votes as they can from their constituents. I cannot, for the life of me, remember what Jack's reference to the 30 mile per hour speedboat was all about-but I'm sure I knew at the time.]

Smyrna Army Air Field, Tennessee

April 20, 1944

Dear Miss,

Busy, huh? Must be a lot going on out there, a lot more interesting than some places anyway.

No news as yet–except for one or two facts that are seed for good rumors. May 1st, huh–well, that isn't so certain after all! Soon as we finish the flying course and link, out we go! That means that more than likely a little over a week will see most of us through. Then there's the fact that we'll be sent out to wherever–and as we finish up flying–not as a group. That goes whether we've completed the ground courses or not. For two days I stayed on the ground because of my cold. There are others that haven't the time I've gotten so far–at that.

Let's you and I forget about the fishing business–time won't allow it. Good fishing, though–and fast!

You hear Kay Keyser now? He's on the radio and I was just thinking about his homecoming in Rocky Mount that you and I went to. Quite a while back, eh what?

So far I haven't heard from Col. Holland and regret writing him while his condition was critical. The B-24 still grinds away, for it's purpose she's O.K.

Still grates and grinds on me from head to toe, flies like an overloaded streetcar, if that well.

Maybe if I can get my travel voucher cashed–I'll be able to call you soon–until then that's about all.

Be seeing you,
Love and then some
Jack

Smyrna Army Air Field, Tennessee

April 25, 1944
Student Off. Det.
Box 422

Well, Young Woman,

No letter today. More mail out than I've had before–at one time. Looks like I'm gonna have to find someone who'll answer these things! No news in well over a week, no radio, no clock, no nothing. Nashville, here I come.

The B-24 is a little more familiar now–O.K. as a means of hauling but definitely out as a combat ship. We've absorbed more about this ship than any other single object–vaccinations included. Formation is heavy toil–and yet it is almost as much fun as the BT. The only phase of flying this here thing that comes natural. 'Twon't be long now before we finish the flying course–then what kind of a pit are we to be thrown in on the other side?

The whole bunch of us are rapidly turning into a slapstick brotherhood. Being shanghaied, we've acquired a "go to blazes" attitude to keep up morales. Lately they've been holding gripe sessions in my room–with anything going–basically I guess we're nuts.

Today my appendix very gently complained again. So far it's nothing serious, so don't worry (in case you might.)

Will you write the Saturday Evening Post and transfer the subscription out there? By the time I get it I've read everything in it and those continued stories keep you guessing too much.

Guess I'd better relax now–so, Be seeing you. Scare #3 once for me and ask him for a kiss. Until next time–no love–no nothing.

Jack

Smyrna Army Air Field, Tennessee

May 1, 1944

Dear Miss,

Your letters have been coming through pretty regularly lately, though it takes air mail about three days. That letter I wrote was the direct product of many things both good and bad. Such a mixture of occurrences is going on that it's hard to keep a clear head. Now I know that you've been writing and the day I mailed that complaining letter–yours came and turned out to be the nicest I've received from you–bar none.

This is the last sheet–last envelope, so don't be surprised if the last sentence is unfinished.

Col. Holland told Harp he would personally try to get me into ATC as soon as he's able to leave his bed. Not for my sake but I hope that will be soon. I finally went to see the CO of my squadron to see what the possibilities are of transferring to ATC out there. The Major is pretty young and consequently impulsive–and wanted to argue instead of advise–so-o since there were other high ranks in the room–I choose to drop the subject–for the present, at least–then the Major–out of a blue sky says, "You're just afraid to go into combat." That's one score that isn't settled as yet. The only thing I could do there was to tell him that if that were the case–instead of trying to continue flying–I'd try getting a desk job as he had–if I was afraid of flying. Naturally that ended all discussion either way. Next I went to Col. Kane here–and who is sitting in the front office but the Major - the Col. busy and a conference to be held (already scheduled) as soon as he was through. Three times I've been to see him since and not once has he been in his office–so maybe it was meant to be this way and luck will stay with me (Knock-knock) through this into something even better than ATC. One more try, though, or at least until I see the Col. In the meantime things are drawing to a close here–and still we don't know WHAT.

Those four leaf clovers you keep sending–now, Miss, the first batch I put in my wallet–the second and third, I ate to keep from wasting them, the physic did me good–but, please, how about one at a time?

Behind in my writing to Mom, Milton, Harold and the Stricklands.

Swat the boy for me and tell him to be good and toughen up.

Lots of Love
Jack

Guess this is pretty dull reading but there is really no news floating around. Next time I go for a walk in these hills–I'll see what can be done.

Say again–I love you–Jack

Smyrna Air Field, Tennessee

May 4, 1944

Dear Miss,

Trying to get me excited? Calling in the middle of the day, still it seems to be much easier to get the call through at that time. Here you've been in the Army two years and still get crazy ideas about overseas. It would be sort of hard to be here one minute and over there the next. How else could it be done so I wouldn't have time to let you know?

The same old grind, everything pretty well lined up–and still they keep holding back on my check ride (Instruments and proficiency.) With those over I'd have plenty of time to get my clothes cleaned and pressed, another pair of shoes and some summer uniforms. The change from OD's to Suntans has already come off and me still in OD's.

The destinations from here indicate either Lincoln, Nebraska or Westover Field, Mass. where we'll probably be given equipment, classified, etc.–maybe given ships and crews–and then to final training phase of 10-15 weeks. 'Tis said that during that period we'll have one day in 10 off the post. Still rumoring (pretty authentic, though) if it's Westover, the training area will probably be S.C. or Ga. In the case of Nebraska–training out in that general direction–Washington State, Utah or some such. That I'll have to let you know when I do. The old wanting out of 24's is building up again–not much possibility of shifting now, though–except to ATC. Man, those light low flying ships really look like the answer to a prayer about now. Still might as well go ahead–get in–get out–get back and get settled. The war and these heavy ships are beginning to get on a person's nerves.

Still have the desire for further education and a job with Biological Survey or Fish and Wildlife - or else Veterinarian–but one thing is certain–what is to really count is that we're happy at it–completely–and living comfortably, at least. Give Jack, Jr. a good background and education - that completes it. Should farming be the only thing that makes us as happy–then it'll be farming. Should selling light planes, or anything for that mat-

ter–fill the bill–then that's what the job will be. I'm getting pretty fed up with having a job that is so exacting and demanding with no space for initiative.

Once more I would like to ask for the thick rubber soled shoes and the whetstones–if they are available. However if they're not available now–let me know and I'll get others–or maybe I'd best do that anyway. O.K. forget about the whetstones. Should we get a chance to get together, please bring the rod and reel and a few baits–the plunker, the pikie, perch finish, the little white plug, the green jitterbug, shimmy wiggler (white and red) the brown and white hair bait and that should be enough.

Harold is at Fort Meade again (where he started) and is in a replacement group–subject at any time.

No news other than that from home–and around here it still stinks–except for Tennessee which is just as pretty a countryside–or should I say, beautiful–as I've seen. So far I don't know anything about ANY of the natives except that some of the women are–ladies–which is becoming a very, very rare species. Not speaking from personal experience now–simply from observations! My first impression of the terrain was red gullies and mud. Now it's the dark green of the cedars through light green of the other trees, no pines. There are more wild flowers and birds to watch than I've seen anywhere–at any one time. This business of liking Nature is turning into a mania–which must prove the fact that I'm a little off–somewhere.

Art telegraphed this afternoon (I started this letter in the morning) and says he'll be here Saturday morning. He's expecting to be inducted at any time–already passed the exams. Maybe he'll have a good time down here–and maybe not–I hope so anyway. Nothing to do but show him the post and take him to classes–and technical demonstrations of technical stuff (he's qualified.) It's so arranged now that he can stay right here in my room (not regulation) but possible. Funny that I'm able to keep him here–but not you–or is it?

The cake you're sending has me suspended, so reach in and give it another shove.

Hold the line for further developments and let's get together.

Love

Jack (Lt. J. M. Strickland)

Chapter Twelve

Savannah

Jack was ordered to Westover Field, Mass. (as luck would have it). No ATC–no small planes!!

When I heard this I knew that although I couldn't be with him in Mass. I could at least be closer to him if I were on the East Coast. So I left my parents in San Fernando Valley and "the boy" and I flew back to Washington, D.C.

(My parents lasted out there a little longer. Then they sold their house and moved back East. They rented an apartment in Takoma Park, MD, another suburb of D.C).

I found a place to live right around the corner from the house in which I grew up. It consisted of one very large room in a private home and I had cooking privileges.

Jack's training lasted several more weeks. Then he was sent to Hunter Field in Savannah, GA. Blanche was quite willing to baby sit (Lucky me!) so I was able to make a few trips to Savannah. On one of the trips Jack met my train and had two tickets on the last bus that was going to Savannah Beach that day. He wanted to show me the elegant hotel that was there. It was even prettier than he had described. There was one hitch, though–he had forgotten to make reservations and we were told there were positively no rooms available. We were in a quandary as the bus had left by then and there was no transportation back to Savannah. We stood in the lobby, trying to figure out what to do. Jack said we could sleep on the beach. I was game for that but expressed my qualms about sharing the beach with sand fleas. (I've always been one of those persons that bugs adore. They ignore everyone else around and feast on me.) The desk clerk must have been listening to our conversation. He asked us to wait a minute while he made a phone call. He came back and explained that the hotel had a large suite that they kept reserved for the Governor. He said he had checked and the Governor wasn't going to be there that night and we could use it. We had never seen anything so luxurious. It had windows on three sides of this spacious room and a spectacular view of the beautiful beach. I don't know whether or not there were other hotels there in those days but there were none that we could see. It was as though we were in an isolated corner of Paradise.

We went back to Savannah the next day and I met Jack's B-24 crew for the first time. They were the nicest group of guys you could imagine. They thought Jack was wonderful. One of the most outstanding was Bernard Sugarman from New York. "Sugar" was the navigator. He was tall and thin, sort of shy, and had the brightest smile you ever saw. Jack speaks of him in "the letters."

Around that time I had been doing a lot of thinking. Since Jack had mentioned in one of his letters from Smyrna, the possibility of having another child, I took that as encouragement and started campaigning for another baby. Again Jack felt that if anything were to happen to him, he would not want to leave me with *two* children to raise alone. I argued that I didn't want an "only" child, as I knew I would probably spoil him. I also wanted two children close in age so they could be companions for one another. It wasn't as difficult to convince him this time.

Jack and crew left Savannah for New York where they waited to get their orders to go overseas. The rumors about their date of sailing were rampant. Whenever Jack was pretty certain that it wasn't going to happen the next day, he would call me and I would get the first train I could to New York. We would have a day or two together and I would return home. This happened a few times. By agreement Jack and I had never said "Goodbye" to one another, however I remember four or five heart-wrenching *"I'll be seeing you"*s before he finally left for Europe.

The troops were being sent over on ocean liners. Jack and his crew sailed on the *Ile de France.*

[Letter from Jack to Crew just before they left for England]

Well, you guys,

Looks like the time is just around the corner when we're going to cease being just a crew in training.

Guess you all are just as fed up as I am with training, day in –day out. We've all done our share of griping in the army and we will probably do a lot more before it's over. Let's get one thing straight now, though. Tomorrow we're going to be dodging the same bullets, eating the same food, getting the same amount of sleep when we can. Tomorrow we cease being individuals. We will be a team in the army, fighting the same fight, griping the same gripes and looking forward to getting home with the same feeling of being fed up with all this. One thing stands out, though, we're still in the army with an assigned job to be done. That particular job calls for all out cooperation between each and every one of us. Tomorrow those who still have the idea of getting through this thing the easiest possible way, well, those that STILL have that idea are letting the rest down. Not only are you putting a harder job on someone else's shoulders–you're selling them down the river. Worse even than showing up with a solid yellow streak down your back. Believe me, brother, you're going to be treated as such if that's the case.

Lately there's been quite a lot of bitching (you're in the army, now.) First, it's flying too much–secondly, it's getting up too early and lately it's paying too much attention to how much work the other guy is doing and forgetting your own.

Most of us have already buckled down, gotten the harness as comfortable as possible and started the load rolling toward the other end. The road is long, maybe around the world––one thing is certain, though–at the end is home–bright and shining.

To those guys on this crew who still think they're in the army just because it's the only place to wait out the war–I've got something special to say.

Every one of us has had a certain amount of specialized training, some have worked at it, learned it–and possibly have done even better at it than was expected of them. Those are the ones that realize there's a war going on and that someone's going to get hurt. They're the ones that have done their best all the way and intend doing the same the rest of the way. To their comrades in arms, they are insurance–not only life insurance but insurance that this thing will be ended as soon as they have dragged the load home–right up to the front door.

The others are parasites, hanging on–dragged through by others. They're the ones who have time to really bitch in earnest. They are the ones who are going to regret it the rest of their lives. Their time is a little more limited than the rest–but on a crew like this, they are putting a time limit on the other guys.

Before I finish this little "sermon" there is one more subject I would like to cover; leaves and furloughs. Naturally all of us expect a little time off now and then. For a awhile it looked as if we might get home and see the folks before we were called to do the job we have been training for. Now that the time is close at hand, maybe we won't get that chance. You are a man now and above all else you're supposed to be soldiers. Starting right now, let's be just that. Being above average intelligence, we should realize it's up to us to do our duty as such and do it to the best of our ability. That way we will get this thing over much quicker and much easier.

Maybe some of us haven't stopped to think what we're fighting for, at any rate there are still a few left in the crew that show signs of selfish ideas about how the war is to be won. The idea that the other guys have done a pretty good job up until now, so why not let them finish it–is out. They will find in a very short while that they're OUT, too, so far as the rest are concerned.

Think it over, soldier, or else you'll be calling me chicken. From now on I'm in deadly earnest, I expect the same of each and every one of you.

Let's hope that when we drop the harness and look around us at the guys that were in step beside us, we'll have the satisfaction of a job well done. You'll know that you won't have to lie the rest of your lives when you tell your children how we won the war.

Lt. J. M. Strickland
(Pilot)

Jack (standing far right) and crew in Savannah, Ga.

Jack and Bernie Sugarman in N.Y.

England

Sept. 16, 1944

Dear You,

Greetings and such. What have you been doing today? Nothing much, huh, just piddling around. Wish that was the way everybody was spending their time these days, no matter how much they griped about it.

We've been on the water for quite some time now and apparently it will take a few more days at the rate we're going. Not the same as in peace time–however don't even try to get me to take another such ride on any boat–unless there's land somewhere right close. Seems I just don't belong in places where there are no trees, earth and the things that go with them.

The weather has been OK so far, although some of the guys were slightly sick the first day out. Nothing but water all around. Sometimes it's fairly smooth in a choppy sort of way and then again there are white caps. Cloudy days it's a deep blue, clear days a pretty some sort of blue. When the waves break it's green and you can see through the tops down to the foam underneath which has been rolled under. Now and then a few flying fish shoot out of the oncoming ship's wake and go darting ahead over the water like little silver darts. There are still a couple of birds following–day in and day out–however they stay off to one side and so low to the water you can't recognize or even distinguish any identifying marks. Once there were porpoises–or else a whale–following parallel–at any rate it was alive.

Since this is a one sided conversation, I'll just rattle on.

Nothing to do–read–loll around and wait to eat. Two meals a day–English style food–yipes. First, breakfast, a slab of fish and liver–every meal whether breakfast or supper has–fish–good enough, but by the time we get there everyone will have had his fill of fish and then some.

We've been getting daily reports on the news but somehow they don't tie in together, so maybe things will surprise us when we dock. They turn on the P.A. system once or twice a day and tune in a radio to a commentator who is invariably English so no one can make heads or tails of his words or phrases. They always give it up as a bad job and click it off. Usually everyone joins in with some such ditty as Rinso White, Rinso White! When he goes off you can hear it ringing up and down the passageways.

So far the enlisted men have given me no trouble - assigning duties or details to the officers usually ends up in a near brawl before everything gets under way.

I can readily understand how and why a person gets to be known as a "chicken." I was trying to keep away from that and because we knew we were going over, I overlooked a few laxities among both the enlisted men and the officers. Consequently now that there is little I can do in the way of punishment or restrictions, some of the guys get pretty "bitchy." They're always the newly commissioned, though, and as a rule the older guys jump on them before I do.

Only one real argument so far and that was with a guy not on my crew. For the first time in a long while I darn near lost my temper completely - guess my hands must have been twitching - twice I had the impulse to grab him and have a good old fashioned free-for-all. Both times, for some reason I stopped the impulse. Finally in the course of the argument he said he didn't like me. It was so simple and childish that from that second on I wasn't the least bit mad–figure it out–I can't.

We've seen a couple of movies so far. "Hellzapoppin" and "Alexander Graham Bell." One corny USO show that couldn't have got on the stage at the Seco, although the 'wenches' in it have kept most of the guys looking forward to a word or two–especially the acrobatic one. Then there are a few, 4-5, who are civilians, why I don't know. One makes Miss Aud look like a bathing beauty and yet she must be having the time of her life, what with the ground forces, sea forces and some air forces with nothing to do but sleep and wander around, eat and wander around some more.

Until now I haven't bothered to write because there's been nothing, absolutely nothing of interest to a fountain pen and paper.

Maybe if there is any way of contacting "Harp" or Harold, we can write you a few joint letters. However, that's to come in the future.

Be seeing you–Love–say it out loud.

LOVE,

Jack

Harvey Holland and Jack's brother, Harold, had preceded Jack to England.

Harold was three years younger than Jack. He was a sweet, shy, gentle boy. When he joined the Infantry, we were all aghast and worried about him. He was the kind of fellow who wouldn't hurt a fly and we couldn't picture him as a fighting Infantryman. He signed up with the 30th Division (Old Hickory) which had originated in the South. He was a PFC in the 119th Regiment. He never qualified on the range with a rifle. When he was ordered to the front he told his commanding officer about this. The officer said, "That's O.K. We'll find something for you to do–like drive a jeep." He arrived in France in time to participate in the Normandy Invasion on D-Day, June 6, 1944. Later Harold was awarded the Bronze Star for action in Holland on September 15, 1944.

Harvey had enlisted in the Army in Aug. '42. He had been given the rank of Corporal. He continued to go to the U. of Md. and one of his duties there was to instruct older non-coms in the use of weapons.

He graduated from college in the fall of 1943 and was immediately accepted into Officer Candidate School at Fort Benning, GA. He got his commission as 2nd Lieutenant, Army Infantry, April 12, 1944. From there he was sent to Little Rock, Ark., to train Infantry troops.

On August 3rd he was sent to the E.T.O. on one of the ocean liners which were being used to transport troops across the Atlantic. He spent two months in Salisbury, England, training troops.

In October he was sent to France as a "replacement combat officer."

Jack did not get to see either Harp or Harold in England before they left England.

Harold with jeep

Harold Strickland in France

Sept. 20, 1944

Back again,

Same news as always which is nil–of course. Just happened to look out the window and there's the new moon. Sort of faint on account of early evening mists but she was there anyway - gone now. Same old moon you'll be looking upon about this time.

We're finally in England and she isn't such a bad place as rumored. Though we haven't been circulating as yet - the countryside is one of the most interesting and refreshing pieces of scenery I've laid eyes upon. Everything is very neat and clean, the stock in the farms appear to be mostly blooded stuff and well fed. The fields are neatly kept and I've seen more than one woman working along side the men–what few there are. They're not there for looks either–doing just as much of the actual hard labor as the men. When a woman helps load grain shocks on a wagon–using long handle pitchforks–that woman is doing a man's job in no small way.

There is a rumor that the towns have very few people about the streets–so I guess it will be a change from the "old country." Should the people turn out to be a little cold and aloof I can readily see why. They've been through more hell than can be described in words. Rationing is still about three times worse than it ever was in the States. Clothing is well worn - patched here and there and for every day business wear the shoes have hobnails in the soles. That was a Scotsman, though, so maybe that isn't the rule in England. Personally I don't enjoy being around most American soldiers and officers when they are off duty. There's too much loud and big mouth talk and within the past ten years there's been a noticeable increase in the extremely vulgar words in use on the streets and in public. Sounds like I'll be a preacher yet–eh what? No, just always has rubbed me the wrong way and among these people over here I can readily understand why they don't personally greet the U.S. soldiers with open arms on sight. The people who have waved at us don't just wave with a sweep of the arm like Americans. Men, women and children stop whatever they're doing and put their hearts and souls in it. They wave until you pass out of sight and it makes you believe they're sincere, as well as friendly, in their own way. Maybe if Harold had been stationed in Britain long enough to have taken time to make friends–and I believe you would have to take time–then maybe he would have liked it better. Maybe I'm jumping to conclusions, too, but from observations they are very helpful and courteous in every way except in striking up conversation–and since Americans try to force conversation along with good old American familiarity, the people present a contrast in their own reserved way.

Back to the hobnails. The country is so darn beautiful that I can't understand why so many Scotch and Irish left here. The typical picture of a Scottish cottage is exactly expressive of that landscape. They're usually built right with the ground, conforming to it–just as much a part of nature as an oak tree. They're brick-brown–or stone and whitewashed, usually half way up a hillside with cattle grazing right up to the door. Rarely any steps–maybe one step up from the ground. The grass grows naturally right up to the stones of the building. There are always plenty of bright flowers–well cultivated in window boxes or close by the houses–let's call them HOMES. The larger farmhouses are usually hidden on a rolling hill surrounded by huge trees, and barns, too, for that matter. The fences are mostly wooden-rail type–and all the roads are like narrow country lanes –though they're in good condition, usually asphalt. The little cottages are always sitting alone–aloof from each other. Though they must be hundreds of years old they are kept so well that you would swear they are new. Since the style doesn't grow old it's impossible to make certain whether they are new or old. Here's hoping (very much) that I get the chance to spend a day or so around such places. From all appearances we'll either not be here or else not get enough time off to travel that far. Even the barns are so well made and kept that they put the American farm home to shame. Then there's still another surprise, game –wild life. They say rabbits know all about arithmetic–come over here and you'll see why. In broad daylight it's no more unusual to see a rabbit, or rabbits, sitting out in the open pas-

tures than it is to see a bird fly by. In two different fields, though I didn't have time to count, they were grouped in open pastures–not too far from brush–in bunches of well over 20. Saw three full-grown pheasants and a pretty good size covey of the fattest quail I've seen–outside of eastern North Carolina.

Saw one Scotsman with a fly rod–and judging from the streams –it must necessitate learning that art and developing it to a very high degree. You'd really have to use Indian tactics to get close enough to the clear stream and throw the hook in.

So saying, guess that about sums things up. I don't think I've stepped out of bounds–considering you know where I am– or the country anyway.

Seeing as how everyone is arguing - and I can't think straight with all this going on–Well–Be seeing you.

Wish I could tell you I love you–just as easily–and as often as I think it.

Jack

Sept. 21, 1944

Good morning, Miss,

How are you feeling today? Running sort of low on cash this month? Let me know how the allotments work out so far as regularity is concerned. Changed apartments yet? How did Doris make out with McKeever and so forth and so on?

Got up early enough to get my name on the pass list so maybe we'll be able to see just what the English towns are like tonight or this evening. Six hours is all the time we're allowed on pass, much of that is spent walking to and from town, I understand, –however, being used to such, perhaps the time can be lessened considerably.

'Twas foggy this morning and almost chilly. Took a short stroll inside the field limits. Certainly would like to be able to legally step out of bounds onto some of the surrounding farms. This morning I got a close look at some of the work horses and have come to the conclusion that old or not, there are some things about the country that haven't been worked out through the years until the customary way is the best way–or whatever. In other words I still can't see why people will keep such huge, clumsy-footed horses on a farm when a good old mule will do the work quicker, easier and without needing a road to walk on. Judging from the size of these animals–each one must eat as much as a team of mules. However–just food for thought. Shows you just how monotonous it gets in these camps at times.

Still can't understand why people gripe so much without thinking. There was a fellow reading the bulletin board this morning–new here–and when he got to the list of off limits establishments, streets, parks, etc. you would have thought he had been ordered to eat bread and water–for weeks. First he let off the usual stream of words that mean nothing except that he must be accustomed to associating with the lowest type of humanity. Then he started saying how chicken the post must be and all the staff officers along with it. Typical!

Wonder just what expressive words he would use if he were 4-F, been unable to (or proud enough not to) buy new clothes, even though the prices were beginning to be a bit absurd. Been under a strict rationing system, working 12 hours a day and getting paid less than a private in the allied army. In this case, say he was in the U.S. and it was the English army that was over-running the country. Wonder just how much hell would be raised when he found that the British soldiers, with such high pay and low expenses, were crowding him out of the bars, hotels, theaters, etc. Well, that's just about the situation over here except for the off-limit places. Every time I think about the rationing program over here and the way the people are taking it - well, it makes the U.S. look pretty sniveling with its attitude of trying to beat the rationing and griping about it, going on strikes at the drop of a hat, etc. What's more, since being here, I can easily, very easily, count the cars (private) that I've seen. on both hands. The buses I could count on one hand. Counting cars, buses and trucks there haven't been over twenty–and we passed quite a few towns of all sizes–over 15 at least.

Maybe the difference between the attitudes of the two countries is the difference in the people. Apparently the British are fighting for a cause–and for their country. From all appearances we're fighting because we're supposed to–since our country is at war–and also because we're afraid some of our luxuries might be taken from us. In other words, the British seem to be fighting to save their country as a whole–while we're fighting as individuals for our personal reasons. On and on, however it's a darn good experience to be able to see just what the other side of the picture looks like. It makes the U.S.–other than the casualty lists–well, outside of that, I'd say she doesn't know there's a war on even yet–and should be glad of it and show it with a little more cooperation with the war effort, and a little less griping–quite a bit less.

Don't get the idea that we've been undergoing propaganda treatment–we haven't, it's just what I've noticed myself and from talking to people–usually children whenever we came in contact with them. Just from the questions they were asked and their attitude of being able to take it, without bitching–these are the reasons for this little episode.

'Nough said

Besides trying to analyze the troubles of the world, I also love you - first.

Jack

P.S. How about a batch of 6 cent airmail stamps now and then?

V-MAIL

Sept. 22, 1944

Morning, Miss,

Looks like this is going to be a long, one-sided conversation. My address pad is inside the baggage, which hasn't shown up yet, so I can't write any of the guys over here. More than likely there's at least one within hiking distance of the place. There are no large towns near enough to get to.

Last night at the "Pub" there was an English couple who suggested I visit Isaac Walton's cottage. The original burned a few years back and the present cottage is a replica. We have only 6 hour passes at a time, though, so there would be little time left by the time I reached the town near the cottage.

'Til now I haven't paused long enough to be lonesome–however I've often wished you could be here to see some of the countryside. You'd enjoy meeting some of the people, too. These walks to and from town aren't bad at all. Last night was rainy though and my consumption of bitters was a little below par, so I didn't enjoy the walk back as much as I did the first night. It's fun though, tramping through the blackness between walls of hedgerows and on back to the post. Most of the time I'm thinking of you and sometimes it's quite easy to imagine that you're within hearing. Sometimes, though, it seems as if you aren't listening. Whatca doing?

Mind if I change a few habits along about now? These people, especially the ladies, resent "Ma'am." They would rather it be either yes or no. The only time they use the word is when talking to a very elderly woman–say 80 or 90 years old.

The people are very surprised when I tell them I'm married. Seems as though, in the middle classes, people cannot afford to think of marriage until they're 25 or 30. Not until then are they able to support a wife, a flat, etc. The soldiers' pay over here is almost unreasonable. The private's wife is allowed about four and a half dollars a week. How would you make out on that? Shoes, clothing, food and candy are strictly rationed. There's no wonder that these people are amazed at the careless way we throw our pay around and I was specifically asked why the Americans were so wasteful. I couldn't give a good answer. To throw away a cigarette butt over a finger's width in length is actually considered a shame and truthfully there's no reason why it shouldn't be, is there?

Sometimes this rationing takes an odd twist. Take toilet tissue, for instance.

Last night one of the fellows waited 15 minutes to get into the john and then turned around and came back out. The guys who have been here for awhile laughed at him when he said there was no paper. Seems that there is not a public such in England with paper. There was a sergeant looking on who pulled a couple of small packages out of his pocket and presented one to Dabney. Turned out to be out of a K-ration package. There are K-rations for breakfast, dinner and supper–the supper package contains paper–foresight, eh what? I've carried corncobs–looks like I'll have to revert–only to paper this time.

There are no stockings for women over here–cotton, rayon or what have you. The town people are extremely pallid and white with no sign of make-up. The country people seem to be a bit more fortunate both ways. Even the elderly women have a little rouge or lipstick on. The younger women use Vaseline or some such on their eyelids. Definitely not mascara. You can tell that even at great distances–I know! Heh–heh.

Guess I've mentioned the following quite often, Miss, but how's our savings coming along? There is so much that can be done with them after the war. That would mean property in our hands–real estate–more or less. Looks as if maybe I'll be able to send even more money home. This month's pay is going to have to last until Oct. 31st mainly because it doesn't look like we'll put in four hours time this month. Consequently the allotment will take practically all of it. The only expense here, so far, is food and quarters and the occasional visit to the "Pub." You'd pass out on one and a half dollars' worth of "Black and Tans," etc., so that won't be any great expense.

This "Pub" business suits me to a "T", maybe because I'm a dull thud–however there's no loud and boisterous noises, no drunkenness, no blaring jukeboxes or bands. Not unlike

"Dickhaut's" back home–minus the jukeboxes and also the sandwiches (fish is the only meat that comes with a restaurant meal) eggs are–well, I haven't seen one anywhere. Well, anyway, the pubs are just nice, quiet places for the neighborhood to relax in quiet conversation or maybe a dashing game of darts.

Be seeing you. Lots of love–Lots and then some.

Jack

V-MAIL
Sept. 29, 1944

My Dear Mrs. Strickland,

Since the opening address isn't just a greeting, but a fact,–I feel better already. There's been a short interruption in my letters–and more'n likely there'll be more from time to time. That's no sign that I'm not thinking of you, though. The fact is that "just" thoughts can be pretty cruel at times, especially at the beginning of the road.

We"ve moved a bit since the last time I wrote, the first one being a pretty good one from all appearances, however this one is taking a little longer to sink in. Be sure to change my old address on your letters and tell Mom about the change while you're at it. More than likely the letters written to the present address will reach here along with your previous ones, possibly before. Repeating the address: Name, Rank, Serial number. 700 Bomb Sqn. 445 Bomb Group APO 558, c/o P.M., N.Y., N.Y.

Since we need a little rest right now, the letters might be a bit dreary, however maybe things will perk up after awhile. We've begun to taste the meaning of war, at last–and believe you me, no one over here thinks it's going to be over quite as soon as the people in the States. Here's hoping we're mistaken.

LOVE

Jack

Jack had been sent to Scotland, originally, and then was assigned to the 93rd Bomb Group at Hardwick, England. On September 27, 1944 the 445th Bomb Group from Tibenham Air Base had the highest losses ever sustained by any group in the 8th Air Force on a single mission. Their target was the Henschel engine and vehicle plant at Kassel, which was in the center of Germany near the Polish border.

They were met by a Luftwaffe "Strumgruppen"–a large pack consisting of more than one hundred heavily armed Focke-Wulfs and Messerschmitts. In a five- to six-minute time period 25 of the 35 B-24s on this mission were shot down and 5 more were damaged.

The next day the 10 B-24s that remained at the base were manned with crews and returned to Kassel and successfully bombed the plant.

Jack and his crew were among those sent to Tibenham to replace the ones who were shot down.

Oct. 2. 1944

Dear Kitty,

That's my wife, in case you're interested. But excuse all this, you see - I'm feeling slightly warm between the ears. However, here we go–I love you–now to start the rambling–however, remember I love you.

First off we're still moping around on the ground. Ground school and such which is essential regardless of whether it's interesting or not. We arrived here just as the Luftwaffe is beginning to make the newspaper reports a bunch of lies–propaganda and such. Watch the papers, Miss, and see about that. We'd have been lucky as --- if we could've been here this summer when opposition was withheld–and the missions short, fast and sweet–more or less anyway.

Don't mean to disturb, there's no need for that–the percentages show that, in figures. What's more the law of averages is in favor of this bunch here–again unless things happen the same as they do in the States.

The boys have buckled down as a whole, up to and including Laforet. I believe he's decided that the name "First Pilot" or "Crew Commander" isn't quite so highly desired as it is in the States, due to duties and such. To top that, we find a common point of mutual interest–namely the planes we HOPE to fly after this tour–providing we must continue flying.

Finally, the first impression of England has worn off. The quietness of the people and their habits become a bit boring after awhile, though I still would enjoy the pubs–I'm afraid long, drawn-out conversations would remain too literary–bookish, etc.

There's still a great difference in Scotland and England. The Scots appear to be the quiet type with a hidden charge of humor and energy that explodes regularly. The English are–the quiet type. The surrounding farms have turned out to be pretty dreary - never anything but brown stone and brick (Of course paint is extremely scarce) however the OLD paint is usually brown. The Scots go for bright spots here and there–just enough. The English viewpoint of life has changed–or at least made up–my mind. Quite definitely, conventions are out. I refuse, again, to live for my job and the money involved. If need be, we're going to have Goblins at all the windows and a hallway for P-51s to pass through, anything to get away from drabness. See how far-gone I am now? What'll I be like before it's over? Have patience, Miss. Keep your feet on solid ground–and lead me to it.

Got my first practice flight a day or so back. These old horses seem to have an extra source of energy over here. What's more, this is the one type of warfare that has moved V-Day up to a matter of years. Just something that is highly essential, but I still wish I had gone into otherwise.

I'm looking forward more each day–and there are plenty ahead - when you and I can settle down to our own way of life–when and where we please. We might piddle around a little at first but it won't be long after this is finished that we get our initial course plotted and get off to a good start. What with savings and bonds coming in at regular intervals, we should have a fairly easy time of it–more so than it might have been.

So right in the middle of all this, I guess I'd better hush up and hit the sack. The guys are hinting about the lights.

Be seeing you.

Lots of love, again.

Jack

Oct. 12, 1944

Dear Miss,

'Bout time you came over and chased this melancholy feeling away, don't you think? These nights that we have to walk over to the latrine to shave–well, the stars and clouds and the fading moon, you can guess who I'm thinking of. Romantic walk, ain't it?

Today was the day of firsts in about every way you can think of. Your first letter since the States and it was written on a young man's first birthday. Here's hoping it's the beginning of continuous mail, however it's probably a far-fetched hope–for awhile anyway.

Yesterday I had one of those pe-culiar army experiences–with a smile thrown in. During chow–it's more or less cafeteria style –except the choice–well I'm walking along holding out my plate. The K.P.s behind the counter put a slurp of something here, a slurp of something there, then slurp a big gob of slush over the whole thing which has run together anyway. Comes dessert–home canned sour cherries–not bad. Then I glance up. My eyes bulge a bit and a big burst of laughter wells up, get red in the face–finally bust out. Since I'm still holding out my plate, the K.P. says, "More?"

"No." Since my mustache is rank enough to mow off now, he didn't recognize me. (Mowing it soon as I get one snap shot) "Don't you recognize me?"

"No, SIR, I mean, Yes, SIR."

"I'm Strickland."

*"Well I'll be a #!?**+!~. What in hell are you doing here, Jack?" So we gab, hold up the line, slap each other on the back. Every time I look at the guy I bust out all over again. You know him, too. Nice looking, chunky, blond, usually a crew cut. No? Well, too bad so I'll change the subject.*

Wrote Harold and Harp yesterday. Have hopes of an answer within two weeks.

Today we ran the gamut, so far as emotions are concerned. Turned on the Bomb run–mind blank–no thoughts–then real-

ize I'm humming way back in my mind, "I love coffee, I love tea. etc." Why'n hell, I don't know. Must have been the Ink Spots I heard on a program a while ago. All this passes through my mind, then, like a dream, thoughts race, thick and fast. Pull it in closer (the formation.) Steady, now. Hell's sort of concentrated up ahead. Here we go. Guess it'll be concentrated down below now. Shame to wreck all those things down below. Hope the people get to safety. (am I soft!) There it goes–just as mean and concentrated a dose of medicine as man can make–almost. Well guess it will bring the end at least two days closer and slow up the opposition against Harold and Harp and all those guys. By this time we're getting out–fast–running, if you please. WUMP–a slight jar and we're clear. Let's head for home now - pretty chilly up here, right foot numb. Funny how the pilots sweat–wet sweat–and their feet freeze. So, turn up the electric suit–adjust the connection and gradually your feet burn a little, thaw out, feel nice and comfortable. Little shack, here we come. That bunk's going to feel good. Wish I didn't have on so darn much equipment–or else the relief tube were closer–oh well, grin and bear it–hope you can, anyway. Surprise, you didn't–I mean, you DID. Back on the ground–now for relief. Everyone chattering at once. "Hey, Skipper, did you see so and so?" (conceited, aren't I?) and now I find if I stand still my knees shake - somewhat like they do under the dinner table, except I'm standing up. Wow! Must be fatigue, eh, what?

Here we are at operations and I get a warm feeling. There's the blond guy, the aircraft mechanic on KP. The corporal's waiting–or did he just happen to be here? Funny, his squadron's operations are elsewhere. Then again, maybe I'm conceited. Makes me feel good anyhow–but how did he know I was up? We grin, swap cracks and move on. There's a lot to do yet before we eat and turn in for a long nap. The guy, in case you're interested, knows you–and I think you'll remember him. His name? Burns!–my former boss at the Goodrich Economy Store–surprised?

By the way, young lady, a few requests which I didn't expect to make–First, two or three cartridges of 20 Schick Injector blades –secondly, about half a dozen pair of those pure wool socks down at Walter Reed PX. Thirdly, 4 or 6 pen light batteries and lastly, some 6-cent airmail stamps in your letters occasionally.

That's about all for awhile. Maybe I won't need anything else that isn't readily available over here.

Let's see, something else now–what was it? Stationery, if and when, try at a stationer's. Ask for Eton's Foreign mail–which is what I'm writing on now.

'Bout time to pause awhile and get in on an argument here amongst the bunks–Wars–why?, how?, basically and such, etc. Quick switch–propaganda–I'm wound up on that so here goes, while I undress.

Be seeing you, Miss. Lots of love–full, rich,–not automatic, lean–and you can quote me.

Jack

[Editor's note: The target for the raid on Oct. 12 was Osnabruck, Germany. The target on Oct. 14th and Oct. 17th was Koln, Germany.

A quote from the *Washington Star*, Oct. 22, 1944–"In the week ending Oct. 15 there were more bombs dropped on German cities (40,000 tons) than were showered on London during the Blitz."]

Oct. 22, 1944

Dear Miss,

Hi today and what's cooking? First off–as is going to be–always–I love you. Feel sort of sharp on that subject–but on everything else at present–feel sort of dull.

We haven't been down so long and those long stretches at altitude sorta leave you fagged–if you know what I mean.

Your letters still haven't caught up so far as the new APO is concerned - however, got three today–after a long pause–and you sound a bit worried about the subject of spare time–beers, etc. Nope, not gallivanting. At that time (when I wrote about the pubs) we had little else to do and after days of doing nothing –we pubbed a bit. Been to town once in the past three weeks and, after a lousy variety show, a guy named Tex and I took a few pubs in stride while we waited a couple of hours for the trucks to come for the run back to the field. Got any suggestions what we should do at such times? The streets are so darn black that we actually had to hold on to each other. (would look peculiar if people could see us–two officers, walking with linked arms) That's the only way to keep from getting separated–unless you walk in file–each with one foot in the gutter and the other on the curb–however, that gets tiresome and if the guy in front stops, the guy in back usually knocks him down. We both fell over a low iron rail at the curb and skinned our shins. Some guy within a ten-foot radius had just rubbed noses with a lamppost. Believe it or not.

Sometimes home seems a long way off–something like a vision you've had in your mind–but never really know whether it's there or not. Just to let the hot southern sun parch you, or the cold winter's drizzle soak through seems almost too much to ask. Whenever I set foot on that soil again, I'm going to walk for miles, cross country, along roads, through towns, swamps, meadows and woods–amen–just to set foot in a good old American trash dump would be interesting and satisfying. Wanna come along?

Now isn't this a hellofa letter? 'Bout time I quit–however, how about a request–namely a Washington paper–suburban edition–one of the bigger papers.

Lots of love–plenty

Jack

P,S. Look in the envelope for hair out of my mustache, which I've removed–completely. It's loose in the envelope.

[Editor's note: The target for the raid on October 18 was Leverkusen, Germany. On October 22, it was Hamm, Germany.]

Oct. 27, 1944

Dear Miss,

Just got back to the base after our first 48-hour pass. (Two of your letters were waiting so that gave me a start on the right foot.)

Since there were a few things I needed, headed for London. Just another big, dreary town, except this one carries a few drastic - or should I say MANY drastic reminders of the early days of the war.

Gilday and I soaked in the leisurely pace of the town and in general–visited the historical points of interest. Since he's Episcopalian, he wanted to attend services at Westminster Abbey. The place is undoubtedly over a thousand years old, however such talk makes me froth at the mouth. The fact is, everything the English hold dear, including some of their customs, seem so darn useless and elaborate. However, it's in their very bones–so I guess it's part of England.

Maybe, too, my mind's becoming affected by all this drab dreariness that exudes from the very atmosphere. Truthfully I'm afraid it's seeping in since it's not fun to write letters any more–or at best, occasionally. So don't be surprised if they drag a bit, both in frequency and interest.

We ran into a couple of very young Merchant Marines from Canada–and it was actually like the first day of spring after a drizzly winter. Their expressions of speech were new and lively and in general, nothing like the deadly routine and inflections of the English speech.

Since we were darn lucky and got a pretty fair room close to the crossroads of the crossroads of the world, there were plenty of nationalities round about. Took my first bath since leaving home –minus four showers–and really enjoyed it. The water was warm, however the room temperature–as everything is–45 to 50 degrees. The tub, though, was long enough for me to stretch out full length and touch neither end–ahhh–such luxury. We talked, we soldiers in general–New Zealand, Australian, African and one young Scandinavian who was rabid about the U.S. He seemed more crazy to get there after this is over than most of the Americans. This is contrary to the usual–although from the propaganda of American papers it's the typical attitude of all nationalities–strictly propaganda. This propaganda by the papers and the Readers' Digest *is one reason I've learned to take all good news about the war with plenty of salt. You know that the Nazis literally destroyed all food in the occupied countries–leaving the people nearly destitute–well, right now the allied army in Belgium is facing a problem–distributing 1,200,000 hogs throughout that country–namely because communications are disrupted and the livestock cannot be transported right now. Escapees bring back tales of cattle in the barns and houses in which they stayed. Such things were supposed to have been done away with three or four years ago, remember? Sweets and clothing rationed, yes. By the number of wild fowl and animals around these parts–there never has been a meat crisis–however eggs and clothing are scarce–or anyway, clothing is plentiful, but strictly rationed. 'Nough said at present–gotta eat and take a short flight around this locality–be seeing you.*

Since this is the following night–somehow I feel a bit more useful–or something–maybe because we flew a bit and a practice mission this morning. This morning the weather got to be pretty serious–and by the time we raced back we were at 750 feet (Close enough to recognize a person) and still unable to see anything except occasional glimpses of fields, ditches and roads. Since we were in formation, wing tip to wing tip–you didn't have to bother with instruments–that's strictly up to the lead ship–consequently, you never know whether you're upside down or right side up. Being the first ship to peel off, I had to really "rack it up tight" in order to start the traffic pattern in close. Truth of the matter I almost believe I dug a ditch around the field with my left wing tip. For a second it was pretty uncertain. I passed through the smoke from a train and had to flick back to instruments while on one wing tip–and that practically dragging the ground. There had to be five flares at the beginning of the runway in order for us to see the field even that close.

By the way–reminds me–that leave at Monroe–and weathered out for three days–just before–remember it? Well, one of those cadets on that trip is here now as a navigator on a lead crew.

Lead crews fly about twice a month though you usually advance a couple of steps in rank pretty fast. I don't like the idea. The crew was worried that we would be one of the lead crews. Due to a fairly lucky and timely incident I don't think there's much danger of that now. Besides the change in attitude of everyone on the crew is now–to drag out the missions over as long a period as possible. That leaves me holding the bag–and looking for a blacksnake whip–on account–while we're here I want to do the job NOW while we're helping the ground troops (usually.)

The reason for not being put up for a lead crew, well, Sugar is now checked out as a navigator–and one day we went up to assemble for a mission–hit wing ice on instruments–and picked up quite a bit of it. The radio compass had an error–which I noticed and attributed to a strong wind–so we were over enemy held territory before all the ships had taken off. The compass error was later attributed to false signals by the Germans. Well, so forth and on though we were about to lose one–possibly two, engines–so-o-o rather than let down on instruments through icing conditions–I chose man-made trouble in preference–namely the possibility of enemy flak and fighters. We ended up just over the treetops–streaking for home. One burst of flak–inaccurate! Turned out to be the only hole in their coastal defense (we didn't know it at the time) so we let down still closer to the marshes–by-passed two villages, hit a channel, got in the middle of it and headed for open sea and home. Once passed over a ship between two villages–one on either bank. Told the gunners, "If she opens up, let her have it and I'll let the bombs go at the same time." Turned out she was abandoned and grounded. Took one last look at the apparently peaceful farms and windmills turning lazily in the breezes and then the fog shut us off from view of the land–relief–slightly.

Later we found we'd been in the flak area–and shot at before the rest of the planes had left England. The channel we came out of was one of a very, very low number that didn't have flak guns side by side. Lucky–and more than likely God had a hand in it, too–though He must have been laughing at our speedy exit.

'Nough said. Now, about you. Outside of what you had weighing on your mind the 12th or 13th, how about getting a check up by a good doctor? Lemme know about it. Then, too, what was it you said about next April–or June–repeat again–yes–or–no? By the way, thanks for the gum–however you keep it. I appreciate the thought but we get a package at the end of each mission and I haven't used what I have.*

Jumping around–looks as though Christmas presents over here are next to impossible–please understand. What with rationing of every little article from toothpicks to miniature flags–that leaves jewelry. That particular line isn't too elaborate, no better than American and prices are from 3 to 6 times higher.

In the meantime, how about opening each envelope and folding them flat instead of slitting one end and pulling up the flap. They'll fit the book better that way and be about the same size as the paper–leaving no gaps.

Thank the folks for the presents that are in the mail and do a good job by Harold in letters and little packages–all along–they help a lot and he needs them worse than I.

Yours truly is in the squadron (smallest) unit - leading the group–leading the wing–leading the whole Eighth in bombing accuracy. In other words–to over look the bragging–I'm lucky enough to be in the leading squadron on the field–the field is leading all the others over here in getting their bombs on the right spots. Catch the buttons, please.

Seems like I could rattle on and on tonight–however nature calls, gotta shave–and that means walking a quarter of a mile over their English lanes to the latrine.

Be seeing you, Sweet. Keep such tales of operations strictly in the family–and where there's no chance of the public, in general, hearing about such things as engaging the enemy (speaking about the let down over enemy territory.) Well, anyway–Be seeing you.

Lots of love–
aimed correctly.

Jack

* [Editor's note: I had written Jack that I thought I was pregnant.]

Nov. 3, 1944

Good morning,

How're you feeling, Miss? See what I told you–paper over here isn't so hot–when you can get it. Next time in I'll see if I can pick up some stationery at a bookstore or whatever. Now, if you were feeling good, that ought to make you feel bad on account of how would I know you have some stationery in the mail, even now–or who am I kidding?

Tonight I got tired of sitting around while people played cards –so I decided to go to one of the barracks and play some records. Got down to facts and made up a list of those I wish you'd get hold of - and store for future reference only. Some of them you might have to get second hand or by begging. I'll list them before they are really scarce. Came across "Gloomy Sunday" and since it has such a profound effect on people in the way of suicide (you remember it was banned for that reason) well, why not translate it and broadcast it to the Germans from the front lines–might as well, since they use everything else. I'll suggest it to the intelligence officer next time I see him.

Oh–the list–here 'tis:

Begin the Beguine (Glen Miller or Artie Shaw)
Song of India
Temptation
Green Eyes
Beer Barrel Polka (accordion - no voice)
In the Mood (Glen Miller)
Tuxedo Junction " "
Sunrise Serenade " "
Moonlight Serenade " "
Perfidia (vocal Andrew sisters, if possible)
Amapola (Jimmy Dorsey or Andrew sisters)
Pistol Packing Mama (Bing and the Andrew sisters)
Blues in the Night (Bing - John Scott Trotter)
Cow-cow Boogie (Ella Fitzgerald - Ink Spots)
Honkey Tonk Train Blues (Bob Crosby)
South of the Border (Andrew sisters)

and what else you think of.

While I was listening, one of them was a rumba–or a tango–or somesuch. Anyway I'd certainly like to be dancing a few of such numbers with you–about now.

H'mm by the way, young lady–about this mail situation. Mighty slow–especially this last week or so–none. I can count them on one hand–maybe starting on the second. They're still coming in mixed batches such as say, one of Sept. 20–and maybe one of Oct. 12–coming together. What kind of service are you getting and what is the average time on airmail? Seems to me you mentioned sending a few pictures and so on. So far I haven't used any–oh, yes–two snaps of the rest of the roll we started. It'll be quite some time yet, I guess–however once they're printed I'll see if I can pass them on–and possibly–have the film censored and send it, too.

Now how the devil can I write–with nothing going on for a week or more and no news from home to hash over? Tried to contact Harp and Harold–McKeever, too (or did I mail that one?)

Well anyway, so far, no news from them. Do you have any?

You're right about "the Boy"–there's no way for me to know what's going on–however, maybe before too long I'll be able to watch him expand. In the meantime, let me know how you're making out. Take care of yourself.

Getting late–gotta bank the stove, etc., so I guess I'd better rush through and finish this up.

Lots of love–spelled the age-old way.

I LOVE YOU.

Jack

Nov. 9, 1944

Hi, Lady,

Now I'll start again. Guess I've started two or three letters that are out moded. Time is still stumbling onward. Bout time we start on missions again. Don't get too excited about rushing through this thing. Three missions and then almost a month of piddling. Really looks like we'll be a bit more regular now. Hope so anyway.

Your pictures came the day after I wrote my complaint about not getting them. Now I can relax and gaze at you two now and then. What's more I don't have to sit back in an isolated corner when it comes to pictures from home. Jane certainly did a good job of tinting them, eh what? Thank her for me, too. They shore are perty, aren't they? Conceited.

Two more days and we'll get another pass. Swore I wouldn't go to London this time–however, got a date–which I didn't have at the time. So-o-o, guess it would be best not to break it. That'll be this Saturday at 0700 P.M. on "Rainbow Corner."" You probably won't mind, seeing as how up to now I haven't had a single date. Not nary a one. What's more, it gets pretty lonesome over here–so, knowing your broadmindedness–I'm going to try to make the date. Should you not approve, speed up those letters, somehow, and tell me about it–and why–and why not.

Here's hoping everything turns out as planned on account of the fact I didn't have too much time to accept the place and the time. Maybe I should talk for you on the date, too. Anything you would like to say is O.K. by me–only there isn't much time to say it, so, let 'er rip. Since the whole thing was done by mail, I'm sorta wondering what the outcome will be.

Whatever the date looks like, sounded pretty eager–or maybe I did, too. Well, anyway, here's hoping and you can hope along with me on account of the date is with Billie–guess you remember the name, huh? Never occurred to me last summer–or you either, that we'd meet again over here–or did you think that in Monroe? I'll let you in on all the details that develop–promise–just so you won't do any excess worrying!

By the way, this paper came as a surprise to me. Though its supply is limited, it'll come in handy until your package arrives. The PX supplied it–most amazing. Still I'd like to get a couple of cans or packages of unpopped popcorn. Wool socks will be appreciated, too. Verify–repetition.

Weather was really raw today–rain, wind and wet snow–the first–and non-sticking, thank goodness. I've gradually acquired luxury–such as can be had over here. My bunk is a lower. Sugar is in the top one and the stove is in the middle of the room at our feet. Light rigged on the springs overhead and a backrest at the head. In other words, I'm in the sack now, pretty cozy, eh what?

Today's mission has just returned–a direct hit just in front of Harold. Well, tomorrow will probably be our turn–hope so, anyway. Looks pretty certain that Sugar's bar will be gold after the 5th mission. He deserves it, too. Mine's still that greenish tinge–for how long, you tell me.

Well, be seeing you. The Ink Spots are lying. (We bought a radio.) They're saying, "This is a lovely way to spend an evening."

Anything you wish me to tell McKeever?

I love you, Miss.

Jack

[Editor's note: On one occasion in Monroe when Jack and I were out for the evening, we met a young woman named Billie. She was attractive, quite voluptuous, and also very interested in Jack. I was pregnant at the time and felt she was grossly unfair competition. I must say Jack did nothing to encourage her but as I sat there and watched, I did a slow burn. Jack couldn't resist teasing me about his "date" with Billie. Billy McKeever, as you've gathered, was our high school friend from Silver Spring.]

Picture of Kitty and Jennis III on his first birthday

SAVOY HOTEL LONDON

Nov. 11, 1944

Dear Miss,

I love you! Bet you aren't even fully dressed yet–lazy? Just piddling around, huh? About the same goes on here at the present –so why couldn't we be together while there're no duties calling?

Today's the day I was supposed to meet McKeever–0700 P.M. –Rainbow Corner, remember? Well, anyway I spent all day trying to get a nice room so that we could relax in style. What gives–it's Saturday, the place is crowded, as usual, only more so –since today is also Armistice Day and that means the British Legion is holding a big annual celebration.

Well, anyway, after calling on the two nicest hotels–1/2 block apart–I got the same answer–no soap. Soooo–followed a course –never tried before–continually walking from one–back to the first–back to the other. Finally the desk manager, tails and all, hands me a registration card to fill out - didn't even wait for me to ask the now aging question. So–all set. That means the bunk I reserved as a precaution with the Red Cross will go unused. Piddled until time to meet the guy, shaved–rushed over and waited. 7 - 7:30 - 8 - 8:30 - 9. Guess it's no use. Anyway, left his name on the blackboard and a note with instructions on how to get here. More than likely he's either shipped out or was unable to get a pass. Sure would have liked to have seen the guy–however, maybe next time.

While I waited (it was mainly the enlisted men's Red Cross building) I made out one pass for some guy, signed it, so he could get through the red tape of getting a room or a bunk - through the Red Cross. Sat down again and another GI (Medics) comes up with 2,000 somethings in French currency - had to have an officer's signature to change it–Bingo–O.K.–taking a chance on $40.00–checked his name and APO–seemed O.K. –Sat down–waited–up comes another guy on pass from France –same story–so $40.00 more. Sat back down and up comes another GI–"Sir, are you the O.D. here?"

"No, just waiting for a guy."

"Sir, the MPs won't let me bring my date in here."

"Sorry, Bud, can't help you." (Any guy who'd take up with the regular run over here–ain't got much pride. So far, no other kind have I seen. Not looking, though–just observing.)

Forgiven? 'Nough of that there–guess I'd better eat–if any place is open. The doorman, who has been shooing the "Picadilly Commandos" (What a tribe!!) out told me of a place that was open. Stumbled on it–pure accident–(English directions are absolutely stir-crazy–"Go down here 3 minutes–or 100 yards (Never in blocks or miles) turn left (probably between 2 blocks to 10)–turn right for about 300 yards–bear VAGUELY towards the NORTH!!!!" Believe you me, that is exactly how they give directions. Then they invariably add, "YOU CAWN'T MISS IT!!!!!!" Repeat these four words to anyone who has been over here and I guarantee you'll find you have an absolutely raving maniac on your hands.

Well, about the restaurant. French, as usual. I remember a little French–but never, in my born days have I heard–or can decipher–the nouns on the menus over here. When I get back - any place with a menu in French–we get up and walk out. This was different, though–more diplomatic and agreeable. The waiter says, "Sir, would you like braised ham?" (I'm nuts by this time and anything connected with the lowly hog sounds good to me. "Yep, and what vegetables?"

"Just leave them to me, Sir."

"O.K., I'll try you."

Good–ham, french fries, spinach, baked beans and green peas. Fine!! I recognize every crumb. "Wine?"

"Yes." (Sauterne is "very dear" over here. Dear means over 4lbs per bottle –or 16 dollars and up.)

"Wine?"

"Yes, a pony of Port."

"A pony?"

"Yes, ##!!, a SMALL GLASS."*

"Yes, Sir–and sweets?"

"What do you have?"

"Just leave it to me, Sir."

"O.K. You're doing O.K., so go ahead." He did "O.K,", too.

Delicious cake of some sort–orange peel and whipped cream. What in Hell's wrong, now? My nose fall off? A Czech, sitting at the next table, is whispering something to his date. They stare–so tit for tat.

Well, that's over. Now to ask directions to the "Savoy–Diplomatic Cross Roads–of the Cross Roads." Here we go again. "Straight through there," pointing through the middle of a bank. (Black as Hades out, still,) "and then bear VAGUELY–"

"Thanks a lot. I got it now. Thanks." Tee-hee–I fooled 'em that time; out comes my compass–luminous, too, and the map the Red Cross gave me. Darn near made it here. Two shillings (25 cents) to some guy–good English speech–and line–for a bed –only wanted 1 and 6 (18 cents) so guess he meant it. Bingo, bumped into some Irish man–started conversation. Guess he was about 45-50. O.K, O.K., O.K., so we had a bitter (beer.) Listen to his tale of woe–give him another beer (He's in the army–Irish or British.) Anyway–we have many points in common–nice friendly chat–he's broke–oh well, finally made it here and still have most of my–uh–allowance.

Now, here I be–all alone. Not much chance of Bill coming in –very nice room–twin beds–paneled in mirrors. A BATH!! WHY IN ---- aren't YOU here? Sure do miss you, young lady. So I begin to tire–guess I'd better re-tire and keep one ear out for McKeever.

Be seeing you.
Lots of love–lots
Jack

Nov. 13, 1944

Hi, Perty,

Back at the base again. Nope, Bill never showed up–and so far–no news from same.

Fact is, no letter today–or yesterday. Nope–nor the day before. However–guess you and I are in about the same boat. Same all around, though, all mail over here has slowed up–drastically–and, as you've been saying, everyone back in the States has been complaining of the same. Your cablegram came today. Don't know whether you really want an answer or not. You really shouldn't worry–however I know how such things go. We've been having a pretty humdrum time of it lately and that's all the more reason why y'all shouldn't be worrying–oh, so you didn't know all that?

While in London I saw a few spots that were the effects of recent explosions. Didn't hear a single explosion–although I'm not too sure whether a couple of jars were loose doors slamming in the hotel or explosions far off. We've become pretty familiar with buzz bombs. Their noise is pretty distinctively a noise all their own. The first one sounded like a P-47–having trouble–since that one, they've all been a bit further off. That first one, though, was just as low as the planes coming in at Selman–over the roof.

Well, anyway, this being over here has started plenty of Americans to commit themselves to some pretty deep thinking. Right now I'm reading a book, "Kamonga" which deals with evolution in a rather off-hand sort of way–and for some reason or other–I've been knocking a few ideas around in my thick skull. I realize now that it's been forming slowly–sort of gropingly–way back before I came into the army. Maybe that's the main reason for my liking nature–and feeling so much a part of it. Really interesting, though, especially since you don't have to really retire to think about it. Every little daily occurrence has its own lessons–if you can only pause long enough to ponder over them a bit.

That comes back to religion–and today a new thought occurred to me. Been sort of hard to just throw off the thought that Jesus was a fabrication. Now, doesn't it stand to reason that he could have lived–just as any other great man in history –only–being an individualist with a brain–far, far ahead of the normal person, he simply gathered together all the religious beliefs of mankind, combined them to such an extent that they could be written–or thought of in a concrete way–instead of in the abstract. This being what all mankind had been looking for –without realizing it. He, being open to all forms of ideas and being able to see the good and bad points–decided to try and bring about a set of rules whereby all mankind could live in peace and happiness, if they would abide by them. So, setting up his theory, he used plenty of psychology and showmanship with a little of the mysticism of the magician thrown in–just because he was brilliant enough to realize that with magic thrown in–it would place him above ordinary teachers and philosophers –and attract the uneducated who were too ignorant to understand–or too bored to listen to his teachings–otherwise. So that makes him a great man, no matter how you look at him–truly, just a disciple of God. Yet he is worshipped–just as much–if not more–than God, through no fault of his own–simply because all the religious opinions were drawn up around him. Most religious sects today, without realizing it, ask of him to grant their prayers, and in ending a prayer usually, along with all their other requests, close with, "For Jesus' sake. Amen." This all adds up to the reasons for my not following any set road so far as religion is concerned. Books and education, including the Bible, (I believe) were meant to start men's minds to functioning–not to be absorbed as fact–unshakable. Most of the people of today have that idea in their minds. What happens certainly wasn't meant to be–and has a deadening effect on their minds–causing a problem–just because some person, using his ole noggin, put his advanced ideas in writing. That's bigotry and that's why I believe in arguing and discussion.

Please, when the boy grows up, show him the way to think–and do–but let him find the final result, himself. Don't let him get the idea that at the finish of school he has finished his education. Show him that he has simply been taught to use his brain. So–comes college–when that time arrives, if he has found no definite ideas of what he would like to do–no college. Let him find out from personal contact with the world just what he's interested in–just what he'd like to study–work up enough interest in that study so that he will appreciate the fact that in going to college–he will not just be teaching his brain to function further–but is taking a short cut through thinkers who have gone before him. They've written their experiences and findings for him to learn quickly–and then continue on his own–with an open mind.

Maybe it's the stifled atmosphere over here that has started me to thinking along such lines, maybe it's the effect of the army, and the contact with men who seem to have closed off their minds entirely–once someone with a strong personality–or teaching has instilled them with a complete idea. That done, they terminate all questions on the particular subject–and that part of their mind is useless from then on. The world keeps rolling and leaves them behind.

Now that brings up the argument that I really like to discuss here in the barracks, most of the fellows enjoy the same–except for one or two who refuse to enter into it. They're not open to discussion simply because they've been taught differently from childhood. They're held prisoner by these teachings–or at least their minds are. That question? Why is the world at each other's throats simply because their leaders have influenced their minds to such an extent that they are willing to give their life for that belief? It's amazing how propaganda has effected the world. Germany has hers–England has hers–and even America has been led off the beaten path–through propaganda. None of these countries have the same system–or even the same reasoning behind the propaganda. Still it's there–and I believe it's the main cause of this mess. Men's minds have been shaped by a few leaders–and then closed against outside argument. Could there, in some way, be a way to educate the world–in a truthful way–I don't believe there would be another war. If men could only understand and appreciate each other's problems.

To back that up, the countries (few and usually small) that are NOT at war are countries that the educational systems are so limited that they don't bother about other people's troubles–

but are content to live their own peaceful lives–earning their living. Not only that, but they're not "world-wise" to be in need of propaganda. Still they're in danger of being overrun–for mineral rights–or any other reason a larger country should covet them.

I've backed myself up a blind alley. I'm afraid that last paragraph isn't just exactly true–however, the idea is in it somewhere.

So, switching the main idea (See what reasoning leads to?) the plane is going to make the world so small that the majority of peoples of the world will be able to widen their knowledge of world troubles. Maybe it's the answer to the education problem. In the process of evolution, here's hoping it turns from the–most dangerous weapon of this age–to the most educational and, hence, tool of peace. Maybe man will continue to absorb his own national teachings, then closing his mind, though. If so, I wonder which animal will be master of the Earth a few centuries hence. Surely, if this keeps up, man is going to destroy himself before too long. More than likely, though, there will be another "Dark Age" in which the educated peoples of the earth will exterminate each other and the most primitive ones will inherit the earth. (Getting deep but it's fun–eh?) Whoever said, "A little education is dangerous" really said a mouthful. Trouble is, no man will ever be able to boast a full education since that's apparently an impossibility.

Looks like man made a mistake along the road when he branched off from the lower animals–and developed his brain–and hands–while the rest of the animals developed teeth, muscles and claws. Along about this time those other things would come in handy. Maybe he should have developed an armor-plated hide and the ability to grow new members of his body that had been destroyed. So saying, who is better off–man or the other beasts?

Pardon this "Bull roar," Miss–things get pretty monotonous–and if you don't ponder over something–well, maybe, you'll go nuts–and if you do ponder over such things–it makes you wonder if you aren't already nuts. Interesting, though, anyway–or don't normal people think so? Got an idea most of the guys over here will be a bit on the odd side, like this here, while they're here.

By the way, young lady, how are you making out with the young'un? Seeing as how you didn't have too much trouble with the first one, more than likely you won't have any more with this one. I'm going to try like the devil to get on with these missions and see if'n I can't get back there in time to sorta help you out–or do you need help? Don't worry about it–like you didn't the last time–and bingo–what'll we have? Now don't tell me you don't know. Let's see–what was that name–the girl's name? Now just in case, the boy's–don't start harping on "Michael"–it just don't sound fittin' somehow. Say, how's Banks' new one coming along? Would it be one Banks too many if there was a third–and a Banks Murray Strickland, too? Your Pop would have four Banks in his family then–and I hear that with even one or two Banks in a family–well, it's considered a pretty well to do family–or don't you follow? Let me know how you're making out–although I can pretty well keep up–from past experience–can't I?–Can I? Keep me posted on the name situation.

Be seeing you,
Love - again - and always.
Jack

Nov. 17, 1944

Hi, Lovely,

What are you keeping so quiet about of late? Looks like nobody's getting mail these days, except the postman. That includes you, too, more than likely, but it aint on account I haven't been writing. Wish you had written on the 5th and 6th–because, after weeks of unbroken silence, the mail postmarked on those days came through.

Your letter about Billy came in after I had contacted him–via mail. Since we didn't get together in London–looks like I'll have to go there again on the next chance. Last night he phoned and after pushing buttons and blowing off a little steam on these limey telephones, I talked with him. Not much said except trying to make arrangements for a rendezvous–although I believe he's a little lonesome, maybe a little more than most guys. He said he had gotten a letter from you but he still wanted any news from home that was forthcoming. You can see why the conversation was mainly on future plans only.

Still no news from Harold or Harp, so I don't know if Harold received the oranges I sent or not. The weather over here is bad enough–but those guys at the front certainly deserve every little boost–and pat on the back–that anyone can give them.

While in London this time, everything was closed for the weekend. There were plenty of little fancy oddities apparent, some useful, some not, but it was good they were closed because the prices are out of the question. There was one store–dealing in sheep and lamb skins–that sold the hides outright and then contracted the job of making them into gloves, slippers, jackets, coats, hats–and what have you. They were novel–practical, too, in a way, but the prices were unheard of.

For awhile I was contemplating buying some riding boots. They're the only things I'd like to bring home from England that I've seen. Hand made and to the individual foot, usually. They're really excellent examples of the best to be had. The darn things are so perfect that it's a pleasure to handle them. But, the price, again, is too darn much and no more riding than you and I do–out of the question. Besides–for me–they wouldn't be practical for anything but riding and there are plenty of good boots in America that would stand the guff better, as well as serving any purpose. Then–I don't have a model of your foot over here–the sizes are all screwed up–and how would I get them back to the States? So that leaves practical presents out. Once more I'm stumped as far as this Christmas is concerned.

There was, though, a Rolls Razor store that had a few razors on display. Interesting as hell–eh? Well, anyway, that's THE razor I've always wanted and they can't be had in the States any more–so, if possible–thanks for the present.

Feel like a heel about all that and the fact that I haven't been able to get you a present. Man, would it give my ego a boost just to be able to get something different for you–just to watch you open it and give me a kiss in return. That would be one of the nicest presents I could wish–and how I wish. Sis, I don't miss you, not much!!!

Well, missions–yeah–missions still slow–mighty, mighty slow –however every chance from now on will be used to the utmost–come on, chances.

What do you say to a few plain old snapshots now and then. They're nice to gaze upon–especially when they are connected with the goings on at home. So far I haven't clicked the shutter since I removed the mustache–guess I'll get started on that right away.

Still–and again–nothing much to speak of over here–especially since Scotland is so far away. Most of the time, time drags. We'll listen to German broadcasts and think about what we're going to do when this is over. Sort of a day dreaming–however, I'm doing a lot of that and sorta planning. Would you like to live in Louisiana or South Carolina? This Fish and Wildlife or Department of the Interior has both assets–and, well, bad points, so, to have something concrete in mind, I'm trying to plan on a nice farm as a home and a veterinary practice as business. By farm, I mean nut orchard or cattle–guess I shouldn't mention it but a goat dairy, too! This flak really gets you! I won't try to sell you on the goat dairy–however, I'd expect a little help in the way of hired hands–and the cost is so far offset by the income that it really isn't a laughing matter. Yeah, I'm serious! O.K., O.K, you can have the plane anytime you want to go into town–or up home for a visit. The house would be our kind of house to the last nail!

Now for the house–long, low and rambling–or don't you agree? Come on then and let me have your ideas

Sure, I'll listen–go ahead.

Be seeing you.
All this and love, too.
Jack

When Harvey found out that Jack and I were going to have our first child, he insisted on being the Godfather of it and of any future children we might have. We were not particularly religious but since Harp was our best friend, we were delighted to bestow that title upon him.

This is a card that Harp sent little Jennis from France.

Card

CARTE POSTALE - POST CARD

Nov. 18, 1944

Hi there big boy,
Certainly hope you're fine and are behaving yourself. I'll bet you're growing to beat the band and eating your mother out of house and home. I know you miss your dad, but just remember that he's up there fighting for you, & your mother, & the most wonderful country in the world.
Let's hope that we'll all be back home before too very long. Goodbye for now.

Your loving godfather
[illegible]

Imprimé en France

G B PARIS

Mr. J. M. Strickland III

Reverse of card

V-Mail

Nov. 21, 1944

Dear Miss,

Still no news from home these many long days. Today I checked at the Post Office and they say that V-mail still travels. Since it's better than none at all, how about sprinkling a few in your correspondence?

So far no packages have arrived–and in the meantime I've more or less decided what the little things that mean a lot amount to. Peanuts,–raw and also salted–popcorn, YOUR chocolate fudge–genuine–old country smoked ham and sausage, uncooked. Then, again, some soft, thick wool socks. While you're at it, send a laundress–I've been wearing this set of long johns for three weeks without let up.

Baths come at about the same intervals–or whenever we have a 48-hour pass and get into a modern hotel. That leaves pajamas–could use one more set of flannels–or somesuch–and I wouldn't be above wearing those with red feet.

Twice I've been to London–the second time was in hopes of meeting McKeever but since that didn't happen, looks like there will have to be a third time in order to contact him. Then, too, I'll need another bath.

Lately this place has been becoming saturated with the kinds of rumors that usually add up to something in the long run. There may be a shift in theaters, one way or the other–However that can mean any number of things so you might as well let your imagination run wild. Don't get in a stew though–because there's no answer yet and there might not be any time soon. Fact is, I shouldn't have bothered to mention it, so don't pass it on.

Last time anyone mentioned Harold was a letter from him in Sept. How about a little enlightening on the subject.

By the way, while you're in an enlightening mood, how about giving me a good report on how you're making out. You on a diet, yet? Got your teeth under observation? May I prescribe one quart of Thompson's homogenized milk per day–no less!

More than likely Walter Reed is a battle in itself–just to sweat out the line waiting for check-ups. That isn't all but I've got to go now. Maybe the mails will open up–both ways–by the time this arrives–however if it hasn't, shoot me a V-Mail–what say?

Lots of love, Jack

P.S. To diet–also 1/2 pint of cream per day, if possible–eh?

Nov. 23, 1944
Thanksgiving Day

Dear Miss,

Happy Thanksgiving to you. Here's hoping you enjoyed your dinner as much as we did. Sliced turkey–dark and white meat –cranberry sauce, dressing, green peas, hot rolls!!, coffee or grapefruit–pineapple juice, pumpkin pie and ice cream. Man, what cramming! Then to top it off,–I polished up a nice red apple, stuck a purple chrysanthemum on top supporting the note "Donated and polished by hut 21" and presented it to our squadron commander! Now maybe we'll get a mission now and then!

In the V-mail letter I mentioned rumors about something big. Well, it ain't so big, at that–however, it's something new–experimental and we're one of the two crews in the squadron–chosen to try it out. If it works it'll be accepted generally throughout the Air Force. Now don't go jumping–it's nothing of especial value–like secret weapons and such–sorta–oh well, I'll tell you about it sometime. This will mean a few missions in quick succession–however it probably won't continue that way too long. Due to general luck, we've not put in a mission in a month now –just my crew, though. Got rid of Wagner yesterday after two or three false starts. Strangely enough instead of raising a rumpus and both of us flying off the handle, I surprised the hell out of me to find that my brain has either slowed up–or else my tongue speeded up. Well, at any rate we had a nice long talk–the outcome being that we both agreed that it would be best if he were off the crew. We parted friends and I dare say I like him more now than I have before. Still the fact remains that he's a very poor soldier and I have no place for him on the crew. That's what I told him and–along with the fact that I intend sprucing up the crew until it was one of the most out-standing on the field, he agreed that I couldn't expect too much of an effort on his part–because of his personal makeup and outlook on army life. Now enters his replacement–guess what!!–the crew, as it now stands–English, French Canadian, Russian Rumanian Jew, Syrian, Italian–all whose parents come from the mother country. That leaves Schultz, Edwards and me with roots in the U.S.A. Now comes Del Pero! whom I haven't met yet. Sounds like Mexican or Spanish. So saying, when we get our ship–definitely–how about "The League of Nations" for a name? Maybe I can find a Chinese boy, too! Let's see now–"Potpourri" –man–oh–man–we'll be at home in any country, regardless! Their difference in thinking is a constant source of bewilderment on my part. Still–we've pretty well whipped up a team and are doing O.K.

Now my navigator, you ask. Well, 'tis a long story. He's a conscientious guy who really accomplished a lot more in a short time than I believed possible. I give you Mr. Bernard Sugarman –"Bombigator" in no small way–with full confidence of the crew behind him, plus the respect of all the navigators and bombardiers on the field. Two more missions and he's promised a gold bar. The usual promotions–if any–come between the fifteenth and twentieth missions. He'll get the honors on the fifth one.

Got three of your letters at once yesterday–first in about a month–and still hungry for more. See what they do for my morale?

Now take the Department of Interior situation. Mr. Lincoln wrote me that he'd looked through the record and considered it interesting enough to see that it got some publicity. Think he's referring to the Ornithologists' magazine. You remember my imaginative idea of transplanting diseased hearts–especially with stronger - longer lived ones? Well, guess what! June 24 Colliers–"Keeping Up With the World" states that the transplanting of hearts in frogs has been done successfully in Russia –now, a frog's life, barring accident, is either 20 or 40 years–don't know which–anyway–maybe some one over here (U.S.) will go one better and say–try transplanting a dog's heart–good for about 17 years with a large turtle's–if he'd live to be even half the age of a normal turtle–75 to 100 years, wouldn't it be worth trying anyway, with an end in view of prolonging man's life and prime of life well past a century? Still–for what? 'Nough said.

Just that second completed a roundhouse discussion that lasted well over an hour and we fly tomorrow–I hope.

Back to Mr. Lincoln–I had all intentions of writing him about some of the amazing peculiarities of wild life over here. Now I'd better go to sleep and do that next chance I get.

Love you - always
Jack

Stop building me up. I'm beginning to feel like a BTO already!

Nov. 24, 1944

Hi again,

Guess I might as well write you again–don't feel like writing Mr. Lincoln or anyone else right now. Maybe it's because I feel like writing you.

Today you wrote (third day in a row!) and wanted to know what Hamm was. Fine thing, you people back there don't know there's a war on after all–or do you?

Well, anyway, there's a country called Germany (Europe) and there are cities in that country and Hamm is a fair sized, well-known city. Still, without a flak map, y'all don't know the difference between eastern, western or central Germany–how could you, after all, since commercial maps make one town look about the same, regardless of location. Tell you the difference some day. Look through the papers for the Eighth's targets–and that's us.

Your letter was concerned with house plans–and about four letters ago, I was writing you about the same. Now I'll get ornery. When it comes to a boy's room–he should have 97% of the say so about furnishings, colors and the positioning of the furniture–he's the one that will use it–and he'll be the one to learn from experience to plan such things in advance–thinking of convenience, looks, as such things come up–making him realize that with a little fore-thought, he could have gotten a better deal. Sorta "since he's made his own bed, he'll sleep on it" idea. 'Course he might not make the best decisions, at first, however it would develop his initiative, reasoning powers and appreciation of his own–as well as others'–ideas. The only thing I'd have us decide on that score is the mattress. Not too soft–possibly a little hard–however, how about trying to train him to sleep on his back–not his stomach. Since I can remember I've slept on my stomach and I've tried to stop it, mainly on account it flattens the chest and allows the stomach muscles to sag and distend until the stomach rests on the mattress. Or don't you think so?

Now, no, I'm not fussing–just reasoning–just want to swap ideas with you. The train set up in the drawer idea–leaves nothing to the boy's imagination–brings out no thought or initiative. It's there, set up–working. Now, on the other hand, through trial and error, he'd find out what hills the engine would pull–whether it was stopped by the weight of the cars–or lack of friction, etc. Then, too, he'd probably be a bit careful about spreading out too far on the floor–on account of having to clean it up eventually–see–fun, eh what?

I definitely think we should be saving everything we can now in order that we'll be able to make a fair start when we build–and include rooms for the kids, away from the living room or any place that would cause them to have to go to bed early–too early–or stop playing with toys–just because we have company. Yet they would be off to themselves and wouldn't bother us–and we wouldn't necessarily have to hem them in when company is about (two schools of thought there,–easily.) Instead of forcing them to respect other people's rights they could see what having their own rights respected by other people would mean–or somesuch.

Maybe it's because–for me–experience has been the quickest, easiest and surest way of learning things. So, I harp on the fact that the brain is not meant to store a lot of reading material - but rather, as an assembly shop–outfitted with what ever materials you happen to have wanted stored there for future reference; used singly or together to form constructive ideas that you've put together from spare parts. That's all so jumbled that even I don't know what I've tried to say. Sorta, give the brain the raw materials and expect it to turn off a finished product, rather than training it to think along roads that have already been explored and completed–or made to absorb, and believe, some finished product already turned out by somebody else's mind, put in a book–read as fact, instead of being used to improve upon. Guess I've really ended up in a circle. The beginning of all this came from the completely dead, docile attitude that seems to occupy the average Old World mind. They're doped by past knowledge and live in the past. That is the major difference between Yanks and the people over here. It's a drastic difference. The average American seems to be a dynamo, built up around the idea that there's nothing impossible and they're in the world to prove it. Sort of a braggart's way of thinking - but healthy and open to reasoning.

By the way, you didn't mention it–but that room picture was heated by a hot air vent about one foot below the ceiling. That's something I've been wondering about for years. More than likely there's reasoning behind it–but hot air rises, so why shouldn't the vent be placed on–or near the floor? Those home magazines have been pretty interesting–especially since I found you–and chased you down–heh, heh–O.K. so I really did!! Back to the magazines–they have some interesting ideas but it's more fun to dissect them–and use the ones that interest us. Keep up such clippings–they help.

Be seeing you
Love,
Jack

Ideas; for a boy's room:
Mexican, adobe - (colorful, simple, deep windows)
Ship's cabin - (old or new) with lighting, big windows, instruments
Cowboy bunk house - Simple, colorful, rustic
Back woods shack (very rustic, simple, heavy)
Pilot's lounge (modernistic, big windows, radio predominating, leather or chrome furniture.)

[Editor's Note: A lot of soldiers devised devious ways of getting past the censors and letting the folks at home know where they were stationed or what battles they had been in. (Harvey told me that when he would write home he would address the envelope to "Nancy Holland." Since there were no Nancys in his family, they figured out that he was in Nancy, France.)

I had no idea what Jack was talking about in his Oct. 27th letter when he said to open the envelopes and lay them flat. He had never mentioned anything about a "book." I did as he said and he had written "Hamm" on the inside of one of the edges of the envelope. I was not too swift on the uptake and when I answered his letter I asked him what HAMM was. I wish I could think of some excuse for being that dumb. I guess I deserved the "mini" lecture.]

Nov. 28, 1944

Dear Young Lady,

Man, it's nice to come in and find a letter from you. Still piddling around the ole home town, huh, buying presents and all that. Whatcha trying to do, babe, show me you know how to pick friends, too? Guess you can understand why I like Jane - or did you know all along? Nope, don't mean to make you jealous (see where my ego is?) but she's one in a million. You said you understood all that but I think you were trying to fool me. Maybe now - you join me in thinking that.

Whew!! I'm so darned tired that I'm dizzy, actually feel a bit on the tight side–not a single swig of even beer for weeks–maybe one (1) about a week–ten days ago. Still the bed seems to be floating.

I saw the Alps today and they're strictly rugged. From up there they should have looked like bumps–but, oh no–strictly rugged, including the long trek back. Looked sort of weird after seeing nothing but whiteness for so long. Still sorta friendly feeling to see the good old Earth there to greet you. Sorta hazy–brown, purple, jagged, snow, that yellow haze in the sky beyond them.

We did a good turn for the French break-through and then dragged back. Seems really funny but when we got back I was so tired and shaking. Darn those hunks of dough called flapjacks, no how. Please–never–waffles or corn fritters–delicious–but flapjacks–repeat–pause–never!! We did have a good supper when we got back, though–pork chops, I love.

Returned to the barracks via moonlight–our moonlight. One difference, though, "Once in a blue moon"–just a saying? Wrong. No, not even weird, but cold, brilliant and beautiful–same old moon. The dark spots were aqua, so were the light–fading to a sea green–transparent and clear. Now the clouds have come in and she's gone. Still, though, she'll be up there and you'll be looking at it tonight. Post-War-Dream–You–me–above the low overcast on a warm summers' night. You'll be slightly awe struck –believe me!! Somehow the moon seems to be part of home–

seems to smile all the time in a warm, friendly way regardless of the season.

Thinking back to Selman–that place Milton told me to stay seems like a part of Paradise. You–me–the boy-friends that we wanted, nature greeting you on every side–and some nice smooth flights. Bit tedious on dark nights–but really fun when the moon shared the sky.

My brain just ain't constructive tonight, so might as well let it choose it's own aimless wandering and relax.

When this is over I want to get right back to nature where I belong. There are so darn many things to show you–to listen to –to see, smell, make friends with, and ponder over. Talking like a maniac? Just you wait!! In the meantime,

Be seeing you, and until then, loving you (and afterwards, too.) .

Good night,

Jack

[Editor's note: The target for Nov. 27th was Offenburg, Germany. Jack sometimes misdated a letter.]

Dec. 1, 1944

Hiya, Babe,

Well, got back today–and once more there you are, waiting for me–a letter, no less. That's what I was looking forward to–too (or aussi)–s'il vous plait. Merci pour enscribe un petit document hui–or somesuch. It all comes back to me now–vaguely, darn it! Now don't go jumping to conclusions. You see, we had a little trouble yesterday. First it was gasoline - then, bingo, #2 engine deserts us. Results? Well, wish I'd paid more attention to my French lessons. We'd already hit Nov. 30th's target and had to drop out on the way back. So landed at Merville in France on three engines. No, NOT SWEDEN–you can't divorce me yet–said nothing about France, did you? So there! Can I help it if the hotel only had one room vacant and me with nine men on my hands. So, to le gendarme–oh, the beginning–whole story, huh? O.K. but first, remember your letter was the most welcome reason I came back today. Then, of course, we were near the breaking point whenever someone offered us food. They had barely enough to keep the spark going, at that.

First we headed for the official emergency field–only to be unable to locate it, though Sugar had me flying over it at least twice, according to the map. Things were looking down–our gas supply was the same and I was afraid of the other three engines since there was no way of exactly determining what the trouble was. Finally chased down a passel of Air Transport Command cargo ships–fired flares, had Edwards at the Waist sending messages with the biscuit gun (hand light.) They finally caught on–changed course, led us over a landing strip and then, bingo, I got them on the radio. "Thanks, buds, thanks a hellofa lot." There was a bit of wing waggling–sort of difficult with three engines–anyway, they circled until we got in O.K., wiggled once more and left. (Makes you like those guys.)

Now–the field–lucky us–was a bomb packed boche field. No, not quite–a very meager detachment of British there–willing to help in every way–but unable to do a thing but feed us–later I found out it was horse meat (BUT NOT BAD!) and a few cold boiled potatoes, our first meal since before dawn.

Tried radio, wireless, VHF–everything–no luck–couldn't contact nothing–if you know what I mean. Gassed up and attempted to determine engine failure. Finally decided what it was–not too encouraging on the condition of the other three. So to town–it's getting dark. One hotel room–draw straws–"No sir, you take it. We'll go ahead and let the police billet us with, or in civilian homes."

Like #!!# you will!! Privileged characters, huh? Forget the hotel–we'll all stay with civilians." So down the street we go, clumping along with our heavy boots and clumsy looking heavy clothing. The police first ask for a cigarette–granted.*

Gilday's popularity zoomed among all the crew. (He speaks French fluently.) Solham pulling one arm–me on the other–Del Pero had him by the collar–see, only two men per house–so who gets the interpreter? The police didn't ask them to take us –they knocked–shoved two men in–and down the street! Finally five of us left. Pulling rank (c.s. aren't I?) I promoted Gilday to temporary Flight Officer–and officers must not mix with the enlisted men! Finally Napolitano and Solham left us–3! "Well, Del Pero, looks like you'll have be alone." Felt bad about it, though, really.

Finally Gilday and I are shoved into a home. Couldn't help it, young lady,–no choice, I swear. This family was grandmere, mamere, papere, and two jeune filles.

Guess I'd better write the rest next week. Gotta go–be seeing you–uh O.K., O.K.–18 and 20 respectively–I repeat–we had no choice.

Very nice family and I ain't kidding. We jabbered–Me, sitting around with a silly grin–nodding and huh-ing, etcetera. Finally told them that I had learned more French in two hours than I had in three months in school–and meant it.

Not much happened. Gilday and I slept in the same feather bed–and, oh man, did it feel good to snuggle down under that feather quilt. They knocked next morning–at 7, as requested. Rough, and I ain't kidding–to bail out in that cold, pre-dawned room. Tried everything imaginable to contact the emergency field for help–still no go–getting nowhere fast. Filled #2 with oil–she'd do for a few minutes. No real weather service–word of mouth that weather was brewing over England. Dadgummit, we aren't going to stay here and rot!

Cargo ships came in–returning to England–O.K. "Gilday, Schultz, Nap, Del Pero–grab your shutes, Mae Wests and all the flak you can carry. That takes about 900 or 1,000 lbs. off the ship–we'll try getting off on three. Tell the base we're coming. Be seeing you."

So off they go–after a little sweating, we followed–feathered #2 as soon as we got our wheels up. Made it O.K. and that's about all–of course elaborations later–for years.

Bought one pair of sabots for shower and general knock around use. Still no presents, Miss–but I love you–whether I can show it or not. That was all I could get in the way of novelties–or presents. SABOTS!

Just think–horse meat last night–caviar tonight–funny war! Caviar was furnished by Koppel, a nice guy from Wisconsin–shack mate.

By the way, another change of crew. Laforet–for one guy who needs two to finish–then Moore–former technical representative on B-24s–that consolidates the crew, at last! Got the feeling growing that we're gonna have one of the best crews over here - especially when we reach about 10 or 15 missions. Moore is green on 24s but has plenty of time in B-25s, and, so I'm told, about 1600 flying hours–more than I have–what do you know? He's very quiet, sensible–think he's from the south or west. I think he's going to be tops once we get started together.

That leaves Schultz–who has developed into a sorta scatter-brain, though he'll be O.K. in flight.

Be seeing you - I'll write very shortly but gotta sleep.
Lots of love

(Il dit) Jack "Je vous aime beaucoup"

[Editor's note: November 30th target was Homburg, Germany.]

There were rumors that Sweden, at that time, was noted for availability and acceptance of "free love." I had told Jack that if he ever wrote me that he had been "forced" down in Sweden, I would start divorce proceedings immediately.

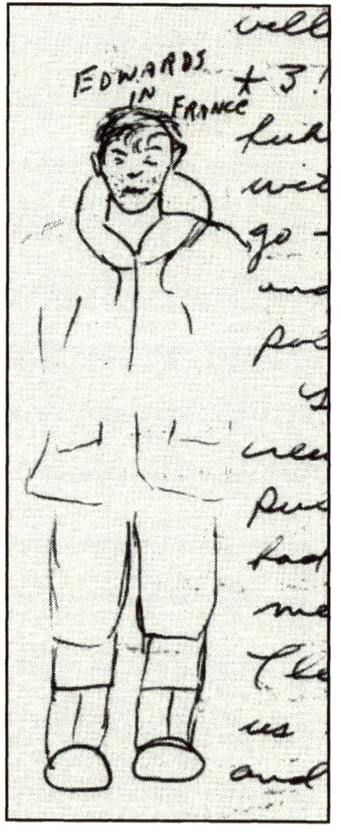

Drawings in letter

V-mail

Dec. 8, 1944

Dear Lady,

My apologies, it's been about a week since I've written. Wrote Harold, Bill, Uncle Richard and more'n likely two or three others. Go ahead strain your eyes for naught. Still not much to write about - or maybe on account of that there are just two types of days over here and they begin repeating themselves. The two types - mission and non-mission days.

Sorta lost tract of the towns we've been to–just don't bother. Might as well forget to count them but, as a hint, not quite half the total number. For awhile things looked pretty promising but everyone on the crew began to get a bit irritable, now and then –so I pushed for a 48-hour pass. Got it, went to London–not much fun–but a bit more experience and opinions were brought about and if I tell you all about such things now, what will I talk about when I get home? I was, as usual, a good little boy. Fact is, and I ain't kidding, some of these guys are beginning to wonder if'n I'm human and I'm wondering why it should be so unusual? Long as I know you're there to greet me, I shouldn't have any trouble.

Went by and checked on Col. Cushing and he's in Paris.

Returned from 48 and found your cable about Harp. Don't mean to hint at psychics or any of that, but for at least a month I've had the feeling he was laid up somewhere–though I thought it would be France. Now it looks as if it will be awhile before I can get to see him–BUT–I intend locating his location tomorrow - and taking it from there. Here's hoping from the bottom of my heart that he's not seriously injured.

Sometimes I'm afraid the war has made me a little too impersonal in my thoughts and sometimes–actions. In trying to foresee trouble and accidents, I find myself deciding who would be best to help and who should wait their turn to be rescued where complete rescue seems impossible.

With us (family and friends) we just can't expect God to spare everyone so there's no reason to let it affect us too much should anything happen. He's been good to everyone I know, so far, and I hope everyone continues the same in His protection. Selfish, aren't I?

Now, since this is likely to drag on and on and I've got a job to do - my share of work here in the barracks–better go. More tomorrow - and probably pretty conceited–Get set.

See you,
lots–pulenty of love

Jack

[Editor's note: The target for Dec. 5th was Munster, Germany.]

Dec. 8, 1944

Dear you,
Dearest you,

Haven't heard–long time–need you–very much–comes the day we're together again–please, Honey–(comes naturally, too) please don't get away from me again.

This business of being away from you just ain't supposed to be! I need you–repeat–you to talk to me, listen to me and head me off occasionally when it begins to be dusk and it's hard to see ahead. No, Miss, I don't mean that the going is getting rougher –I just need your hand to hold on to occasionally, just for reassurance, for my ego and peace of mind in general. Come on now, give out–show me the way through this little stretch of woods–won't you? Please, I'm actually pleading and in case you're interested, I'm neither lonesome nor melancholy; fact is I feel good–the kind of feeling that makes you want someone else to share it with you.

We just returned from another pass to London. My new co-pilot, Lieutenant Moore and I went together this time. There should be another name for him besides co-pilot on account of that word just seems to make a person less capable. For some reason good co-pilots are few and far between, consequently the average conception of that word is first of a person with little experience. Moore is from Jacksonville, 29 years old, married and verging on that state of mind that men get into when they're most dependable, because they're sorta settled in one frame of mind and settle that mind on the job at hand until it's done. He was flying in the Navy for quite a long time–supposedly a couple of thousands hours there. Then he's flown B-25s to the tune of 1,600 hours. I hope he has as much faith in my capabilities as I have in his. 'Twould be selfish to hope that he would go all the way through his missions with me–however at present I hate to think about having to start all over with another guy about the 15th or 20th mission. We've had one mission together and it's amazing how much of a load it takes off my mind to know there's a guy right beside me who believes in playing this game as safely as possible–as monotonously as conditions permit–without having an uncontrollable desire now and then to hit a few hot licks for the benefit of what audience might be on hand. I don't have to sweat when there are ships coming from all sides–he believes, as much as I, in keeping up with what's going on–on every side–and in the blind spots, too. There's a sort of teamwork there–somewhere–that tells me just what he sees on his side, consequently all I have to do is keep the plane clear from where I can see, which comes naturally. What's more, in the emergencies–and we have them occasionally–there's complete trust in his being able to cope with any of them without me having to fly formation, watch the engines and stay tense during the period when a fraction of a second might mean losing an engine. In other words, when I'm flying that's all I have on my mind now–he takes care of messages, the crew and the engines–which shows to go you–that a good co-pilot has to be as good, possibly more so, than the so-called first pilot is.

Well, anyway, we went to London together. Missed Bill again –this time I think he has gone on over.

I've been having a pretty good time–or I did in London this time–fact I haven't sworn not to go back expect to meet someone I know–as I did every other time. First time–curiosity–second time–to meet Bill–however this third time I'll change my tune.

I talked with such a huge variety of people–their hopes, opinions and what have you–every walk of life–every type of character, including the bluffs, the low in mind, the egotistical, Yanks, rebels from Washington State to Biloxi, Mississippi. Stranger than fiction I ended up with the --- NAVY!! Four guys–each different–ranging from Ensign to something or other way up. Two were perfect gentlemen–without being dull thuds, two were wolves. One–the one that left a more vivid reaction in my mind than anyone has in years–is–A Mormon with no hush-hush or whisperings–the most perfect gentleman I've ever met. Funny, but for the first time since I can remember I had a feeling of deep and genuine respect for a guy. It's a hellova thing to try and explain–however it gave me a big boost to realize that there are a few such people left. Can you understand?

What's more, while we were in their apartment (the four guys' apt)–they waited, actually waited on me hand and foot–real bourbon, cokes–in coke bottles, popcorn, which I showed them how to pop–and if you think I don't know how–ask me to prove it sometime! Conceited as Hell, and I admit it. He was the equivalent of an Army Captain and wrote down the address when I left–with a genuine invitation to stay there any time I was in London. The apartment was actually luxurious (the Navy, you know)–three bedrooms, two baths, living room, fireplace, kitchen, electric range and frigidaire–it's amazing how much a guy misses those things–that only women are supposed to miss.

The key to the whole thing was–they apologized, time and time again, for being in such a comfortable position. The reason for being so darn nice to me was that they had been in a few trials themselves, not so long ago–and knew from experience just how much I appreciated it.

While in London I visited one of the most famous clubs in the world (I didn't know it at the time) and after that, one of the most infamous–and unknown–because if it was known, it wouldn't be. Now the first–Run by–"Old Red"–maybe you've seen her on the newsreels. She's famous the globe over–and I've never heard of her, consequently I got into an argument through a chained door and ended up getting my ears burned up by the most professional bit of swearing I've heard in my life–without being insulted once. Moore, a friend of his (a Captain) and I were taken there after hours by a cabbie. The door was closed. I knocked. It opened about three inches–stopped by a chain. No one in sight. "Hello in there. Any possibility of getting a round of drinks?" Bang!! "Who the hell do you think you are, coming along at this hour?" "We're Americans." "I don't give a ---- ------- --- --- --- etc. who you are. What do you want–a round of drinks, four guys? Well, you can't get it now and I don't give a --- -- -- - (100) if you are American. Get away from that door."

Well, I'm mad. "If Americans aren't welcome here what's the idea of the American flag in porcelain on the door?"

"It's none of your - -- -- business. Get away from that door."

"O.K., I'll get–but first I'll tear every sign of that flag down and if you intend stopping me, don't say I didn't warn you of that. Regardless of your sex, nationality or prestige you'll regret it if you try to stop me."

About that time the Captain said, "Tell her you have wings." I did. The door swung open and she asked us to come in. Told us it was after hours–and she couldn't help us–though she'd give us a quart of Scotch in the morning if we'd come back. She had straight copper red hair–a hideous face–no eyebrows–but two thin penciled lines, instead. She begged us to take the two guys who were there out so she could go home–we finally did. The cab driver stuck his head in to tell us that the meter was still running–and were we leaving or staying? She lit into him –called him, among other things, a stinkin' yellow-bellied Limey and used a phrase, which since then I've found, she used on a three star general who didn't have wings, "Get your -- out of here." There were short snorters on the walls totaling over $2,000.–even $100 bills. There was an Admiral who came by not so long ago to present her with Japanese and Chinese bills (The only two countries she didn't have.) She invited him to one drink–he finished it–and then, "Get your -- --- out of here." He did.

Truthfully, I think she's insane. She just recently started admitting paratroopers. No one without wings is allowed inside–except once–for the Admiral. She is rabid on Limeys–and to mention a woman or anything pertaining to them is suicide. She finally told us a place to go–though she'd rather we didn't. It was black market and the prices were unheard of–we went. I'll tell you about that dive someday. No signs of lice yet but the general appearance of it suggested rats, roaches, fleas, lice and everything else. Once inside everyone lost all interest in any kind of drink - fact is they couldn't have killed our jubilant spirits quicker if there had been tuberculosis, leprosy and such on all sides. We left and turned in for the night - much the worst for the experience–and never again will any of us pay a cover charge before we see what lies inside the door. Strictly, we were on the up and up the whole time, so don't think about that again.

Just what do you think about all these ravings, Miss? I had to tell you all about it–and now tell me things–just rattle on.

I love you,

Jack

V-MAIL

Dec. 13, 1944

Dear you,

who doesn't write often. Your V-mail came today on the installment plan. First installment only!! Gives me something to look forward to, though. Man, I'm glad to hear you're situated where you can see the sunshine occasionally. Nice walk to the folks' house, too, eh what? I can almost pick the house because I carried mail there in '39–or was it '40?

Now, will the censor think
that's a map of over here,
or did he come from
Silver Spring, too? [Editor's note: See following page.]

By the way, got a box from Banks with some delicious candy in it–in man-sized hunks, too. I guess I'm blowing my top but there are so many little things that I crave from time to time that you would think it was me carrying that there baby instead of you. While I'm thinking of it, what was the girl's name?–and what if it's a boy this time? How do you look–showing yet? Yeah, I know–you're gaining weight that can't be attributed to family growth.

Now–back to the requests–save the list and maybe the guy up there at the Post Office will let you use it from time to time. Now, darn it, I've forgotten most of them–good think, too.

1 - Sausage–smoked, country or kosher salami–yeah, with garlic
2 - Nuts–salted, raw, pecans, peanuts–anything
3 - Popcorn–un-popped
4 - Pickles–<u>sweet</u> and olives, if possible
5 - Pretzels, <u>Lance</u> crackers–Toastees, etc.

Anything else you might think of but some good old smoked sausage would taste good. Say a package two or three times a month. I think we'll all go nuts when Christmas packages cease arriving.

Seems like I've forgotten everything I had in mind so guess I might as well quiet down–main reason is I've got to make this sack from top to bottom. So I'll continue soon. In the meantime take care of yourself and Keep Me Informed, darnit. I miss you - and your building my ego up and besides that I love you, it's high time you returned it.

P.S. or else!!!

Lots of love

Jack

[Editor's note: During the war there were regulations about sending packages to the men overseas. One had to have a written request from the soldier for any items sent. The package was then taken to the Post Office, with the request, where it had to be approved and was officially stamped. That was so the request could not be used again. That is why Jack seems to be making so many requests in his letters.

Dec. 11th's target was Hanau, Germany.]

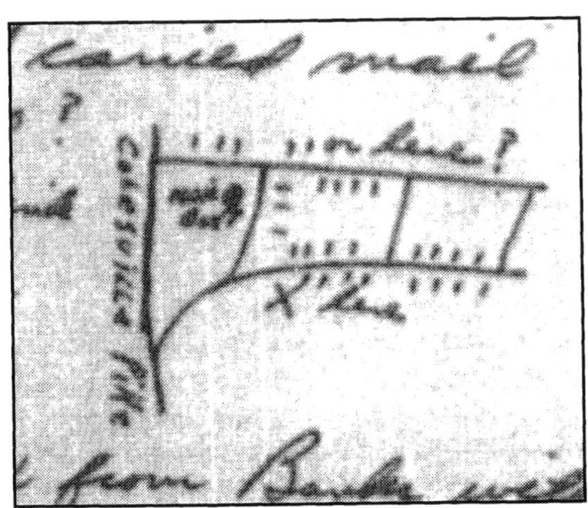

Drawing in letter

V-MAIL

Dec. 17, 1944

Dear Miss,

Your second installment in V-mail arrived yesterday. No other letters have arrived these past three or four weeks. Must be devoting mail facilities to packages and V-mail.

We've been stood down for three days running in order to celebrate this Group's 200th mission party. Quite a celebration, if you like scotch, beer, gin, and rum–which I don't. Now with bourbon or rye it's entirely different–so while it was quite an explosion 'twould have been better with the latter liquids as primers. Still it was pretty drunk out last night and water played a big part on the field's menu today.

Now, down to business–you keep dropping occasional bits of information on this landlady deal. Now, is that nice? Either all or nothing at all. If it isn't already settled, you can go the Courts and Boards of the closest army base and let them handle it - or to save lots of red tape you can proceed as follows; Legal assistance can be obtained in any of the following manners–providing, of course, you haven't already proceeded to put professional aids to use–which wouldn't hurt anything. The aids below have already been set up.

1 - Personal or civilian attorney

2 - Member of the Advisory Board for Registrants (Established in each county, pursuant to Selective Service regulations)

3 - Member of local bar committee on war work. (The American Bar Association has been responsible for the organization of such committees to provide legal assistance to soldiers and their dependents)

4 - Any member of the Army who is a licensed attorney.

'Nough said, I'd say for you to write or phone the Maryland State Chairman of the Bar who will refer the matter to a local bar committee on war work. His name and address: B. Harris

Henderson, 231 St. Paul Street, Baltimore, Md.–or just ask any attorney in Silver Spring who the local attorney is that has been assigned for such cases. Go ahead–get it over with–and sue, if Mr. Murray advises. But do it now.

That about covers everything at present. Especially so since I'll miss mess if I don't proceed now.

If you please–got any smoked sausage links handy?

Yep, still love you.
Jack

I do not have any of the letters that I wrote Jack when he was overseas and my memory on some things is hazy. I vaguely remember having a financial conflict with my landlady and decided to move out. I'm pretty sure it was settled amicably and I had no need for the lawyers or agencies that Jack recommended.

In November I moved into a nice house in Silver Spring near Jack's mother and the Clements.

It was owned and occupied by a woman named Mrs. Beckerman who worked downtown. The house had been designed so that the upstairs could be finished off as a second floor. Mrs. Beckerman has started this but had to halt the construction because of the wartime scarcity of materials and labor. She told me that people knew her house was empty all day and had been coming in while she was gone and stealing the copper wire that was partially installed upstairs.

She wanted very much to find someone to share the house and keep an eye on things. I seemed to fill the bill. It was a nice arrangement

Which leads me to the incident I mentioned earlier about my "moment of truth" when the situation finally arose and I thought I might have to defend myself.

One winter morning several hours after Mrs. Beckerman had gone to work, Jennis and I were alone in the house when I heard a noise upstairs. I listened and heard the noise again. Having mentally prepared myself for just such a situation, I got my gun and stood at the foot of the stairs leading to the closed attic door. My son, who was 19 months old at the time and could speak quite clearly, was fascinated. He kept saying, "You got a gun, Mommy? Lemme see de gun. I wanna hold de gun, Mommy." I was badly frightened and as I tried to quiet him, I realized, and faced the fact, that I could not have pulled that trigger if Gargantua had opened that door and stood there.

I called the police station and in no time two policemen, wearing high boots and carrying pistols, arrived. They checked the attic and it was empty. They said the noise was the snow sliding down the roof. I had heard snow sliding off roofs all my life but it just shows what fear and imagination can do.

I felt like an idiot, but the Officers were very nice. They said, "Never hesitate to call us if you think something is wrong. We'd much rather come out 100 times and find nothing wrong, than have you not call the one time something is really dangerous."

Since then, on the few occasions when I thought someone was trying to enter my house, I have not hesitated to call the police. They've always answered promptly and have been equally as nice as those two men.

Dec. 23, 1944

Dear Miss,

Got back from an exceedingly long mission today and found that you were pretty much on the ball during November. Maybe the mails just happened to congregate while we were away and the results–all at once were pretty impressive. The mission came to an end this afternoon–or something over a hundred hours on one mission–mind you!

Seems that we took off Tuesday morning–and back here Saturday at dusk–what think you? No, nothing secret–nothing unusual–except that we were lucky to have found a place to land. For awhile it looked like France again–but, no, we got across the channel O.K. and there were a few spots over here still open, so down we came. We had to stay that way until this afternoon - and even then I didn't see the ground from wheels up until we neared the base. Some stuff and of all the places to have been stuck. Some Limey village out in nowhere. Things were looking up today for the first time–fact is we've been invited to a dance by some very hospitable nurses. Hospitable? Yep,–you've never seen a mothier bunch in your life (Us.) The guys were wearing everything from electric Suits in a variety of shapes, colors and fit down to oil stained suntans and heavy boots–no shoes. Three days beards, no soap or towels–finally bought tooth brushes and shared a large tube of paste.

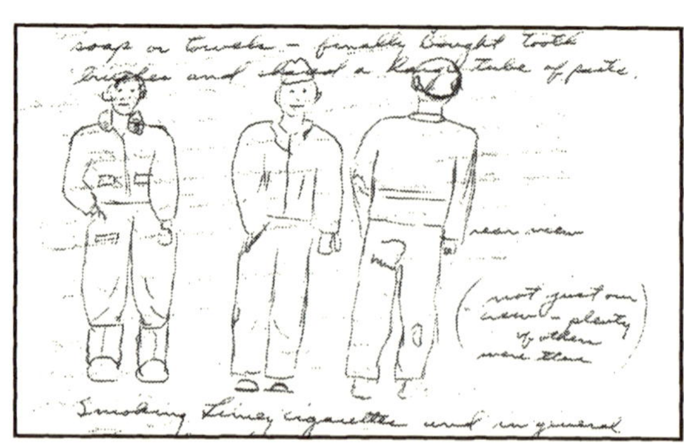

Rear view (not just our crew plenty of others)

Smoking Limey cigarettes and in general, a bunch of hoboes.

Soon as they found out the set up they immediately insisted in giving us all their rationed cigarettes that they had on their persons. Nope, didn't get friendly-over the feeling of brother - sisterhood of all Americans over here. Played one game of ping-pong with someone from Lancaster-she had to catch her bus shortly-and gave me a package of Luckies-my first American cigarette in three days. You'd have to smoke a Limey one to appreciate such generosity! Before they left they invited the whole gang to the dance tonight and said they'd have everything O.K.'d by their Colonel (speaking of our appearance.)

The Red Cross hostess promised us a Christmas Turkey dinner and general American Pow-Wow Christmas. Naturally, after starving along all week-both food and cigarettes. We left there this morning-so it goes. Still glad we got back-watch the smoke over there next week-they need it and bad!

Now, let's see-Robin? No-doesn't sound just right, somehow-what was the girl's name we decided upon at first? The name. Then there's Allen-Allen what? First or second name? Murray would make a good second. How about other firsts, too? Let's see-Otha-Millard-Clay-Vinteus-oh well-Hayward-Miles -what then? Buster-Randolph-Herman.-go ahead-take your choice. You can see our minds have gotten pretty much in a rut over here-war, you know,-Harvey? Uh, girls?-Fortress, Havoc, Hurricane-Now take that there Havoc, interesting, eh? 'Nough said, you suggest for awhile.

Now-the sack-tomorrow, you know. Be seeing you and wish it were now.

Lots of-yeah-LOVE
Jack
Your husband, you know, scatterbrain

More shortly when I don't need the sleep.

[Editor's note: Dec. 19th's raid was on Ehrang, Germany. Fog had closed down the home base so they had to spend 4 days in Southern England.]

Dec. 24, 1944

Ole Gal,

Everybody's had it today. Something tells me the heaviest blow ever dealt by warfare was dealt today. Yours truly or our gang placed 6,000 lbs. on the dot. Jerries had it, and what's more–since sun-up–we're still not completely landed yet–the guys are still droning in–and it's been dark an hour. I'm dead tired so until tomorrow–lots and lots of love, Jack. Let's see–yeah, Jack, that'll do. Sweet dreams for you and me and that's Christmas Eve. Night, Miss.

Now, let's start over. This is the 26th–too tired on the 25th, you know. Not much going on, we missed a good day today–maybe tomorrow. The boys over there at the front are at it without let up, but if this weather keeps up, it won't be long before this little business reaches it's climax, then it's going to swing one way or the other–but fast.

Somehow I can't get down to the grim business of savage hate that's supposed to go along with warfare. The Germans, as a country, affect me that way but when we hit that town day before yesterday I couldn't help but wonder what they thought about this Christmas Eve. One second there was a town down there, cold and barren with snow covered hills all around. Blink your eyes and there's nothing but a pile of smoking rubble. The town wasn't much larger than Rockville; fact is you might call it "Bitsburg." Quite a bit more compact and populated than Rockville.

Christmas has come and gone and I don't believe I've heard "I'm Dreaming of a White Christmas" once this year. The frost over here gets so thick that it looks like a heavy, wet snow. Every twig on every bush is outlined with half an inch of frost. Even the mesh fences seem to be white lace. What's more, it lasts day after day. Thick enough to break the twigs and eat the frost thereon–Yes!–Frost!!

By the way, thanks, Miss, thanks for the presents. Most of the candy is tucked away for future reference. The cigarette lighter is in my pocket right now, something I need more than some-

what. The things that are really worth their weight in gold here abouts are the things that come in handy at pre-sack time when everyone is in whatever they sleep in and standing around the stove, prior to rushing into the sack. Onions are plentiful over here - but no mayonnaise to complete the most delicious sandwich of them all! Hint, you know. Potted ham, we have–K-rations–we've gorged on them so much they're almost too much to even smell. The things we have are good–and plenty–on that we can't complain but it's monotonous to have corned beef (Libby's) five times a week–and then try to make a sandwich of it at bedtime. Sooo–once more a list;

We have	*We wish*
corned beef	*cured sausage – fried sausage cakes*
cheese	*(They'll keep in jars – cooked.)*
spam	*sardines – mustard - mayonnaise*
	popcorn – nuts – hot dogs
	whole milk – but how would you send it?

There I go again – wishing – and all it would take is a trip home – for say 80 years.

When I get home - what? Wanna go to school? Wanna try the Department of Interior? Wanna try farming? Now take that farming business. It would take quite a few years of hard work. One thing I've found out about me over here is the harder the work–the more interested and energetic I become. So, consequently–in the case of working for us–at something I'm interested in–eventually we'd come out on top–but would I be the only one who would enjoy it? There's no doubt in my mind–whatsoever–that we'd end up with the nicest home, the cleanest and best farm–the choicest stock that can be had. Sounds hickish, doesn't it? Well, maybe so, but it wouldn't be that way. First place we wouldn't be slaves to a certain crop–like the farmers usually are–tobacco, cotton, etc.–crops with the most demands, which will be soy beans, peanuts, corn and truck vegetables and fruits. Fine beef and pork–with horses as a sideline and hobby.

Enough variety so that regardless of crop failure–or prices–

there'd be plenty of other markets on the other stuff. Then if–and when–a depression came at least our quantity and quality of food would be assured. What's more, with planes developing as they are, it would be fun to branch off with a small–select resort–or if nothing else, a restaurant with our products on the menu. Sounds daydreamish but every time I start thinking about veterinary or Fish and Wildlife they seem mighty uncertain and farming comes up again. Naturally I see only the brighter side just thinking about it - but the hard work involved only makes me want to dig in and get started all the worse–call it a challenge, if you may.

No, it wouldn't be cut and dried at first. First off, there wouldn't be the dreaded monotony of city life and hours. Secondly, there's no better place on Earth to raise children. Thirdly, no boss. Fourthly, the plane would keep us in touch with home –no matter if we lived in South Carolina, Louisiana, the Ozarks or close to the Gulf–say Mississippi.

Maybe this will all wear off but it certainly gives me a wonderful feeling to dream and plan. Right now we've got at least a start on savings and by squeezing a little maybe we could save even more. 'Bout time I started getting eager again about promotion–I've thought about it–more and more, and a raise could mean that much more–clear. I could get along on less over here, easily,–especially if I knew it was being duplicated back home. Fact is I've loaned 2/3rds of a month's allowance out already–so that really puts me ahead next month! Just how much could you save if I could boost the allotment $75 or so? No stuff, now, just how much could we count on saving each month?

Now back to the farm. We can be choosy–now–about its location: Pretty particular–so it'll be a little harder to find. First–fertile–like Louisiana or the valleys of the Ozarks. Then, thinking about the restaurant or Resort end of things. Close to beaches and or–hunting and fishing reserves–South Carolina or Mississippi. Duck hunters spend most extravagantly–so bayous or streams. Once more S.C., Miss., La. Foolish, or is it? We could have a small landing field close by–in fact the restaurant could overlook it and the countryside at the same time. So to consolidate all this into a picture–or dream, as you would–here goes:

First–though couldn't be complete for a few years–take a long, low rambling home (modern plumbing, heating, lighting) fit into the countryside with a nice view of lawn–with a river or marsh in the distance. The land in between–grazing land, unbroken by cultivated fields, place the garden off to the rear–or a small orchard or grape arbor. The fields in the rear of the "homestead." The stables and barn below the hill to one side. Then take the farm and place it to one side of a marsh (or a definite rise of ground) or in view of the sea shore (might necessitate sandy soil, though)–or a river. Just beyond a small coppice you may eventually find summer cottages, a restaurant and a landing field. Put yourself near the house–a couple of kids outside and then we'd all settle down to enjoy life. Maybe there's a special movie–a circus–in Columbia, or Rocky Mount, or New Orleans–let's take a hop down and relax from the toils of farming for awhile. The lights on the field can be set for a definite time to come on–and go off at dawn, so we won't have to worry about getting back at any particular time. No more than a hundred dollars would light the field–probably 1/4th of that amount, so don't jump on me about that yet.

Rosy picture?–or aren't you even interested? O.K.–if you are –if you are, don't forget the first spell of hardships–or maybe we could be sufficiently close to a small town so that it wouldn't be too hard. Then we could start the farm and stock and then build the house–complete in its entirety. Move out to the farm–free from everything we don't like–close to anything and everything we wanted. The boy would grow up broadminded–good schooling–and clean minded, too–without losing touch with the world, as so often has been the case in the past, speaking of boys raised on a farm.

You can put the dream aside now–close by, if you like–let me know about it, though.

Better crawl in the sack–need to rest for tomorrow again. And again, you can see what we think of during off moments–but always comes tomorrow–so–be seeing you.

Love, and more love,
The farmer.

[Editor's note: When Jack wrote that the town was small, "you might call it Bitsburg." I thought he was using an expression like "Podunk." Years later I found out that the target for December 24th was Bitburg, Germany. On December 28 it was Homburg, Germany; on December 30, Auskirchen, Germany; January 2, Glutz, Germany; January 3, Pirmasens, Germany; and January 5, Somerheim. Germany.]

Drawing on bottom of letter

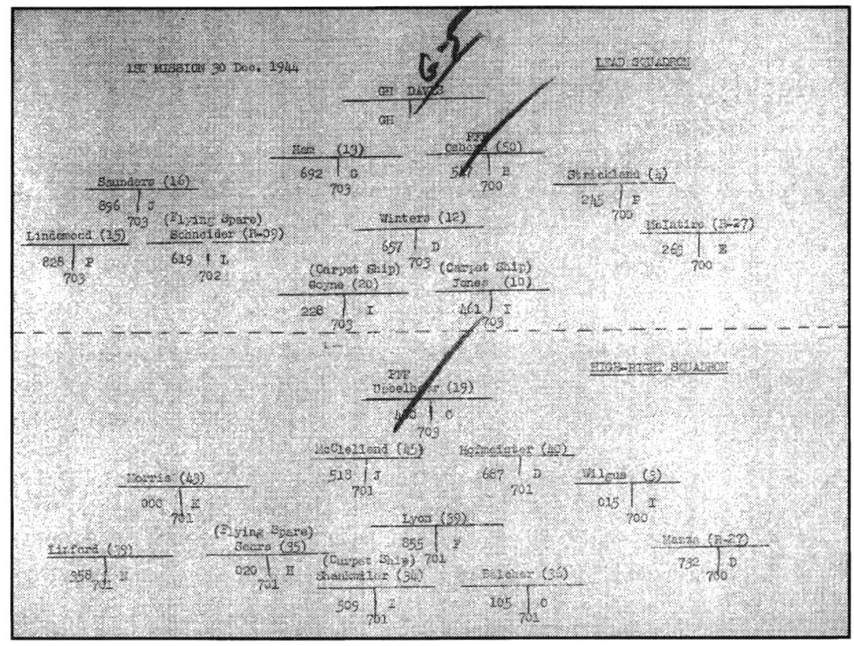

1ST MISSION 30 Dec. 1944

LEAD SQUADRON

GH DAVIS
GH

Ham (13)
692 G
703

PFF
Osborne (50)
547 B
700

Saunders (16)
896 J
703

Strickland (4)
245 F
700

Lindemood (15)
828 P
703

(Flying Spare)
Schneider (R-09)
619 L
702

Winters (12)
657 D
703

McIntire (R-27)
268 E
700

(Carpet Ship)
Goyne (20)
228 I
703

(Carpet Ship)
Jones (10)
461 T
703

HIGH-RIGHT SQUADRON

PFF
Uppelhoer (19)
480 C
703

McClelland (45)
518 J
701

Holmeister (40)
687 D
701

Morris (43)
000 K
701

Wilgus (8)
015 T
700

Lyon (39)
855 F
701

Linford (39)
358 N
701

(Flying Spare)
Sears (35)
020 H
701

(Carpet Ship)
Shankwiler (34)
309 Z
701

Belcher (36)
105 O
701

Manza (R-27)
732 D
700

Flight orders: December 30, 1944 and January 2, 1945

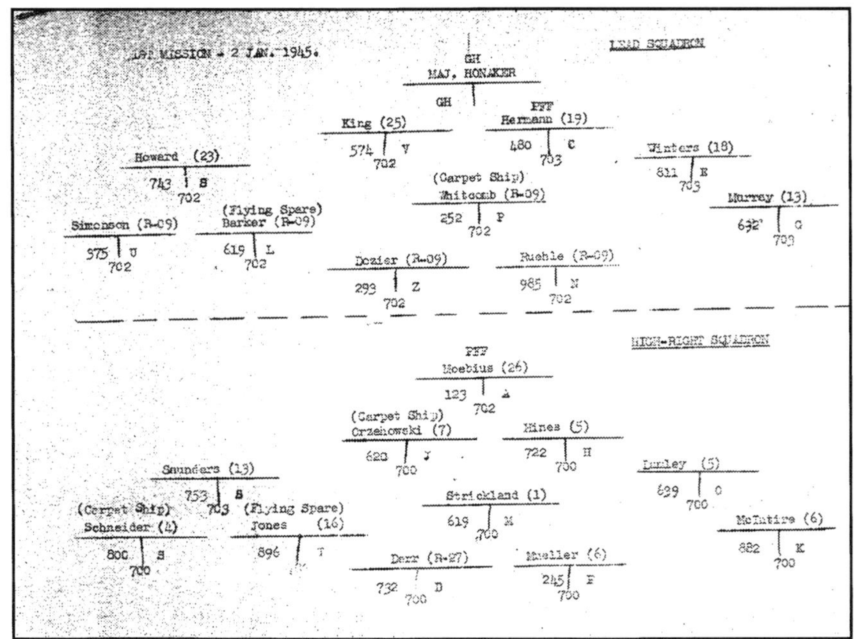

1st MISSION - 2 JAN. 1945.

LEAD SQUADRON

GH
MAJ. HONAKER
GH

King (25)
574 V
702

PFF
Hermann (19)
480 C
703

Winters (18)
811 E
703

Howard (23)
743 S
702

(Carpet Ship)
Whitcomb (R-09)
252 P
702

Murray (13)
632 Q
703

Simonson (R-09)
375 U
702

(Flying Spare)
Barker (R-09)
619 L
702

Dozier (R-09)
293 Z
702

Ruehle (R-09)
985 N
702

HIGH-RIGHT SQUADRON

PFF
Moebius (26)
123 A
702

(Carpet Ship)
Crzehowski (7)
620 J
700

Hines (5)
722 H
700

Saunders (13)
753 S
703

Durley (5)
639 O
700

Strickland (1)
619 M
700

(Carpet Ship)
Schneider (4)
800 S
700

(Flying Spare)
Jones (16)
896 T

McIntire (6)
882 K
700

Derr (R-27)
732 D
700

Mueller (6)
245 F
700

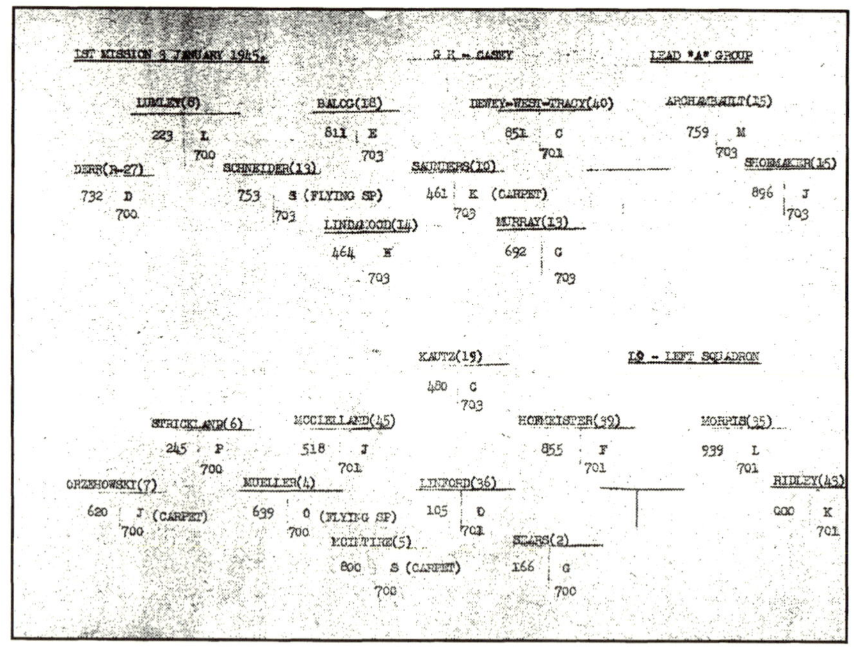

1ST MISSION 3 JANUARY 1945. — G H - CASEY — LEAD "A" GROUP

LUMLEY(8) 223 L 700
BALOG(18) 811 E 703
DEWEY-WEST-TRACY(40) 851 C 701
ARCHAMBAULT(15) 759 M 703
DERR(R-27) 732 D 700
SCHNEIDER(13) 753 S (FLYING SP) 703
SAUNDERS(10) 461 K (CARPET) 703
SHOEMAKER(16) 896 J 703
LINDWOOD(14) 464 H 703
MURRAY(13) 692 G 703

KAUTZ(19) 480 C 703 — LQ - LEFT SQUADRON

STRICKLAND(6) 245 P 700
MCCLELLAND(45) 518 J 701
HOFMEISTER(39) 855 F 701
MORRIS(35) 939 L 701
ORZEHOWSKI(7) 620 J (CARPET) 700
MUELLER(4) 639 O (FLYING SP) 700
LINFORD(36) 105 D 701
RIDLEY(43) 000 K 701
MCINTIRE(5) 800 S (CARPET) 700
SEARS(2) 166 G 700

Flight orders: January 3 and January 5, 1945

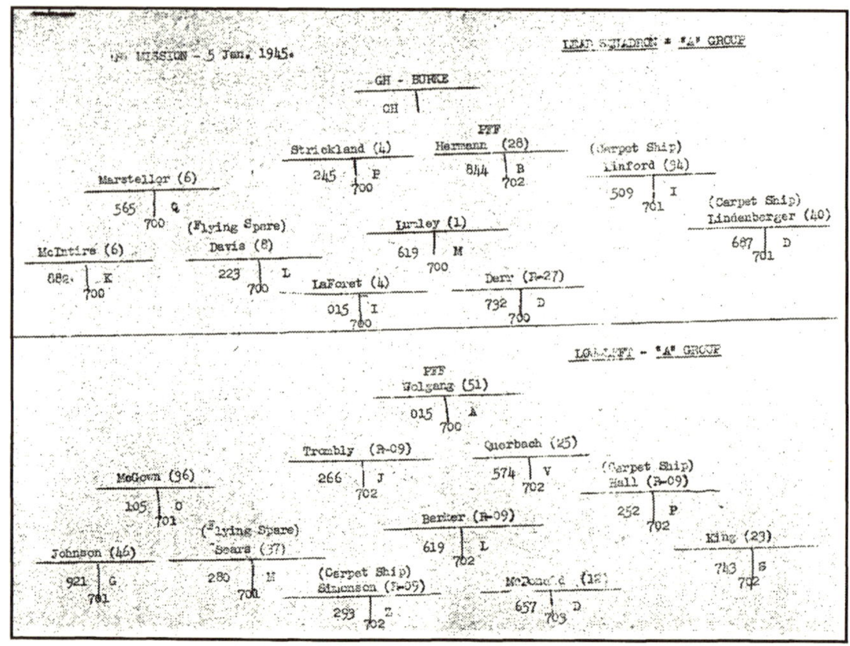

MISSION - 5 Jan. 1945. — LEAD SQUADRON - "A" GROUP

GH - BURKE CH
Strickland (4) 245 P 700
PFF Hermann (28) 844 B 702
(Carpet Ship) Linford (34) 509 I 701
Marsteller (6) 565 Q 700
(Carpet Ship) Lindenberger (40) 687 D 701
(Flying Spare) Davis (8) 223 L 700
Lumley (1) 619 M 700
McIntire (6) 882 K 700
LaForet (4) 015 I 700
Derr (R-27) 732 D 700

LOW LEFT - "A" GROUP

PFF Wolgang (51) 015 A 700
Trombly (R-09) 266 J 702
Querbach (25) 574 V 702
(Carpet Ship) Hall (R-09) 252 P 702
McGown (36) 105 O 701
Berker (R-09) 619 L 702
King (23) 743 S 702
(Flying Spare) Sears (37) 280 M 701
Johnson (46) 921 G 701
(Carpet Ship) Simonson (R-09) 293 Z 702
McDonald (12) 657 D 703

Jan. 11, 1945

Good Evening,

Well, young lady, you know how it is. Your birthday approaching and I still haven't found anything that you'd appreciate or can use. Since first hitting this place I've been on the alert for a certain type of tableware–knives, forks, spoons, etc., but until now–no go. Silverware and jewelry, once more, is neither of such wide variety or interesting as that in the States. What's more the prices are above American even including the tax. Their tax on jewelry over here is rawther miserly–being a mere 100% tax. Porcelain figurines and vawses are elaborate antiques–by famous masters–but somehow they all leave me cold. O.K. well sometime, sooner or later, I'll find something and bingo! In the meantime (and just in case) here's hoping you have a happy birthday and each one after that even happier.

Now, off we go again–more'n likely things will slow up again –for awhile, anyway. Yeah, dragging on, but even at that I'd feel like I'd sorta cheated on Harold when I get home before he does. Yeah, I know–sure–the second sooner I can be with you, the more thankful for everything I'll be.

The slow down this time shouldn't be a lengthy one–just a short period–possibly a week or less (I hope) of training which will end when we become proficient on still another phase of this birdman's war.

Let's see–what all have we done lately? Well–about a week ago they "chose" us to fly the precious pile of junk on the field, known as the "Bunny" because it has a picture of Bugs Bunny on the nose. Usually it's referred to as the "rabbit." Well–it's precious because it's about the oldest B-24 in the E.T.O. and they're trying to make a record with her. Now the mission–supposed to be next to the last before she's sent home for a publicity tour–maybe you'll see her. The number of the mission? #99 and we felt the same way! The first time we didn't get off the ground, on account of complications on the field–jot a note down to ask me about it later. The second time–up we go and, young lady, I babied her just the same as we do our dear ole P - for Peter. Well, over the Zieder Zee–no!–quits–so back we come

–yelping for our own plane. Twice our plane was flown by another guy and it just gets under your skin to see someone else using her a bit more carelessly than we think she should be. Anyway we got her back–sweetheart that she is, and it felt like putting on an old pair of gloves after trying some that had fingers too short and seams too coarse.

So, off to another tale. There was a guy who came over with us, he was the first to give me trouble–train from Savannah to N.Y., flew one mission and refused to do it again. He led a pretty miserable life around here and the night of the 200th mission party some drunken–uh–officer called him–among other things–yellow. He had to be pulled off–and then–it can be understood–started crying. I got mad enough to bust anyone who spoke to him–and finally another guy and I put him to bed. Next day he volunteered to fly with us. OK–OK–finally done–he was as nervous as a cat but since I was about the only guy who had anything to do with him, he said he'd try again with us. The first time it was a "milk run." The next mission–we more or less had it. The flak–every bit of it–was practically in the cockpit–and so was God. Got a few nicks here and there and once the ship bucked hard enough to make my aching seat–ache even more. Sorta gingerly like, I slipped my hand under my clothes–nope, not wet–for any reason. The guy, in the meantime, hadn't let out a single peep–cured!! .   I hope.

Everyone felt in much better spirits than usual when we got back. While I hadn't told the others why he was riding with us, I think everyone on board knew all about it. I walked to the barracks with him after supper and he was so darned happy that it affected me the same way. I saw a Limey, hunting rabbits - so, he takes a shot–misses–big old me got a hold of the gun while the Limey was looking in hopes he'd wounded one. Lickety-split, out comes another–whoom–got him–first time I've shot at one with a shotgun–used to do it with a rifle–but the Limey was amazed that we'd even shoot at one running. (Why, shore we do!)

Take it as you may–my old bonnet–the original–won't go on anymore–even sideways.

Well, anyway, we'd picked up a spot of flak in #1 and next day the engineering officer wanted to know all about it–seems the engine should have quit hours before we got back. That's our sweetheart for you–she's made me fall in love with the 24. Every man on the crew has the utmost faith in her. Fact is, sometimes I kid them and tell them we're flying so and so and right away you can see their faces fall–and if I don't set them straight–sooner or later–someone comes out with, "Hope they scrub this mission." We decided not to name her until we finish and then it's going to be a respectful one.

Due to circumstances we may have to give her up–it's almost impossible that we don't–but anyway, here's to success! By the way, she's also the one we landed in France with–later, on the ground, we realized we had plenty of gas to come home on. Still just to prove her mettle, she came out of there from the ground up on three engines–no trouble at all.

Harold wrote me on the 13th and that pretty well spots him because he mentioned our bombing just three miles in front of him on a certain date. He's exactly where I thought he was but that's not encouraging because that means they bore the brunt of the pushback. Wish I could let you know the differences in satisfaction of strategic bombings and the tactical ones where I know we've given the ones just in front of him a good stiff jolt.

Got your cable about Harp a couple of days back and I've been trying to get down that way without interfering with our duties too much. If these blokes over here had let it come through a couple of days earlier, I could have seen him while we were on pass. As it was, I got it about 3 hours after our pass ended. Just in case I miss him, give me the low down. Roy Edgar wrote me about the same time–wanted me to come up but that, too, was out, especially since Harp comes first under the circumstances. Fact is–next to Harold, he comes first anyway.

Blank goes my mind–so guess I'd better say "over." Young woman–guess by now you realize–thoroughly–that next to you–I love me best–think you can stand it–again? Well, anyway, keep telling me the news, both babies, you, the new quarters–and how much for rent? You've probably guessed you've got a miser on your hands. The more I make, the more I want to save –because when this is over I'd like to have a good substantial sum to see us through until I can start pulling the same in civilian life. How much do we have now? AND how much each month?–not sporadic–please!

Saving Love, too–for you
Be seeing you,

Jack

[Ed. Note; The first raid in which Jack flew the B-24, *245P* was October 22, 1944. This was the Liberator that he and his crew thought of as "our plane." He was to fly it in 10 more raids, including the one on March 24, 1945.]

Jan. 15, 1945

Well, Standby,

The mailman was good to me yesterday, one big bunch of mail from nearly every one of the family except Doris and Mom. Seems like I have three cousins in France, one in England, one on the ocean and all of Uncle Otha's children are building ships, what a family! Between the Stricklands and Uncle Sam there's quite an armed force on hand. Ollie, Jr. has the Purple Heart, Uncle Clay's son, Ronald, has the Silver Star and others. Harold tops everything with his Bronze Star, two citations and Expert Infantry Badge. Oh well, guess it's gotta be since it started back before the Revolutionary War. However I've got an idea not very many of them enjoyed it even though they must argue to live, apparently.

So much mail and so many questions–wow–somehow I've got an idea it will be a long time before I catch up–if'n ever. Your "V's" came today.

Still having tooth troubles–among others? Hate to see it happen that way–are you sure you're paying close attention to calcium foods–not just the tablets? OK–OK, but there must be something that could be done except fillings.

Oh-oh, the name? What? Again? Don't any of those others suit? Banks Murray Strickland sounds O.K. Then, in case of a girl's name - you struck a hidden chord somewhere, but is it ethical? Kitty Lynn Strickland, eh–what's that you're saying?–yeah–the middle name usually is a family one, huh? O.K.–your try again. Kathleen, Carolyn? Both are purty but so is Daisy, Poinsettia, Nasturtium, and Oleomargarine yeah, name her Oleomargarine on account of there's none or no other butter. 'Tweren't me, Miss,–Moore thought up that one.

Now Kitty Lynn is about as close as I can come unless Lynn Murray would do.

Things sound pretty normal back home–sounds good–tis good and oh how I wish it were the same all over the world. Next time you all hear from Harold, especially after Christmas, let me know–definitely. Some people back at home still seem to think that we're coasting on to victory. Most of the letters among the boys over here seem to have that thought in them now and then. 'Taint so, in any way. Those guys over there are still wallowing in snow, mud and ice–day in and day out–and we continue to hit them from above–and in both places they hit back in no uncertain terms. Fact is, on the ground it was the Germans who were forcing the fight from before Xmas until even now. Maybe it'll be the final round–with a decisive knockout–and then, maybe it'll be another "Tony Galento"–no quitting until forced to. Propaganda has the German people down and out, dejected, beaten. Their farms don't show it anywhere, and then, too, they are definitely better off than any other country in Europe as far as food and clothing is concerned.

Miss, it's rough–rougher still at the front. Harold wrote and asked if it was true that we went home after 35 missions. Before that I was eager to drop those loads as quickly as possible and get back immediately. I'm still "eager" to do the same, but with the most effect possible. For awhile it appeared certain that I'd be home before the eventful month. Now, well, 'taint so sure. I'm still trying–yes–and it isn't exactly impossible, but–O.K., here's the clean break, Miss. From time to time I heard the rumor–but since I've asserted that (I thought) it wouldn't be –well, Group has made us lead crew. That means five missions less - but usually (not always) that they'll come slower. Here's hoping that it turns out for the better, though the responsibility is going to make me sweat. The only time I've ever wished I was leading was once or twice when one of the Majors here took the formation through an overcast that appeared thin. The other time was when the flak was tracking us and he took no evasive action. Leading a Squadron isn't so bad–leading the Group will make me lose weight. If and when it's the whole Division or more, I will have had it.

Sugar has changed to another crew - too good a Bombigator to waste on a bombsight. Now I have two Navigators, a Bombardier and before long, still another officer. The enlisted men are outnumbered. This page should be burned as soon as you read it–yep, that's an order if I ever gave one. It'd be best not to let anyone know about the change in crew–nobody.

Now is the time for all good wives to come to the support of their husbands–give with the morale support, Miss.

We're lucky they waited this long, fact is, we might be lucky–plus. We should start out after one practice mission. Instead of starting out new, everyone on the crew has had experience in his time–on actual missions so that will take a big time lapse out of the training.

That leaves one thing–here's hoping God still believes in me enough to give me the ability to do this job like it should be done.

Now, guess I ought to finish this up and grab some sleep. 'Bout time I shaved up, too. Sometimes in looking ahead it seems pretty short before we approach the end of our tour over here. Here's hoping that's the way it is.

In the meantime–see what I mean when I say we want to have an occupation that we both enjoy? Once I get started, I try my darndest and if it were something that neither of us wanted, it'd be a heckofa life to lead, wouldn't it?

How about some comment–good or bad–and by the time you get this and send an answer –we should be feeling pretty chipper about the whole thing. Good luck. Take care of y'all.

Lots of love,
And how I'd like to show you I mean it!
Jack

Jan. 22, 1945

Well, Miss,

How long has it been since I dropped one of these here lines? Wasn't so long ago since I told you about the slight change in status.

Well, anyway, since then I've flown–yeah flown. Col. Fleming called for a pilot to go with him to the diversion point–place where mission was to land on account of our being socked in at the base, well, anyway, we go up there on instruments–land–spend the night–next day clear as a crystal–remember Crystal? Well anyway we spend the day and that time could have been used dropping our scoring bombs on the target range (for crew records.)

So forth and so on. Got a darn good–excellent–chance to compare our planes and methods with the RCAF planes and methods of bombing. They've got something there–in the Lancaster–better know as the "Lanc," fact is I've developed a slight craving for a few missions at night with them. Things were going well enough so that it looked as if I'd at least get a chance to fly one–nope–back home we go. One swell day wasted and, next day–snow, rain and wind–slight gale. Seeing as how I'm waiting around to see how we work as a team–well, seeing as how–I've been running around test-flying ships, checking new crews and finally checking out on a new instrument landing system. Back when we weren't doing many missions I spent quite a few hours on that system in Link. Now it comes in handy. Won't be long before it will be getting us missions when most of the others are stood down. Then they started me checking out other guys in the air. This here new fangled thing is a honey.

Well–again–Cousin Roy Edgar finally got tired of waiting–came up to see me. Same afternoon I had one of the not too unusual pains in my side. This time it wouldn't go away when I pressed against it. Oh well, when we first came over, one of the surgeons at the first base told me it was the hangover from a dose of lead poisoning at one time or another. Not serious since pressure relieved the pain. Yeah, and so on. This time they checked me–punched, prodded, scratched, etc. "Come back in two hours and we'll take a blood count - but don't eat." So I sit and watch Roy Edgar eat steak (which we seldom eat)–go out at nine–more rain–sleet–wind. By this time I should know the base in the dark, so I struck out. Luckily I was wearing a field helmet–raining, you know. Plodding along, head down, and crash! I ran head on into some big, bulky object. Backed off–looked–couldn't see a thing and no trees were supposed to be that far out in the road. Went back, got a flashlight–came back –Jeep! Sometimes it gets dark over here.

Once more started out–got to the hospital–more punching, prodding–this time no blood test. "Get in the ambulance, pick up your class A's and toilet kit."

Here I be after more punching and prodding and two blood counts. Meals in bed!, heated ward–um–um, I'm lazy, you know. and my conscience isn't bothering me on account I think I'm doing the right thing by staying here under observation for awhile or so–say a couple of days. Roy Edgar tried to check the box on the card for mental observation. We had him laughing so hard that he got stomach cramps, so they tried to give him a blood count, too. He really cut loose at that–for awhile it looked as if he had brought me over here for an appendix operation and he was the one going to have it.

Army Forces Network is now playing, "You Always Hurt the One You Love."–eh, what? Reminds me–got the film O.K. Nice going–R. E. saw the boy for the first time–thanky ma'am. I'm going to hang onto it for future showings. Made one of the guys over here pretty homesick–besides me, of course–but there'll come a day!

Got a letter from Harold–think it was mis-postmarked on his part. Dec. 4th. Told me lots–including the fact that he is just about on the spot that I thought he was–being on the spot–he said they had shifted to buck the counter attack–so I'm hoping he should have dated the letter Jan. 4th, instead. More than likely that's the way it should have been because I think the letter he answered–I sent the latter part of Dec.

From that word "latter" on was written today–which is the day following yesterday, I think. Time just IS over here–any-

time–doesn't make much difference one way or the other. Got to feeling weak, dizzy, etc. today–same as once before when I was in bed for awhile, remember? Sooo, got permission to get up and took a good little tramp round and about. Snow's about 2 inches deep - looks like more coming tonight. Rabbit tracks thick as fleas - with quite a few pheasant tracks. That's something I've been intending putting down for future reference. There seems to be an over abundance of all kinds of "varmints" yet there are an exceptional plentitude of rabbits, pheasants, quail and partridges. Get around to figuring it out someday, I guess.

Now that I'm back in bed again, I've almost made up my mind to ask them to go ahead with the operation though I hate to think about starting in at this age, and definitely I hope they use the latest methods which tend to prevent cutting through the stomach muscles–more pulling them aside–more or less like digging through straw. I've talked to some of the surgeons and they claim that's the method in use now - but I think they're just pulling my leg or somesuch just for conversation. Well, maybe I can talk it over with <u>*the*</u> *surgeon - if'n when. They should definitely know today or else I'd like to get back with operations until something definitely turns up one way or the other.*

They haven't really caused sharp pains–but there are other symptoms–still no fever or nausea. Trouble is, I know they're there–sorta like a small lump–so I should say "it's" there. When it does start aching, it's more of a contraction of muscles in that immediate spot. I've been wondering if making up your mind to lick appendicitis without an operation will help. The appendix was at one time a secondary stomach back when men ate rougher food. Wonder if there are a few more remnants of muscle in mine than are left in most people. No–I mean yeah–conceited–but why does it feel like contracting muscles? Maybe I can concentrate on it and it will force whatever is initiating it back into the channel. Damnit, I've been eating enough butter since I got into the army to prevent this from happening–for years–or so I thought.

Still another worry–or fact, is that I'd enjoy the operation a heck of a lot more–on sick leave–at Walter Reed–when I get back.

Lastly, the only reason I dislike having it out is because I still intend doing a lot of paddling, riding and climbing around yet–and I hate to think what might happen if my stomach muscles are weakened. 'Nough said, I guess–see my thoughts are all too much on me right now–or more so than usual. Don't worry about it, though–I'll be O.K. either way and I'll leave it up to the surgeon whether it stays in or not. If it comes out, it shouldn't take too much time to recuperate–besides I've got a lot of work to do.

Don't you think it's about time you elaborated on Harp's condition - it stays in the back of my mind constantly and I've been watching for an opening that would let me get to see him. It would be great–if it's got to happen–for me to get down to see him and have it done there–eh what? Not impossible but almost so. There are about two hundred miles in between–near that anyway. Don't try to figure it out though. I don't especially want you to know. Shortly thereafter it looked as if maybe I'd fly down. My squadron C.O. wanted to go to London–we got it all arranged–I was to drop him off there–spend the night, and pick him up in the morning. Took a little finagling because they won't clear us to land elsewhere except in an emergency–or for reasons of duty. We intended taking off–local clearance (just to fly around)–land down there and call them. No, guess it wouldn't be too much trouble–Major Burke, the squadron C.O. would have been responsible. Turned out, though, he was called in by the Col.–meeting–lasted all afternoon, so–no go. In the meantime I'd gotten a skeleton crew together–class A and all - big flop!

Say, young lady, how do the names sound now–your choices and mine–or the ones you chose and I arranged? Kitty Lynn (I'm liking this one)–Lynn Murray-Banks Murray?

I should be writing Mom, Harold, Harp and Bill now - thought maybe I'd finish this, though, because it might be a bit difficult tomorrow and the next day - or so.

Keep writing–you're doing fair–'twould be excellent but they keep coming in bunches. More than likely it'll be some simple tie-up, though, and it'll take a few weeks.

Mom's package finally arrived, peanuts and all–yummmm.

They'll probably be there when I get back–hope so anyway. Still going strong on those "5th Aves." Roy Edgar brought me a bottle of stuffed olives–some his mom sent him. Uncle Richard sent me a large can of canned pork–bet a dime it's the same as that in K-rations–it'll come in handy either way. Now how about some plain old soda crackers–saltines or Ritz? The Vienna sausages were both welcome and delicious. It's only the potted meats and Spam that are least welcomed.

One guy in the barracks got a can of pork sausages. Put it <u>*in*</u> *the stove for heating. Shortly thereafter, the can exploded - the stove jumped a few feet and a big cloud of steam came out. Everyone was quiet–writing. Sugar had his legs around the stove. He and Laforet jumped up at the same time–Laforet beat him to the aisle so Sugar huddled up in a corner–cursing–we roared–Laforet didn't stop until he was outside–then turned and poked his head inside with an expression to match the incident. See, nobody's getting jumpy yet. Don't bother us–bother us. Well, anyway, thanks for the film, the packages, letters and love. Here's hoping, again, you have a Happy Birthday ad infinitum. Right now all I can return is the love. Someday I'll catch up on the rest.*

Be seeing you

Jack (does sound foolish, doesn't it?)

P.S. I feel like writing on and on, only there's nothing to say. Picture, as soon as I look normal again.

Jan. 24, 1945

Dear Miss,

First off, I'm sorry–yep–I apologize for not writing more often. No,–can't promise to do better however, I'll try. So long as the letters come in you can feel assured that it's because there is something going on to write about. When they slack up–'taint much going on. Good enough? Now don't go spreading rumors over here that you're writing too much. Sometimes they are fairly regular and then again it may be a week–or more–between. Sometimes? Most of the time. Keep sprinkling in the V-mail. They are faster and definitely come all the way by air. Don't slack up on those long, homey ones, though, because they're the ones that really count–the other fill in the long waits.

Them there movies, Miss,–just like a trip home–'cept you better stop making me jump when the boy gets into such a position to be able to fall into the creek. Yeah, you did, too–less than the wink of an eye away.

Tell the guy I certainly do appreciate all the trouble he went to, to take and develop those films. Some day I'll make it up to him, one way or the other; he certainly knew just where to aim that there thing, didn't he?

Lt. Col. Cushing wrote me a nice little note–got it today. Congratulated me–as he said, a little late–wanted to know why we didn't let him do that the night you and I were over there to see them. Harold wrote, too–well past December–and they're still doing a great job over there every day. He's added the cluster to his Bronze Star. I have hopes of seeing him–when and if–we get a rest leave. Maybe–maybe–I can get a day or so off for him and we'll possibly get down and see Col. Cushing.

Guy just came in–was going to Paris–ended up right in the middle of Harold's area–dab-nab-it! Maybe my rest leave will be spent in the front lines–fine rest!

Should get a chance to see Harp Monday–certainly hope so, anyway. Should I, I'll let you know all the data.

We finally got our target bombs away–good bombardier that. Now we're in line again, but I'm going to take time off enough to see Harp and by the time we're due a leave–we'll be having time enough in between missions for that. Certainly did feel good to be up in the blue–I mean, gray–again. Fact is, I've been feeling good ever since.

First day here I felt the same as I did when I decided it was the south and fishing that I needed. For awhile it had me worried because the longer I'm in bed, the worse I get and there's definitely no place over here that would have substituted for the Congeree and Santee rivers down in ole South Carolina. Then I would have been up the creek.

The surgeon said that the organs in question were sometimes more retarded in degenerating, therefore better able to handle such troubles because of the muscles still retained in the walls. See what I mean? Now, let's hope there's no more such troubles over here.

Got those pajamas, etc. right after I received your letter stating they were on the way. Yum–yum–that candy takes me back. Now, young lady, can you do as good a job on everyday foods–well, those cakes weren't bad–not at all. O.K., try biscuits now –then fried chicken.

Hey, gal, once more, Happy Birthday - I guarantee - either I'll get you a pretty fair gift or else I'll make up for it in a way that will keep you from thinking I forgot it.

Thought about this plan–or had this here idea about Dec. 24, 1941–say, no, that would give it away. Should I be able to send you something on time - according to what it is–don't you dare try to undo the last seal until I'm there. O.K.–once then–but once only–so plan that once before you do it.

Mom's letter was among the ones waiting when I got back here. Certainly puts the icing on the cake when she writes. Guess she's pretty busy and with all that reconstruction going on she must enjoy turning everything loose occasionally and spending a little time off in town now and then. Did I understand you to say–once–that she brought Pat and Betty up and that gave you a chance to go to Silver Spring? Did you mean that when she came to see you, you left her in charge of the boy and went downtown? Doesn't sound like you meant that–or maybe you're pretty busy after all.

Now that's no way to write somebody who is holding some good old country sausage over my head? No, so don't keep a holding it, Miss–please.

So saying, off we go–hmm–hmm, I mean, after shaving, off I go to the sack.

Be seeing you
Lots of love
with added improvements daily
Jack.

Photo of Jack in England wearing wedding ring

One of our high school friends, Don Carroll, was a photographer.

He came to see me one beautiful fall day in 1944 and brought his movie camera.

He wanted to make a film of Jennis and me for Jack. He entitled it, "A Day at Home."

The film started with us leaving our house and going to Sligo Park (a wooded area near our old school.) I pushed Jennis on the swings and let him slide down the slides and he played in the leaves. He picked up one leaf and as we crossed the little bridge over the creek, he threw it into the water. As Jennis and I watched, the leaf hit the water and ripples circled out from it. Don super-imposed a picture of Jack over the leaf.

It ended with us coming back home.

Don did an excellent job and it was a lovely little film. I sent it to Jack.

I think one of the guys over there must have kept it to remind him of the U.S. and home, since I never got it back.

Jack worried about not getting me presents for my birthday and Christmas. But he did manage to send me (via Harvey) several pairs of silk stockings and a bottle of Chanel #5.

I never could figure out just what he was talking about when he mentioned the present for me that he had thought of December 24, 1941. (That was the day he gave me my engagement ring.)

I had never given him a wedding ring because he had not wanted one.

As he had promised me, he had several pictures taken by a London photographer. It took me a long time to notice that in them he was wearing a gold band on his left hand. I'm pretty sure *that* was his present to me.

As you've gathered, the mail going to and from Europe sometimes took weeks to reach its destination. I lived for Jack's letters. Our postman arrived at the house at exactly the same time everyday. I had never listened to soap operas but there was one (whose name I forget) that came on just before the mailman delivered my mail. To help the time go by before he came, I would turn the radio on and listen to it while I waited to see if I had a letter. To this day I can still sing its theme song, although I have no idea what the story line was. I also remember when I *did* get a letter from him I would open it and scan down to see if he told me he loved me and then I would go back and read the whole letter.

And there was RATIONING. Because the military had top priority for all commodities, there was a scarcity of just about everything. Each person was issued two books of ration stamps a month. Lard and cooking fat were used to make medicine, synthetic rubber, soap, gun powder and other essentials, so the Government asked housewives to save their used kitchen fat and turn it over to their butcher. In turn they were given two red stamps for every pound they turned in. Not only did you have to have the designated number of stamps to purchase almost anything, but also you considered yourself lucky if you could find goods to purchase. If a store happened to get delivery on anything that was scarce, the word spread and in no time there would be a line for two blocks in front of the store. The supply would quickly run out and if you were at the end of the line you were out of luck.

So most of my days were spent in waiting for the mailman, taking care of my precious baby, writing letters to Jack and taking the bus into town to try and get groceries. I didn't have a car and also being pregnant made it awkward trying to manage a one-and-a-half-year-old toddler and carry packages on the bus at the same time. Occasionally Blanche would volunteer to walk down to my house with Pat (who was Jennis' age) and Betty who was a few years older and stay with Jennis so I could have an easier time shopping. I was very upset when Jack chastised me because he thought Blanche had come to visit and I had taken advantage of her and made her baby-sit. Unfortunately misunderstandings took a long time to get straightened out when our only means of contact was slow mail.

Often each of us had forgotten what we had written by the time the other had written back.

445 Bomb Gp.
700th Bomb Sqd.
APO 558, U.S. Army

Jan. 24, 1945

Dear Colonel Cushing,

The mail service from here to your station was much faster than I had expected. Sometimes it takes Harold's letter a month to get there. One of his letters arrived with yours or should I say THE letter. Since the breakthrough I've been "sweating him out" because I knew he was more or less Johnny on the spot. He's probably been having it rough as you said. That fact takes my mind off the few worries that we have. From time to time we've been directly over him, those missions certainly give one a sense of satisfaction. That's especially true when we see what we hit. The guy seems to be rolling up quite a record and since it's the Infantry, that takes in a lot. He has two citations, Bronze Star and the Expert Infantry Badge. His latest letter added a cluster to the Bronze Star. Guess I'd better settle back comfortably and be satisfied with the back seat!

Mom wrote that he'd shifted positions slightly however he's using his old address. This is it.

PFC Harold W. Strickland 33562034
Co. B, 119th Infantry
APO 30, c/o P.M., N.Y., N.Y.

Thank you, suh, for the congratulations and best wishes. Seems like those wishes have already been at work. Now I realize that we were pretty young to have been married, fact is, I realized it then. Guess I'm old enough now to know that it wasn't a mistake and I don't believe there will be any reason to think so.

We two are three now–# three is one year four months old; walking, talking (more or less) and from what I hear, getting into mischief already. He's a he and it doesn't take long to realize it when you see him.

I'd like to be able to see you sometime and it might be possible any time–that's one thing we can't tell in this outfit. That is, I'd like to see you at a time when you aren't too busy. You've already been doing some important work in the Army. Fact is I hear that you are probably in line for decorations on the typhus work alone.

I'm sure Harold would like to see you, too. I intend trying to see him when and if I get a "flak leave." From the look of things, I'll be able to get over to him. Maybe if he could be relieved for a few days we could drop down and chat for a short while about things in general. Mom hasn't written about seeing Mrs. Cushing since last fall so maybe we could all catch up on the home front.

Sounds good, anyway–now if the Russians will oblige us.

Chow time now–so off to war.

Good luck,
Jack

[Editor's note: Col. Cushing had been a neighbor of Jack's in Silver Spring. He was stationed in France at this time.]

Jan. 27, 1945

V-MAIL

Back again,

So soon, too! Here I sit waiting for a train. Strictly Limey atmosphere. Cold waiting room, small coke fireplace at one end, benches against the walls–four of them! I'm the only American present and at first everyone sat and stared at everyone else, now they're beginning to talk a bit. Since it's hard for me to understand them, it's seldom that I converse. Met a guy on the train, though–first Limey conversation I ever really didn't squirm through. Guess it was because yours truly was doing the talking and he was interested. Usually conversation material is pretty slim and their expressions sometime seem to have no meaning. Subject–differences in wild life over here and over there–consequences? - he's going to mail me a book–by a Limey Naturalist–should be interesting–eh, what?

Say, miss (with a capital M) did you know automobiles roll on tyres and you aren't shown anything–you're shewn? Did you know I like you lots? Did you know I met a guy from Durham that knows Shoaf and Judge Womack, too?–plus Shoaf's younger brother–plus remembering your trip down there? Anyway, you don't know him, do you? Swell guy–married–Tarheel (gentleman) name of Huckaby.

Meanwhile, lots of love (train coming)

LOTS

Jack

V-MAIL

Jan. 29, 1945

Hi, Sweets,

What's cooking, young lady? Sho do miss you especially right now (more than usual.) I'm on a train–yep, that's what all this static is about. Been with Harp two days and nights.

He's feeling fairly chipper though his injury isn't exactly to be taken easily. The use of his left arm and hand will probably be pretty limited unless one of the advances in surgery can take care of it. There's a decent chance of being able to do quite a bit in overhauling that arm.

Better get down to bare facts on this page. I wrote Mrs. Holland for Harp and then gave a pretty complete report of his injury in a letter of my own. Due to the "bright" spirit in the room I might not have written as serious a letter as I should have. Well, anyway, after it was mailed Harp asked me to NOT write the folks the details. Will you please–right now–DON'T FORGET–call Lois and ask her to get the letter first–take my part out–read it and then do whatever she thinks best. The letter is addressed in my hand–censored by Harp (theoretically.) It's an airmail envelope like this–

Please don't forget–or put it off until tomorrow.

Now, once more, here I be alone. One whole compartment to myself and the train is practically deserted anyway. Not much left to do but listen for my transfer point and think of you. Snow's on the ground and it's snowing again. About two or three inches on the ground now.

This part of "Merrie old England" (quoted from a maniac) is much nicer than where our base is located. The houses are generously built–like those back home, landscape clean and people much more warm and friendly than the people at home base. Maybe these people are just more urban than those back there.

For the first time I've gotten mad at the lousy Huns - Gritting Teeth Mad! Those stinking --- -- -- deserve cold-blooded, savage murder. MAN, WOMAN and CHILD. Every one of them can't be to blame except that each and every one could have done their part in avoiding war and can do something about it even now. This viewpoint didn't come from seeing Harp. Mainly because I've gotten an idea of how German home life and conditions are, compared to any country over here. I'm just hoping that the Allies unleash every weapon of war ever invented. The Russians are the only ones who seem to know what this is all about. I've never felt any pleasure in having to kill them–rather liked to doubt if I had–but now, I'd like to get any of them in the sights of any gun and blast them until–well –just a pile of gore. For awhile when I was particularly worried about Harold, I tried to figure a way to get into a ship with triggers under my finger.

Here's hoping the mollycoddlers back home who keep repeating–be lenient, warm, friendly to them–show them they were wrong–that idea just won't work into their minds with the conditioning that they've been through. The only thing (in my mind) is to show them just what an average–or below average–bunch they are–then school them. Do you think Russia will have to worry about Germany attacking her again? 'Nough said. More when more paper is at hand.

For all this–I still miss you–mainly on account I love you more'n somewhat. So forget all the above and think about this,

Lots of love–all three,

Jack

Lieutenant Harvey H. Holland

In October 1944, after spending two months in England training Infantry troops, Harvey was ordered to France as a replacement combat officer. He was in the 90th Infantry, 3rd Army, commanded by General George Patton.

Paris had been liberated August 25th. Most of the country had been taken back from the Germans and they had been pushed to the northeast border of France. The Germans were ordered to hold this part of occupied France at all costs. In order to hold this territory they had erected hundreds of pillboxes from which to fire on Allied troops and they were fighting fiercely.

At this period of the war, it was said that an Infantryman averaged two weeks of combat before getting wounded or killed.

When Harvey got to France he was made First Rifle Platoon Leader (a platoon consisted of 50 men). "Willie" and "Joe" types, who had been fighting the ground war, looked at this skinny young man in a big helmet, and wondered what they had been sent. It wasn't long before they found out. (Willie and Joe were characters depicted in the cartoons of Bill Mauldin. They were scruffy, unshaven, hardened combat Infantry. The cartoons appeared in "Stars and Stripes," a paper distributed to the soldiers overseas, and the troops loved them.)

By nature Harvey was very methodical - the characteristic that enabled him to graduate from college in three years and from Law school in two years. (He later became a very successful private practice lawyer in Maryland, D.C., and Virginia.) He would stay up all night, planning the next day's maneuvers. He would have a plan A, and if that didn't work out, a plan B, and if that failed, a plan C. He insisted the squad leaders inform each of the troops of these plans. He said to tell them, "We're not here to be heroes or to die. We're here to stay alive and help win the war."

One of the first maneuvers involved crossing a small river via an old bridge. Harvey did not like the looks of the bridge and ordered his men to wade across the river instead of using it. There was much grumbling as it was cold and their boots and clothing would get saturated, but they obeyed.

Shortly after that another platoon faced the same situation. They used the bridge. It was mined and blew up as they crossed, killing and wounding several men. The "Willies" and "Joes" decided this young man knew what he was talking about. After several more incidents of this nature, Harvey had won the respect and admiration of all of his men.

Harvey's division had liberated Dillingen, a coal-mining town that the Germans had wanted desperately to hold. They were now between the Mozelle and Saar rivers. The job of the allied ground troops was to take out as many pillboxes as they could. The fighting was intense and the Germans were throwing everything they had at the advancing GIs.

He ordered his men to dig foxholes. Because they had taken a number of prisoners who were constantly trying to escape, the orders were to remain in your foxhole after dark - anyone seen outside of a foxhole, friend or enemy, would be shot on sight.

The Germans were bombarding the Infantrymen with artillery shrapnel and were shooting the Red Cross personnel who came to help the wounded.

On the morning of Dec. 8, 1944 Harvey and his 'runner' were kneeling inside their foxhole. They were under heavy artillery attack and at the same time were being attacked by German ground troops. He and his "runner" (a man who took messages back and forth between Harvey and his men) were firing at the Germans.

He told me it was said that, "You never hear the one that gets you," but he remembers distinctly the sound the one that "got him" made as it came toward him. He dove down on top of the "runner" but had not managed to get his left arm all the way inside the foxhole. His arm was hit by shrapnel. He looked down and could only see his upper arm and thought the rest had been blown away.

Then he felt something touch his head. It was his left hand. He realized his elbow had been demolished and his forearm was bent backwards and hanging by one muscle and (Thank God!) an artery.

He looked at the "runner" who was not moving, and thought he was dead. Finally the guy gasped. He had the wind knocked out of him when Harvey dove on top of him. The soldiers had been issued kits that, among other things, contained morphine. Harvey, like many of the men, had previously given his supply of morphine to troops wounded on the field.

When the medics got to him they had no medicine or painkillers to give him, so all they could do was put bandages on his arm and leg. Harvey said that at first there was no pain, but later it arrived with vengeance.

Around the fifth day (December 13) Harvey and a few of his men, including the 'runner' who spoke fluent German, devised a plan. When it was dark they used a flashlight to signal the American soldiers on the other side of the Saar River. Two German prisoners, hoping for favorable treatment from the Allies, volunteered to carry Harvey down to the river on a litter. There were a number of old, deserted, metal boats on the riverbank. The Germans put Harvey in one and rowed him to the other side where the, now alerted Americans, had a jeep waiting.

They drove him to the 106th Evacuation Hospital in France. This was an emergency set-up in the lobby of a partially shelled out hotel. The operating theater was in the mezzanine. The inside of the hotel had not been completely destroyed and Harvey remembers seeing crystal chandeliers and other remnants of the once lavish establishment.

Here Harvey was finally given some morphine and had the first of a dozen or so operations on his arm.

In this makeshift hospital there was a multitude of wounded GIs.

To differentiate between the severity of the guys' wounds, the medics would put colored toe tags on them.

Harvey got a RED tag, which meant he had top priority to be evacuated. He said he felt sorry for the other guys but was delighted to know he was to go out on the next hospital plane. The weather was so bad that the planes couldn't get in to them, so it was a few more days before he was taken to the 141st General Hospital in England. There he had a number of operations to try and restore the nerves and tendons in his arm.

This is where Jack visited him.

On March 11, 1945, Harvey was sent to McGuire Hospital in Richmond, VA, where he stayed for a little over a year. The doctors removed more than 200 pieces of bone and shrapnel from his body; however, he did not lose his arm. Between operations Harvey attended the University of Virginia Law School in Charlottesville, VA. He entered the spring of 1946 and graduated the spring of 1948.

I asked him about his decorations. He got a battle field promotion to First Lieutenant, a Bronze Star and, of course, a Purple Heart. He was offered more commendations but wasn't interested. He told them, "Skip the medals–just send us more ammunition."

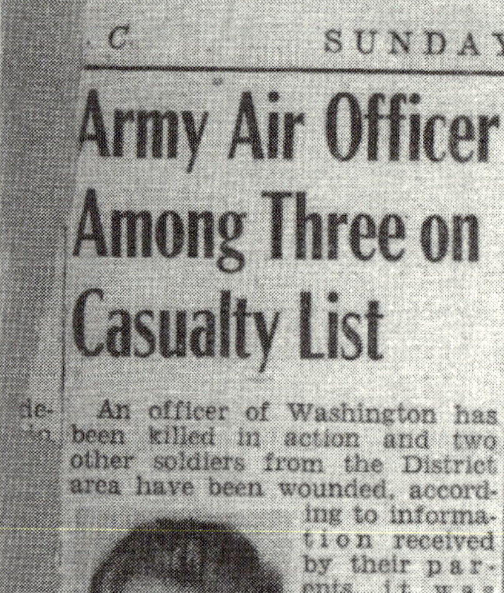

C SUNDAY, DECEMBER 31, 1944

Army Air Officer Among Three on Casualty List

An officer of Washington has been killed in action and two other soldiers from the District area have been wounded, according to information received by their parents, it was learned yesterday.

Lieut. H. Holland

KILLED

Second Lieut. David Osmond Ryon, A.A.F., 24, son of Mr. and Mrs. N. E. Ryon, 1835 Upshur Street NW. (Killed in action over Yugoslavia on April 17, 1944.)

WOUNDED

Second Lieut. Harvey Holland jr., 21, son of Col. and Mrs. Harvey H. Holland, 1804 Piney Branch Rd., Silver Spring, Md. (Wounded December 8 in Germany.)

Pvt. John Ghikas jr., 19 son of John G. Ghikas, 628 G St. NW. (Wounded November 24 at Schmidt, Germany.)

Recovering in England

Lieutenant Holland is recovering in a hospital in England, his mother reports. His father, a colonel in the Army Air Corps, is home on leave from overseas service.

Lieutenant Holland was graduated in September 1943 from the University of Maryland, where he was a cadet officer. He entered the Army October 21, 1943, and received his commission the following April at Fort Benning, Ga. He went overseas in July and has been serving in an infantry division of General Patton's Third Army.

News article about Harp missing in action

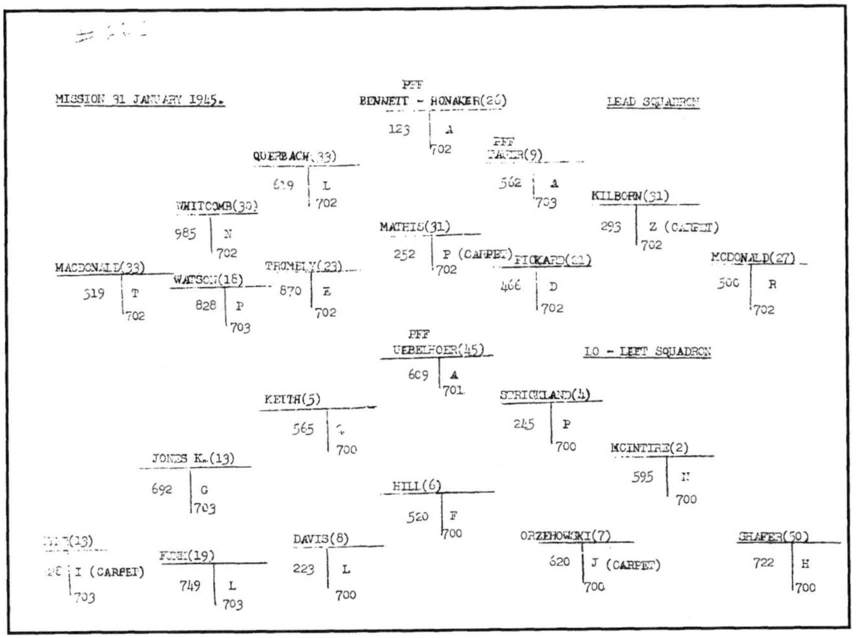

Mission of 31 January 1945
Target: Hallendorf, Germany

Feb. 1, 1945

Dear Lady,

Guess that's good enough for a start. Now to take it from there might be a different question. Truthfully, there's not a heck of a lot to write about but I just felt like writing you, seeing as how I'm "wore" to a frazzle right now–sorta slumbery, too. Man, it would feel good to be 'home,' wherever that would be–and ready to turn in.

Been giving that quite a bit of thought lately and trying to decide just what course to take over here. Doesn't hurt to try to climb on up the ladder and when I finish up the first tour maybe I'll have a little choice in the matter. So far I've worked it down to two alternatives–IF–I have any choice at all. The first is to return to Selman and root some of those combat-shunning wheels loose from their "set-ups." Second, and maybe you won't like this–trying to dig hard enough to be able to move on up through this little organization until I get into division headquarters as weather ship. That, in case you're wondering, is a P-51. Say, I'd better quiet down. Anyway I have confidence in my ability to handle the job and what's more, it would be one way of getting that single engine in front of me once more. What's more, I would strictly be on my own with no one to worry about and free to resort to any course of action, so long as I got the job done. Recently I climbed into the 51 and it felt like I was astride a rail. It would almost be like learning to fly all over again. Now, to get that little job, I'd have to volunteer for a second tour. But that would mean top priority on a trip home–via air –and 30 days leave. The second tour would be counted in flying hours and not missions. There's a big possibility that, otherwise, I'll be railroaded to the States–a few weeks leave–further training, more than likely, in one of the larger bombers and then on out the back door–say, San Francisco. Fine way to talk about it–I would much rather be in the Pacific than over here but I've had the cure of such ideas. I've even left the door open to the idea of test pilot out California way–if it could be swung –or in fact, anything ex-

cept instructing pilot cadets. I'd rather go into the other theater than try that.

We just got back from another diversion (landing at base other than our own–weather.) This time it turned out to be a base for "Aussies" in the RAF–or RAAF. Their hospitality was almost too much and their quarters bordering on luxury compared to ours. Fact is I was awakened from a deep sleep of peace by a WREN and found my shoes had been shined while I slept.

Lately I've had a change in actions, somewhere, and I believe it's that my outlook on duty over here is beginning to narrow down until it's almost too serious. Lately I've noticed it mainly in the crew's reaction. There's something there that wasn't. Their little personal gripes don't occupy the usual importance they used to. One thing in particular is their reaction towards those "commandos" over here (females.) First they bragged about their ability to get along with them. I hate the sight of one and didn't take long to tell them so. Within a few days they started making it a point to tell me how they had told one at such and such a place to taxi on–they weren't interested. That's been going on for months now and if they notice them that much, I'm sorta suspicious of whether they're sorta doing things on the Q.T. or not. Still it isn't exactly my business so it isn't up to me to check on them.

Say, Lovely, it's been some time since I started this essay. I miss you more and more or maybe it's because I just keep visualizing the day when we'll be together again. Somehow I keep imagining how it will feel to hear your voice and how it will feel to touch your hair and all the–here I go–curves, etc. Oh-ho–so those curves are fading, huh?–OK–then at least I can compare the kid's kicks with the kicks of number three. Somehow or other I think it'll be a gal–fact is, I'm sorta hoping it will be a gal this time. It isn't often I allow myself to think about you–us–my wife. Somehow or other life without war seems so far fetched and distant that it makes me wonder how I happened to be so lucky as to have had a reprieve from combat so long.

Combat is so concrete–so close at hand–so real that it gets to be a habit to think under combat terms. Somehow or other it seems to be a relief to find you're over Germany where anything can happen–just sit there and drive on. God has been so good to us that's it's almost sacrilegious to even curse when things go wrong. I actually catch myself apologizing whenever I make a slip and use His name in vain. Flak has become so much a part of flying that without it you get nervous in anticipation. Faith in the power of God becomes so strong when flak begins to thicken that you actually feel like taunting it to do its darndest.

Lately the war has taken a turn for the better from all outside appearances. Consequently there has been a tremendous lift in spirits over here. There are no actual reasons for basing the idea, but it almost seems as if the end of the war is just beyond the brow of this last hill ahead. The German people, for the first time, are being rooted from their homes but the area where this is true is so small that it would be a mistake to believe that it will mean the beginning of the end. Maybe if the Russians can keep driving past Berlin–and the Americans can make a definite break through–then when the civilians have to crowd together–then when they discover the conditions of the railroads, the amount of damage in neighboring towns–then MAYBE there will be reason for becoming optimistic. Before that time comes, though, anyone who predicts the surrender of Germany is a fool of the lowest form. We've got to hit them now, harder than ever before, in order to keep things moving towards the end of the war - every pause means the end will double it's distance from our present position. People become used to anything with time and if we give them a chance to observe the amounting chaos in Germany and get used to it, they will never know when it's time to call it quits. Consequently they will continue the fight long after they're licked, technically. They're more or less licked right now but the average German doesn't know it. So it's got to be definitely and violently brought home to them. This might happen soon–and then, it might take quite awhile–at any rate, the end of the war will be determined by that factor more than anything else.

That's my idea, so you needn't believe it necessarily to be Gospel from authorities that know more about it.

Latest reports from back home say that Selman Field–along with most of the other Navigation schools–has closed down.

Where to go when I finish here? We still have months left to think it over but it doesn't hurt to try and work it out now. ATC is still going on and more than likely, so is Douglas and Lockheed–with their jobs for test pilots–which might be overrun, though.

Don't mention it to anyone but I'm going to try and see if there are any possibilities open for a position at Bolling or Camp Springs. What those jobs might be, I don't know, however I intend putting out feelers pretty soon. Once more–shhhh–absolutely!

Lately I haven't had any mail from home–and you. I know it isn't because you're not writing but are you sprinkling in the V-mails occasionally? Strange as it might seem, the weather is affecting you and me because that is the major reason for all this delay.

Maybe parts of this letter seem a bit unusual to you - I only hope I'm not beginning to show signs of the ETO. Let me know if you think so–and in what way.*

Lots of love,

Jack

[Editor's note: ETO stands for European Theater of Operations. The January 31 raid was on Hallendorf, Germany]

Feb. 5, 1945

Hello, Gal,

Now just where do we go from there? Just wanted to speak to you–nothing to say at all–so now? Finally after weeks of waiting, three of your letters came through at once and then today, as usual, the cupboard was bare–entirely. I always put your newest letters where I can reread them but somehow I never get time enough and they pile up unless I move them further back down the line. More than likely if it takes as long to get the next batch I'll have a chance to look them through again.

Your birthday has already gone by, by the time you read this and I hope you enjoyed the day from beginning to end. To be truthful, I don't know whether I sent you any presents or not. Fact is I'm just as interested–as I hope you are–in what I gave you on this birthday. I have a good idea of what I gave you, still I'd like to know exactly what the presents were like–if you've gotten them. Maybe they'll have to wait until I get home–and if so, I can make a promise that you'll like what I hope I'll be able to get for you. Round and round we go, so–be sure and let me know should you receive such. Understand?

Say, how about stepping out somewhere tonight? We can start with something nice but loud–like the Statler and finish up on the quiet side before we turn in–Four Corners would suit me–how about you? Sho–sho, it would be easy enough to get someone to let the boy spend the night or vice-versa. Oh, the other? Well, the women would be envious–whether they showed it or not–and as for the men, any of them would like to be in my shoes.

Guess what, Lady that I love,–of all the things to seep into my consciousness–comes "Begin The Beguine." So nice that it's almost classical and now they season it with just a little swing. Sometimes the world treats a guy with a soft touch–eh, what?

Your letter about Mrs. Holland's anxiety about Harp's condition came right after I'd written you the facts. I still think it would be best to let Lois read it first and then she can choose who and who shouldn't get the facts. Let me know how it goes and if possible, I'd rather Harp didn't know I wrote the details. I'd already mailed it when he asked me not to, so I didn't say anything. You can get the news from Lois.

Now about this time I find I've run out of news. Harold hasn't written lately and I'm looking forward to hearing from him. I sure do wish that they'd figure he's had enough action and include the boy on some of these rotation plans.

That rotation stuff occupies a big place in the men's minds. There were two Marines down in the Pacific who captured a Jap. He knew no English so they proceeded to coach him on one sentence, then turned him over to the interrogators. He marched in, saluted and beamed "My name is Sako Myungi, where do I stand in the rotation plan?" Truth, so help me.

Now look here, Lady, I'd like for you to get those letters through to me, to heck with all this postal system hold-up. I'm still looking forward to talking with you–I've been looking forward to that every waking hour. Sooner or later that day will come but unless there's a big change, and although it's almost twice as close as it was at one time, it's still a good way off. Still I can hope, can't I? These rumors that get out at least once a month don't help one's patience much, though.

Those jars of nuts were excellent and so was the fudge. Now, if you're a good girl, you'll send more on account of I gave about half to Harp. If they wouldn't consider that a formal request–maybe this will do. Please send me nuts, fudge, mayonnaise and anything else that the postman would like for a bedtime snack. Maybe he can suggest such, since I don't know what you can get over there. While you're at it, Harold likes those things, too. Ending with a request–my! my!–but I love you.

As simple as that–as elaborate as that.

Jack

Feb. 8, 1945

Happy Birthday
today!

Now if I were at Forsyth's and this were a few years previous I would give you a rendition from the original singing telegraph boy of Silver Spring.

Yesterday's mail was in a pretty good size batch once again–so that means more days–weeks of waiting. Now the batch before that I really did enjoy–however, yesterday the guys kept pestering me all through the reading and when I finished I didn't know whether. Most of the time when mail does come through I wait until I'm not busy–relaxed and alone, if possible, before I open your letters.

There was something that I intended–let's see–must have been the fact that from all appearances I won't be home next May–fact is, with all the breaks ever dreamed up, I won't finish this tour until the following month–or even more–you can't be too sure, so let's keep the fingers crossed. Truthfully speaking, if things continue rolling over the continent anything might happen any day, but that, too, could go on that way for months.

To really keep up with the war–to keep both feet on the ground you need a fair-sized true-scale map of Europe. Then if you'll keep a day-to-day movement of the east and west fronts marked –you can use common sense instead of letting the headlines build you up–to a gradual let down. I still say they've got to jolt the German civilians and the harder and more savage the jolt, the sooner the end will come into view.

Today it was announced that the population of Germany was beginning to feel the effects–but just like anything else–it doesn't take such effects long to wear off–unless they're constantly felt - with a greater intensity each time.

One prediction may I make? Unless both fronts move fairly fast within the next two months–the end of the war will come close–in big spurts–fast advances–and then another long, dragged out finis in the Bavarian Alps. But that still hinges on the next two months–we're so close–yet so far from Victory.

But if the jolts come hard enough–and fast enough now - you just forget that above paragraph.

Now as for those future plans that we're hashing over. First plan, I guess, are the names. But first let me say something that may not make sense right now–I hope it never does, the very suggestion makes me shudder–skip it–but my blood is racing around a bit too fast right now. Both the names sound swell to me–Lynn Murray for the gal and we'll hold the boy's in readiness–however don't get completely set on it even at the last minute –how else can I say it? Don't think I'm finally nuts, Miss. I shouldn't leave things just hanging that way but that's all there is to say right now.

The plans? There were the plans for the future. When it comes to working for the Dept. of the Interior, there still is a chance of being left flat, suddenly. I've been trying to gradually work up an acquaintance with Mr. Lincoln so when the time comes I'll be able to know what kind of jobs are open and just what is expected and the chances of salary increase according to experience. Then I'd be in a position to choose whether to study extensively for the job or not, otherwise I've just about settled on the idea of learning the veterinary business. Something that I would hold on to as a reserve, no matter what came up. I'm still hanging (very tenaciously) on to the idea of having a good bit of fertile land to do with as I please.*

The feeling may relax after awhile but I want something concrete to hang onto and call home. That feeling, of course, is brought on by the present state of affairs. The yearn to roam has sort of quieted down, too–at present anyway.

Back to the original subject–that leaves the scientific research angle–on the natural life in the globe. Usually that interest boils down to their habits, peculiarities and why they have both. It's fun to examine an animal and try to figure out why it's built that way as well as studying the marked differences in all animals–just curiosity–mingled with a little awe at the efficiency of Mother Nature. Naturally the more you get into such subjects the more interesting they get. The value of this comes up all along the road, especially where medicine is concerned.

Back to the farm–oh yes! Well, just in case depression and all that follows, you can still remain on a good diet–and healthy. A farm situated in the right place would serve to satisfy the exploring instinct and if located near some of the places I'd like to be–the field for exploration (amateurishly) and research of everyday wild life would be unlimited. So you don't like the backwoods, eh? Jumping to conclusions again. Once more - the home would be plenty close to modern conveniences such as stores, theaters, gossip and bridge clubs. The home itself could easily have every convenience of the city–plus–the more valuable part of being able to enjoy the conveniences of the country. What's more, I don't think you'd ever feel lonesome–because if we could build like I intend someday–there'd be visitors in plenty–plus, the city.

Now that I think I can put my finger on it, I've discovered just what kind of people I like and it's the simpler–usually uneducated (formally) people who live a life that doesn't depend on machines and man-made diversions in order to have–not only a happy life but a full one. Just what blind alley have I backed into this time? I don't know. The people that depend upon passive entertainment–artificial forms of recreation and such always seem rather dull and monotonous for all their so-called education. They depend too much on someone else to lead them, to form their ideas about all the major problems and so on and so on. Have you ever seen a monotonous animal? They're all different. Yep, guess I must be eccentric–rough, ain't it? At least I could be an ordinary moron.

Now what are you thinking? Don't look so scared–'taint often I get violent–seldom hurt anybody.

Now <u>our</u> farm. Well, in the first place if you don't already think I'm crazy, it won't take long. I won't wait to say I'm serious–I'll say it first.

Goats–those comical, vile smelling things–they aren't considered that in Switzerland! First, why?–namely because of the low cost and upkeep. Secondly–not much competition, so far. Thirdly –$1 a quart ain't hay for milk. Ever hear of tuberculosis? Ever hear of Sanitariums? Their demand surpassed the supply.

So far as I know there are two, possibly three, goat dairies in the States. One–the most prominent one is owned and operated by a millionaire, started out as a hobby. His stock is thoroughbred-dairy, modern in every respect. Besides, you like Limburger cheese, don't you? Anyway, who said I was going to do all the work? To make money it would have to be large - a start would be fairly easy.

Next crop–(Back to the farm)–Nuts–and I'm not! Why waste meadows on grass alone? Oh-oh, snag–remember how goats don't live on grass? O.K. then you'd know I was nuts–but that would take care of one pasture–thrives on the worst kind of soil–builds it up at the same time–a perennial plant, too–no cultivation after first planting, all set for an indefinite time after three months. Now, will goats eat it–and what kind of milk? Trees could grow in it–and wouldn't affect it by shade. O.K. figure in the nuts at 40 cents a pound–better make the milk 60 cents and the nuts 25 cents. How much do we have now–250 goats–three quarts each–hmmm–now 250 trees–how many bushels per? Huh?

And then the other livestock–enough pigs, some mules, a few horses. Wild game for restocking purposes.

Dream castles, I guess, young lady–nothing else to do right now–but–wouldn't most of it be possible after a start?

O.K. so let it ride. We can talk for hours regardless of which one ends up in the asylum.

So, until tomorrow and I think maybe I could write pretty soon–remember I still love you–even as a farmer's wife. This was more or less an argument–just because you gave me something to argue about.

I love you–no argument,
Jack

P.S. Pecan trees–800-1,000 lbs. per season–so there! (per tree, too–big tree)

P.S. No, the promotion was a Christmas present–finally. However–called up for lead crew about the 5th–I didn't know it at the time.

[Editor's note: When Jack lived in Silver Spring, he met Mr. Lincoln, who was an official in the Fish & Wildlife Division of the Department of Interior. They had many mutual interests and kept in touch after Jack entered the Army.]

Feb. 9, 1945

Back again,

Just as I said I'd be–see, young lady–I do miss you–and what's more, enough to think about you most any time.

That long epistle last night was funny, wasn't it? Well this time maybe it will be just as funny–maybe a bit more logical, though.

I read an article in Jan. Coronet entitled "the great dismal swamp"–capitalized words, though. Well, anyway, it took me back to that neck of the woods and at first reading I felt that my privacy had been violated. Funny how such places seem to become part of a person simply because he feels at home there.

Right off the bat, I wrote Mr. Lincoln a not too business like letter about the article and I'm waiting now to see just what the letter will come to. Mainly–I was asking about the possibilities of setting aside both Ole Dismal and the Okefenokee as federal reserves–just as they are today–and to remain that way from now on–no "improvements" and no roads and highways so that the public might sit in their automobiles enjoying the scenery and killing it at the same time.

Somehow I've never met anyone who actually did enjoy being able to live in such places. By that I mean, being so overcome with the beauty and wonders of the place that it actually made you feel your own life blood inside your veins.

Kitty, don't think I'm changing or getting homesick–I've just never tried to explain to anyone just how–or why–such places brought so much pleasure. There is one guy–possibly two - who seem to have the same feelings. Both of these guys–in fact, all three of us used to "piddle" around in the swamps down Carolina way–but for all our mutual likes, it was seldom we came out together. Each had his own ideas of where he was going–and though we must have noticed most everything–each one would be attracted by his own interest. So, within minutes, we'd become so absorbed in something that from then on we'd be more or less alone.

The only person who ever took such goings on seriously was

Edna–Karl's sister. She died not so long ago so I know you don't remember her. More than anything else I remember she used to listen to my ravings as long as I cared to talk–and at the same time wished that she were a boy, or man, so she could see the things that I described. She painted fairly well and the swamps down on Mr. Byron's farm were just full of raw material when it came to painting. Two scenes I remember still stick as if I'd seen them yesterday. One was a group of huge flowers on an open glade within the swamp–somber black on all sides. The other was a group of tremendous oak trees way down in the swamp. The only time I got that far was during a drought and once when the muck was frozen. There was one more, too, that I wish I could paint until this day. There was a log cabin - ancient–shingled and with a stone chimney and fireplace. Exactly as if it had been built by the early settlers. One room and a very narrow stairway, leading to the attic. There were two buzzards that nested beneath the stair–and–(I've cursed myself then and many times since) I shot them, simply because I'd never had a close look at one. They used to sit for hours–one on the chimney, one on the opposite end. There was one gnarled peach tree at one end and the flowers that had once been a garden had spread all around - even into the swamp two blocks away. There was a spring at the edge of the swamp and it, too, had remnants of cultivated flowers–even more beautiful because they were the ghost of a woman who had lived there at one time.

Can you understand, now, why I've always wished I had the knack of blending colors in painting–or for that matter, even the power to sketch?

Some day <u>soon</u> I'll be able to afford a really good color camera and then I won't have to carry such scenes in my head.

By the way, back to things making you feel at home–as if part of you remained there. There's one town–and only one–which affected me that way. Strangely enough I was never there–Natchez, Mississippi. I used to fly out of my way so that I could get a look at it. Still more strange–a sort of pub–not just a bar –in Holyoke, Mass. Every time the guys wanted to go out to a nightclub or some such, I usually dragged them down there. It was old–dim, but clean and massive. The building was a bit out of the way–beside an old freight canal. It was there that I had my first lobster. One interesting episode was a dinner given by a local ward boss. Their education and their speeches just didn't cooperate. We–a bunch of impolite nincompoops–practically split a gut laughing–which didn't help the speakers' assurance any. They finally broke up–but I'm sure there were plenty in the bunch who appreciated the fact that we must have cut at least three hours of flowery wind–with a beery odor–short.

Ho-hum, yeah, I'm ashamed–no, no gals–O.K. I'll tell you all when I see you–but that's <u>all</u> anyway. Say, young lady, you're through being suspicious of such goings on, aren't you?

Fine thing, to sit me down and rave on and on–but, so help me, there's not much news.

There was something I left out of the letter last night–what was it? Oh–for one thing–I could use some more stationery–and also, some dark ink–even black–but good ink–can't use Parker's 51, either.

That business of attempting to predict whether I'll be home in time or not–just can't be done. It's possible about as much one way as it is the other–there are too many factors involved. Weather is only one of them.

Back to the sack about now, I guess. Request officially–stationery, either brown or white–ink, either black–if stationery is white–or green, if brown. Yeah, I'm crazy.

Hey, before you go,

I love you.

Jack

P.S. Thanks for the nuts, cookies, mayonnaise and such. Watch me enjoy them.

Feb. 12, 1945

Well now,

I proceeded to get writing material together, so off they go with "Begin the Beguine"–and now, "I'll Walk Alone." Yeah, it turned out to be a very popular song–still it must be strictly a woman's song–I've never seen where there was anything special about it yet. When it comes to songs, it's a toss up between "Tumbling Tumbleweed" and "Begin the Beguine." I believe the first affects me more than the latter. Could be because it's played so seldom–at any rate, it really gets me down in a hurry - and takes me right back where I belong.

You asked me how it was that the fellow who rode with me was able to say whether he would fly or not. Well it happens now and then that a guy is built in such a way that he cannot control himself when he is caught in a tight spot. His first mission was a rough one, consequently when it came time to go on the next he was unable to force himself into the ship. For months he was around the base–instructing on ground trainers and so forth. Some of the guys either ignored him completely or otherwise let him know that so far as they were concerned, he was lower than the lowest. That made matters worse–though he finally got up enough nerve to try again. His pilot refused to fly with him. Followed another long period of dejectedness.

He was the first guy to give me trouble when I was in charge of the shipment.

Besides being a wise guy–I didn't like him. Soon as I saw why he had the attitude, I realized that it wasn't exactly his fault. Well, anyway, it came to a head one night at the club–our 200th mission party. Some yellow-bellied rat called him 'yellow' to his face and then left while other guys held this guy off. He finally cried–so I got hold of him–took him back home and got him in bed. The Squadron Commander consented to let him fly with me–if he would. Next mission we were all set to go - he showed up, very quiet. I hadn't told the crew anything about it - but they knew. We were all set to go–and he was very pale and tense, fact is, he was sweating–you could see it on his face–the mission was scrubbed. He admitted then that he didn't think he would have gone through with it–in fact, he couldn't force himself to stay in the nose of the ship–even on the ground. So, as the story unravels, I spent most of the time with him until the next mission–we never quite got around to discussing the problem at all. Then, bang, we're off on a mission. He was scared–that was apparent - but he never whimpered once–did a good job. Upon landing he wanted me to go with him to get the "shot" of bourbon that is rationed out after missions. I refused but promised to go with him when we had a pass coming up the next day. Well, shortly thereafter (he didn't bother to get the "shot" that time) we went up again. This time all–well, anyway, it was about the roughest we've had it yet–strictly a running strain on the nerves. I decided it was then or never–so began to call out the flak bursts–the crew took it up–and we had a running report on the nearest flak–and the flak ahead that we were going into–no turning. Finally he chimed in with his own comments on how accurate it was–the ship actually buckled now and then–but somehow it was fun and he was cured if he ever will be. When we were finally through the stuff I called the whole crew and asked them if they knew whom to thank for pulling us through. They knew alright and I imagine every one of them breathed a prayer then and there–at any rate–I did. God really seems close at times like those–and I do quite a bit of thanking Him–through my oxygen mask. That day He must have been close by because it seems like He heard my thanks the first time–hope so anyway.

We came on back. Everybody got out jabbering and chattering, looking the ship over–and he was one of us. Turned out that our pass started next day so I had to keep my promise–we got the "shots"–ate dinner –and got the chance to go hunting in the dusk. Ordinarily everyone is completely pooped when they get back but I felt about as chipper as possible.

We were put up as lead after that–he was taken off the crew and since then he's flown one of two with other crews. From all appearances everything is O.K. now.

Now to tell you off. Just the other afternoon I was passing the Limey's field and I heard this guy call me so I hopped the gate, the ditch and crawled through the hedgerow–he was hunt-

ing again. Got off a shot–missed. My turn next so I proceeded to espy a rabbit on the other side of the hedge row–I snuck along –got a clear moving shot–got him–one shot–AGAIN, so there. Apologize, young lady!

Now this longevity stuff–a "fogey" in other words. Every three years the army adds a certain small percentage to a guy's pay - it can add up after awhile. Mine starts next month. I might wait awhile longer to increase the allotment and then, maybe I won't wait much longer. Now that you can cash in bonds at any bank, maybe it wouldn't be a bad idea to increase them. Continue a small checking account though, and some straight savings wouldn't hurt. Well, anyway, I'll wait and see how everything adds up–and take it from there. There's no wasting of it going on anyway. That penny foolish, dollar wise business certainly makes a difference. Over here it's even worse because it just doesn't seem to be real money–paper–or metal. They all add up to odd amounts and you can spend a lot without thinking about it. Limey cigarettes are about 2′6, or two shillings six pence, which equals 45 cents–if there's any sense comparing it to American money. Ten shillings come about as close to one denomination as possible–2 bucks–and you know how fast they go. Outside of rations there isn't much worth buying, Passes bring up a problem, though. One pound = approximately $4.03 but they buy about as much as a dollar bill in the States. 2 pounds, ten shillings for a hotel room seems like nothing–but if you stop to think, it's equal to $10! consequently we usually stay at a Red Cross supervised house. Usually three or four army bunks in each room, army blankets, too–BUT clean sheets. You pay for the bed only - four shillings or approximately 80 cents. Scotch–per drink (all you can get outside of gin or rum) is usually 4 shillings–maybe 5–just a few measly coins like dimes but they add up to 80 cents or a dollar. No, don't take up the argument–I repeat–I don't drink any more than I did in Monroe–none at all–or in clearer words–not a bit more than then. Beer–and liquor included.

Say, lady, my moods change quite often and your letters remind me of things that I was turning over in my mind weeks ago. Now I'm entirely out of the future plan mood but–I've found that in snatches here and there, I've formed more views to questions that more or less had me baffled when I first tried to figure them out.

This business of choosing what road to take now–so we can have things planned in advance–that way, when opportunity knocks–you feel right at home and are able to get right into a sensible conversation without hemming and hawing. Told you I had written Mr. Lincoln so I can find out if he's interested enough for me to put a little time on it.

Finally, all told and with things outside my vision likely to come up at any time, I've arrived at the following conclusion. Naturally, as time goes by, other factors will have their effect.

First, I want a farm. Second I want a little certainty of the future–regardless of the economical conditions–and value of knowledge dealing with the objects or subjects that hold a natural interest for me.

The army will furnish–or partially furnish–me with the possibilities of becoming a full-fledged veterinarian. That in itself would be one means of livelihood.

The Fish and Wildlife deals a great deal with diseases, parasites and biological factors that influence the wildlife. Being (I hope) a veterinarian–would prove valuable–almost as valuable as special biological training–which would be picked up anyway.

I intend writing the Army Correspondence School for information on their courses on Biology and Veterinary, too. I'll choose between the two–or both, and at least get an idea of which road is best. Then, too, most of the foremost colleges recognize the Army courses and count them–or their value–up in terms of units–or college terms.

Then comes the farm!–that could be run at the same time I was practicing the Veterinarian profession.

So, present conclusion–Veterinarian with both roads open–farming and, or, biological work.

I'll compromise–it'll take hard work–unlimited–and I'd be outdoors. But after a few years' start I think I could relax a bit and keep going forward with hired help or sharecroppers. There are too many people tied to farm work that aren't capable–or not interested-in doing anything else. There's not one of my uncles who actually works on their farms. One used to-but he had to, to keep the still going, without letting everyone know about it. He's the uncle who has stayed young and is still enjoying life equally as well as any person I've ever known.

Still sounds easy, doesn't it? But, after all, I've worked on farms every summer until I was 16 - I know it will be hard work -and I still think it would be worth it.

You say you want to enjoy life-well all you have to do, to do that, is to get a goal in mind-and start digging to get there. You can't plan enjoyment of life-and if you don't believe me, look at the people who should be able to do anything, but hunt for enjoyment-does their lot seem to be a happy one? Once more, this active-passive theory-or active recreation and passive recreation theory-if you're trying to reach a certain goal-it's fun all the way. If you just keep an eye out for a means of enjoying life-you'll never find it. Maybe that's why courtships are ever lasting in a person's memory-while marriage turns out to be a different thing entirely for some.

Wouldn't it be fun to start on either the farm-or Veterinary practice-and ride all the ups and downs through? Don't you think you would enjoy the friendships that would spring up on all sides? Instead of a town being an every day affair, wouldn't life be much more enjoyable if you were more detached from it and could look forward to a shopping trip, rather than dreading it, etc.? Now, how about the kids-they wouldn't be hemmed in by the neighbors' likes and dislikes, they'd have something to do besides going to a movie for recreation. On the farm-they'd have plenty of active interests on all sides-they could do what they pleased and the variety wouldn't be limited-neither would everything come to a dead end in the way of lack of interest in the people on all sides. Neither would they come to depend on books alone to develop their minds. Oh well, guess I've gone into detail enough.

Now give me an idea of just exactly what you would consider an enjoyable life.

Here I've written the usual lengthy essay-the guys here in the barracks thought I was kidding when my first letters were over two pages long. Now they've just resigned me to a fate of insanity.

That brings up the subject of stationery–I mentioned that last time. Unless you can send me some soon, by the time this letter arrives I'll have about–wrote out–my supply.

Be sure to let me know what Lois and Mrs. Holland had to say about the letter. Should you see Harp anytime soon, tell the guy I want to hear a good account of everything. While you're at it - ask him once more for John's address.

Here comes, "And the Angels Sing"–such a feeling of peace and contentment. That was popular back when your road and mine kept converging and diverging with plenty of bumps thrown in.

I can't wait to get a start on seeing how the boy is making out. I'd sho like to be there so he could get the idea early–that there are a few men in the world. More than likely, even when this is over, I'll be pretty busy for awhile–but I'm hoping things will go pretty smoothly by the time he becomes hard to hold down. There's another factor in the farm's favor and working for myself as a Veterinarian–No, I don't intend starting him on any particular road–but I do intend seeing that he knows there are things that are right and wrong–and the only difference in the two <u>*isn't*</u> *that you'll have the fun of being chased by the cops if it's wrong–and no feeling of satisfaction or accomplishment if he's right.*

Say, when's this thing gonna cease? The letter, I mean. It's about time the mail was sorted out–and from all appearances there should be another batch in. Don't forget the stationery and ink. They're the only means I have of telling you I love you –so you'd better send plenty.

Be seeing you,
Lots of love,

Jack

Feb. 25, 1945

Dear Miss,

Hi, again, after that pause. I'll probably be back on the old schedule of letters occasionally–and sort of irregular, too.

I'm mighty glad you had such a nice time on the 8th. More than likely you had a more enjoyable time than if I'd been there. See–somehow I've sorta lost out somewhere on being entirely civil. By that, I mean, it's quite an effort to really relax–turn loose and have a good time. Don't worry about it though because after all, being in the grind so continuously gets to be a habit–over here–you can't just up and throw responsibilities off your shoulders whenever you like. They still remain there in the background.

'Scuse this scribbling but I hurt my right hand about a week ago and it's been sorta weak and uncoordinated ever since. Especially the thumb–more of less sprained the wrist and some of the joints and muscles. Just bad enough to require soaking in hot salted water at first.

Say, have you been reading the news of the past few missions? These low level bombing missions are just what I've wanted but as luck would have it, we were just rounding out our training for the lead–maybe in a matter of days we'll start chopping down on the total missions.

Call just came–gotta fly–check our ship or something. Be seeing you later.

Mar. 1, 1945
Or thereabouts

Yep, we had to fly–check a ship for the next day's mission. Electrical equipment went out and since it's no fun flying without instrument lights at night, no radio, no nothing and above an overcast–well, we landed quite shortly after take-off.

Since that time we've been fairly busy which is GOOD! Do we 'set' some more or are we on a winning streak?

The moon has been beautiful over here all winter–always there seems to be night clouds to set it off–but always it seems like a cold, distant moon–not the same old moon back home. Quite often it's a green moon, like tonight–pale green–just a slight tint of green, in fact.

Hey, remind me to tell you about this letter that was cut in half for a period of days. I'd rather not break the spell right now–or have I already done so?

Let's see–you've written so much and asked me quite a few questions to boot. Right now I'm too lazy to try and remember what they were–and since I should be sleeping–it would be best not to get that past bunch of letters out and start rummaging through them. One thing I can remember is–Lynn Murray –or Pamela. It's LYNN MURRAY so far as I'm concerned–sorta lady-like. Which do you say? O.K. then, that settles it!

Hey–uh–blank mind–what was I about to say? Oh, if I should ship home a box of trousers–plus a few books–mostly cookbooks–would you be offended? Too much? Fine thing to send and I haven't even sent a present home yet!

Speaking of presentations–that picture will be forthcoming soon–if I can get two or three things lined up in time - might be just a few more days–or a week or two waiting. The waiting list is so long, you know, and with the war going on (yes, 'tis, too) I just can't find enough photographers, film and paper to keep up with the fans requesting a handsome portrait of me - Oh, man! For you, though, since you're my one and only - I'll make an added effort just as soon (I promise) as possible.

Got a note from Harold not such a far piece back–so at present, my mind's a bit more at ease. Somehow it seems that God has been so good–for such a long time–without any thanks except words–that, after all, He holds the whole thing in His hand, maybe someday I–we can show our appreciation by helping those that haven't been quite so fortunate. There it is–the whole thought–just live the right kind of life–and in the meantime, to keep from being too self centered–help make the world a happier one for the other guy.

Say, toots, you don't think I'm nuts, do you? By the way, have you ever gotten up before dawn–heard the birds singing, felt the night slipping away with the breeze–fly up to where the sunshine paints the sky and clouds, before earth bound humans even get a glimpse–then travel hundreds of miles completely detached from the earth by a carpet of white cloud–drop a few tons of death and destruction on a town of every day people–because they've threatened your way of life–then return–see the grim colors of sky, high mountains sticking through the white carpet beneath you–return to earth–as the kids and people are beginning to retire. Dusk, quietness and moonlight. Such a beautiful world we live in–and what do we do to show our appreciation? War certainly is Hell and this one is weird and unworldly. We humans are such damn fools, aren't we?

Sometimes I feel like telling the world what a bunch of fools we are–even if I could–it'd be just another fool–popping off–so there you are–where are you? Round and round.

Nope, I can control such thoughts and there's no need of you going nuts trying to figure it out–just show that you appreciate the fact that you're happy and living in the best country in the world–and then try to repay Old Mother Nature–and God–for being so generous.

Rantings and ravings–I know–but just shows to go you–just how many angles there are to every question, if you want to go nuts trying to figure the goings on in the world.

You know what–I'm just tired enough to get into one of these here meditating moods and that means too tired to think in the usual roads of the human mind–so ought'n I stop? Yes–I ought.

Hey, I love you–and if you'll stand by–I'll write soon–when there isn't quite so much meditating going on.

Lots of love
Be seeing you,
Jack

[Editor's note: February 26 target, Berlin, Germany; February 27 target, Halle, Germany.]

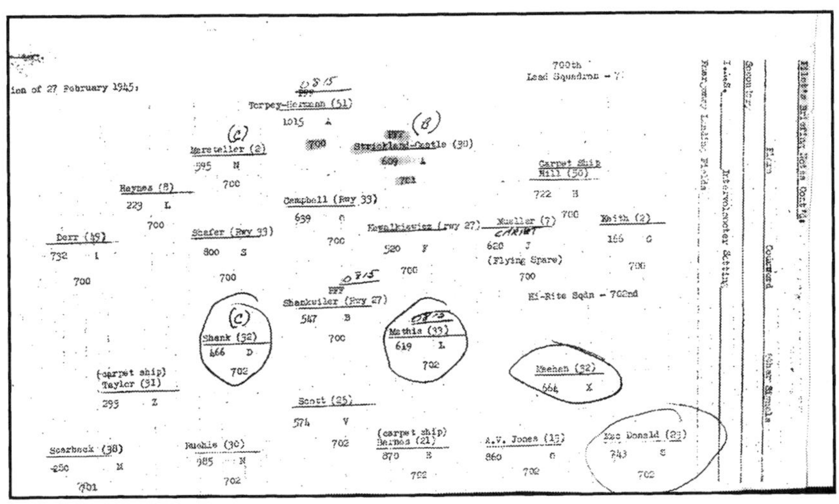

ion of 27 February 1945;

700th
Lead Squadron – 7

Torpey-Hermann (51)
1015 A
700

Strickland-Castle (30)
609 A
701

Mereteller (2)
595 N
700

Haynes (8)
229 L
700

Campbell (Rwy 33)
639 O
700

Carpet Ship
Hill (50)
722 H
700

Derr (49)
732 I
700

Shafer (Rwy 33)
800 S
700

Kowalkiewicz (rwy 27)
520 F
700

Mueller (7)
620 J
(Flying Spare)
700

Keith (2)
166 G
700

Hi-Rite Sqdn – 702nd

Shankweiler (Rwy 27)
547 B
700

Shenk (32)
666 D
702

Mathis (33)
619 L
702

Meehan (32)
664 X

(carpet ship)
Taylor (31)
295 Z

Scott (25)
574 V
702

Scarbeck (38)
250 M
701

Ruchie (30)
985 N
702

(carpet ship)
Barnes (21)
870 E
702

A.V. Jones (13)
860 G
702

Mac Donald (23)
743 S
702

Emergency Landing Fields

Intervalometer Setting

Flight order: February 27, 1945

Although I loved planning for our future, I knew that the long, rambling letters Jack wrote were his way of coping with the effect the war was having on him. I guess each individual had his own way of keeping the demons of war at bay. As time went on it became obvious that Jack's letters were changing. He asked me several times if I had noticed any change in him. I did not tell him that I had, but it was apparent to me that the pressure he was under was getting to him. I could imagine him coming back to the base after a mission of death, destruction and danger and trying to put his mind into the future–thus tuning out the horror of the present. This form of escapism was essential to his mental health but the reality in which he was living was making it harder for him to ignore, even for a little time.

I had lived in constant fear for him ever since he started flying but I could not dwell on it. The only thing I could do was to continue writing him loving and encouraging letters daily. As he mentioned, sometimes they arrived in batches and he didn't have time to read them all in one sitting.

March 2, 1945

Still Waiting for me, Miss?

For over a week now I've been intending on writing a letter ever so often and somehow things don't work out that way. Remember when I said plenty of letters meant not much going on? Still works that way. The usual trouble is having to go to bed early, the usual time for letter writing. Tonight I have a fairly early start, however this letter will probably be a short one.

I certainly hope we keep on rolling even if it does mean a slow up in letter production–possibly a shut down. Would you mind if they were even less than a page long–and V-mail, at that? Not just because I have two more sheets of stationery but mainly on account that there is too, nope not too much (hope it keeps up) but just a "BIG DEMAND" for sack time.

Why, for awhile I had been thinking of getting in touch with some of the schools back in the States–feeling out the future possibilities. I've definitely decided on Veterinary study–and the degree that means the course is finished. Got hold of a bit of literature from the Army Education Branch of Special Services. The study would definitely fill all the requirements–regardless of which field of work–ahem–profession–I ended up in. That's including private veterinary practice. Now comes the rub. The schools with the profession listed among their diplomas–limit the enrollments for that particular study, to state residents. New York, Penn, Kansas and Texas are the major ones. So–Texas A & M takes the spotlight. If I have to apply heat, maybe I can even get some from outside sources–something I've never had to do yet. Texas would suit your desire to be away from everyone and on our own. It's in the south (look at a map) and living conditions, schools and people would all fill the bill. Close to the Gulf, large towns, airlines and La., too. Bryan, Texas is north west of Houston–between Houston and Waco. Look it over and what do you think, Ma'am?

Man, how I'm looking forward to getting back and you and I–yep, and the kids–taking a little time off to run along a nor-

mal road for awhile. I know these last letters have sounded a bit funny–but I'm busy–or pretty busy and have to rush through them–see? Still a long way to go but quite a bit closer than a month or so back. So to bed–and then to start trying to get around to another letter soon –just to remind you that it's LOVE I'm sending,

Jack

Tell Mom and the folks Hello and I'll catch up sometime soon.

Be seeing you.

[Editor's note: The March 1 target was Ingolstadt, Germany.]

V-mail

March 7, 1945

Hi! You been worried?

Somehow I just can't get around to letters. Sorta hard to tell where censored comes in and where it doesn't. There really isn't a heck of a lot, out of routine, going on. We've been shifted to another squadron–the old one still rates tops with me–but–we'll just have to see.

Moved barracks–more monotonous energy sapping. But all that counts these days are the missions–so that's the main reason for not writing–just no interest in anything else. I sent a lot of clothing today that I haven't had a need for–however you might iron the summer uniforms for future reference–I HOPE! maybe by summer–huh?

Got Art's V-mail today. Heard from Harold last week–Bill, too. Harp home yet? Thankee, Miss, for the olives. Really swell to get back to the taste of civilian food. Well, guess this sounds monotonous–but wait until we start a real, honest to goodness conversation. First sentence–Hi, Sweet–I love you.

Jack

Mom's birthday March 25

[Editor's note: Sometime between March 2 and March 7, Jack was transferred from the 700th Squadron to the 701st, which was made up of lead crews. The March 3 target was Madgeburg, Germany.]

R E S T R I C T E D

HEADQUARTERS 2d AIR DIVISION
APO 558

GENERAL ORDERS)
:
NUMBER 92)

E X T R A C T

11 March 1945

* * * *

AWARDS OF THE OAK LEAF CLUSTER TO THE AIR MEDAL

* * * *

Under the provisions of Army Regulations 600-45, 22 September 1943, as amended, and pursuant to authority contained in Paragraph 2b, Section I, Circular 56, Hq European T of Opns, U.S. Army, 27 May 1944, and Letter, Hq Eighth Air Force, 23 September 1944, File No. 200.6, Subject: "Awards and Decorations", an OAK LEAF CLUSTER is awarded to the following named Officers and Enlisted Men for wear with the Air Medal previously awarded.

Citation: For meritorious achievement, in accomplishing with distinction, several aerial operational missions over enemy occupied Continental Europe. The courage, coolness and skill displayed by these individuals in the face of determined opposition materially aided in the successful completion of each of these missions. Their actions reflect great credit upon themselves and the Armed Forces of the United States.

445TH BOMBARDMENT GROUP (H)

JENNIS M. STRICKLAND 0797634 1st Lt Silver Spring, Maryland

* * * *

By command of Major General KEPNER:

FRANCIS H. GRISWOLD
Brigadier General, U.S.A.
Chief of Staff

OFFICIAL:

/s/ George L. Paul
GEORGE L. PAUL
Lt Col AGD
Adjutant General

CERTIFIED EXTRACT COPY
Rudolph J. Birsic
RUDOLPH J. BIRSIC,
Captain, Air Corps,
Adjutant.

R E S T R I C T E D

Oakleaf cluster to air medal

March 14 - or so -1945

Hey, say, Miss,

Getting tired of V-mails? Well, now, according to you there is stationery and ink on the way. Bet this letter takes weeks over the normal number–didn't it?

Things over this way are still in the same tracks more or less. You no doubt know that Jerryland has been undergoing a rather intensive period of being hit these past few weeks. Still, as I said before, unless we rush them from both sides–not in two months, now–but within the time it took this letter to arrive, well, it'll drag on. Feels good to be optimistic now and then and wonder if it won't be over before long. Don't seriously consider that though–it's like running up the last hill after a hard race –and then finding there are hills on the other side–stretching on to the horizon. Lately things have been happening pretty fast, at that, but while they're interesting (in a way) and hardly important, either I'd rather wait and tell them–or else we just aren't allowed to go into detail.

Radio Bremen–Germany's main propaganda station beamed to us–is admittedly off the air tonight–the announcer says "due to circumstances beyond their control"–so they're filling in with recordings, orchestras and for once, no propaganda what so ever –may be another trick, though, to appear efficient and well organized - they'll probably come across shortly with "Radio Bremen is now back in operation." They're not kidding, though–this guy is really new. He just played a recording of Richard Crooks and his orchestra. In case you didn't know, Richard Crooks is strictly a vocalist–baritone–they also played "Show Boat" by Victor Herbert's orchestra! Trouble is, it was "Old Man River." They really aren't that dumb–something smells somewhere–and it ain't in Denmark. Now to really cause even more consternation–they've picked up the BBC program and are piping it back–courtesy, you know–rather than let guys down that can't pick up other stations with good music. Still fishy - though the music is genuine enough but the announcer is definitely a Jerry. You ponder over it! I'll just keep it in the background and remember it in case there's an explanation. Women vocalists now and they're the same mismatched rabble that occasionally come over Bremen radio. No, they aren't piping BBC back–that was another lie–why? What's cooking?

Oh–just back off another 48 hour though it ends tomorrow noon. Somehow I've gotten into the habit of spending half of a 48 in London–that suffices and then the rest here comes in handy because we always have practice missions or some such–the afternoon we return off pass.

Told you I was going to be a h-a-r-d man, remember? Well, I've done that. Got rid of Solham–he was good as an engineer –O.K. personally–but I just couldn't keep pushing him all the time. I miss the guy and more than likely it causes me more worry than it did him. He took it, though, with no hard feelings.

Back to the pass–I looked around all kinds of shops today. Just–shopping around, but there's nothing I've seen over here that is worth the packing and, I repeat, the prices. Variety and quality are all out of sorts with those in the States.

Bought a book–child's, I think–I used to read them way back when I first started reading. Yeah–that was years ago! I think John would enjoy it, so I'll bring it someday–or send it if I have reason to make up a package within the next month or so. The book takes place (story) in England and Sweden–but the name suggests otherwise. "The Cat of Pine Ridge." I was hoping the occupants of the compartment on the train thought it was a mystery novel. Don't think I fooled anyone, though–the illustrations don't strike your fancy as being part of a mystery novel.

(Hey, the program is genuine BBC now.)

Say, toots, have you been noticing any change in me? Sometimes I feel like I've changed in a few ways–maybe it's because there's a lot more thinking to be done in this job–and quite a few odd moments to do it in. Maybe it's just another phase of branching out as an adult (That's us) anyway my thinking apparatus likes to idle along continuously–sort of recreation, more or less–like a good argument.

Been idling long enough, I guess, so I'd better start wrapping this package up.

Still haven't heard from Texas A&M. Guess that'll come one of these days.

Oh well, anyway,
Be seeing you,

Lots of the old love–renewed.

Jack

March 17, 1945

Well Hello There,

See, your package did get here just as you said it would. Now you have the honor of receiving the first sheet to be used. Please note where ink (red) has rubbed off on the bottom of the page.

Now, what gives? Letters have really slowed down lately but maybe that works both ways. Consequently, I've assisted here and there with V-s. When we're busy–or otherwise have reason to be tired–I might use them quite often. 'Til today I've been pretty lazy–no energy, ambition or what have you? I say "til today" because we were on a routine practice mission–by ourselves–and when it neared the finish, I got the urge to "mess around a bit." Now, as you know, most such urges, I overlook–push them in the background, etc., etc. This time the urge hit me just as a B-25 passed overhead fairly close. So on the impulse I threw off the automatic Pilot with one hand–racked up the old hoss into a chandelle after him. He ducked, kept going–didn't want to play. So we droned on–everybody keeping well out of the way–then at the field they told me and a C-47 in the pattern to keep circling until they changed runways. Ah-h duck soup–him with no place to go–me with more speed but less maneuverability. I chased him around the field and the old crate finally caught him–edged in–close formation. He didn't like. His co-pilot kept motioning–not so close. Finally he stood up, leaned around the C.P. and started violent action to keep me away. Like a kid, huh Some fun–heh-heh. I hung on until we got the OK from the tower–he peeled off–me on his tail–landed. We'd chatted a bit back and forth on the radio about a guy he knew at the field–generally cluttering up the air–but the tower seemed to get a little refreshment from such unorthodox goings on so nobody felt bad about it. We got together on the ground and I gave him the lowdown on the guy he knew–end of this little episode. Oh well, been feeling good–or fairly good–ever since–sorta crazy feeling, you know.

Say, babe, you wouldn't endanger our lives by talking too much should I drop a hint now and then, would you? Oh well, in that case, skip it–no, nothing doing–forget it, woman.

Oh well, still love you just as much–maybe more than last time. How are you and the burden making out these days? Better than hot summer time, isn't it? Still that means you'd better take better care of yourself on account of ice–snow and such. Don't tell me you're in bed with a cold on account of I won't like it much–it'd be a sure sign you're not taking care of yourself as much as you should. We've gotten those names narrowed to Lynn Murray or Banks M. S., haven't we? Keep me posted–I'll reserve one ear for that purpose.

Doing the logical thing, let's assume you're up and about when I get home. The usual thing is 15 days (I think) at a rest hotel–family included–about 50 cents a day per person. The two I know of are Miami and Atlantic City. Then follows 30-day leave–I hope. Now, what to do–when, where and how? What are your views?

Jerry has been feeling his oats lately so far as the Luftwaffe is concerned. Just got back from outside–no moon but still fairly light. I heard one or two pass in the distance, but for a couple of weeks now, we've been left pretty much alone. There were a bunch of new guys in not so long ago–had the same idea we did when we came over–"maybe we'll get into combat before it's ended–maybe not." 'Bout 2 A.M. they got their answer. No more talk about it being a pushover from here on in from them.

Now is that a plane or is it a truck? Plane–has he passed or is he coming?–sounds a little to one side so it isn't any use going out to see. Just looked across the lounge–one of the new guys sitting there–pen poised, ears pricked up, strictly in a "poised" position, we grinned–and he resumed writing. Rough in the E.T.O., ain't it? Writing–he jots a few words, stops, stares at the desk–listening. So it goes. Nobody's the least bit jumpy–but after awhile–they get that way, just because it's natural to stop at the least provocation and take inventory of the hums, slamming doors, and distant booms that go on constantly. Comes again–now, should I or shouldn't I? See, I did, along with some of the others–Nothing but the stove roaring up the chimney. See what I mean? Mighty quiet in here. More hums–and what the devil–jump up, relax, jump up, relax. See where the jumps come from? No one is afraid–they simply don't want to miss out in case there's shooting. Whenever they've come at night–very few guys bother to get out of the sack. Same with buzz bombs–except maybe you'll find some of the guys up on the roof–and in the trees–watching them–providing it isn't too late to bother. Haven't seen one since the first week on the base. Heard one or two pass. Felt others hit but outside of London, haven't heard the explosions–and only twice there. Repetition–Rough in the E.T.O., ain't it?

'Bout time to turn in now so guess I'd better say–good night, etc. That, of course includes the facts that I miss you, that I love you and that I daydream now and then.

Lots of love
today and tomorrow
and forever.

Jack

[Editor's note: V-1 Buzz Bombs were pilotless flying bombs propelled by pulse-jet engines. They made a loud noise.

V-2 rocket bombs arrived silently]

March 20, 1945

Hello, there,

See, he did have one after all!! Now, what have you been doing that I don't receive any letters this past week or so? Miss you–I sho do.

'Bout all we can do is keep plugging away at that total number of missions, same as we keep plugging away at the lowly Huns. The end still hangs on that position of the front lines. Here I sit with two cigarettes going while you all eke along on what you can get. Once I got out a fresh cigarette–started to light it and realized that in order to do that I had to lay down one that was half smoked!

Sounds like I must be going batty, eh what? Truth is, I start doing something and become so preoccupied that I forget everything else.

I don't know why it seems as if there's nothing to write about –same old excuse of routine happenings, I guess. Maybe there'll come a day when my reminiscing of what's going on at present will almost drive you nuts. Could be, huh? Spring's edging up the same as it always does this time of year. The only thing that really attracts attention about that, though, is the bird songs that are in evidence at dawn and dusk. The countryside is peaceful enough but so darn English that even that becomes monotonous at times. Then, too, something that kills all pleasure in enjoying Nature and her moods is the fact that the whole countryside over here is man-made. What few areas there are–are hand planted. The marshes are small–more or less controlled by man and to top that–made of black gooey mud. They seem more or less oblivious to it all.

Back in the colder days we flew up to Northern England and passed over the most interesting part of the country I've seen. Takes me to say that, I guess. That was the day I flew with the Colonel to the place where our group had been diverted on returning from the mission. We were both "sweating it out" in the soup when it finally began to break up. We passed over a huge area of high ground that was more or less a mesa. Fifteen hundred feet high–flat on top, rocky and gullied. No trees at all–scrub bushes like parts of Texas. Not a road, very few cattle paths, not even a shack or wisp of smoke for miles and miles. There was snow on the ground and apparently a pretty fair gale blowing across the country. With all it's wildness and loneliness it made me feel good to realize that there was something over here that still stood up against man's will to control everything he touches. Now, over in Germany, it's a bit different. There are farmlands–not hedged in–but wide, flat and rolling. Then there are forests and hills that must be beautiful on the ground. They're pretty well scattered throughout the country, too–not just here and there. The Hartz mountains are just about the most refreshing bits of Nature in this part of the globe (Europe.) Ho Ho, listen to me jabber.

One place I would like to go is–ahem–uh, Sweden. Begging your pardon, Ma'am. Now once there was a possibility and I was a bit worried about how you'd feel if–after all that jesting, hemming and hawing we did–we had to pull in there–rough, ain't it? Well, so far so good so don't worry about it. Besides all that there, there's no doubt in my mind–whatsoever, that I could spend a week on a desert island with Hedy Lamar–or what have you–and have no need of a guilty conscience afterwards. Now, how did we get around to such an isolated subject? What's your favorite vegetable? Yeah–you can't polish it either–you have to use a hammer. Two years old?–you're crazy, it's blue even if it is March. Whatinhellsgoingon anyway?

Uh -oh, oh well, ask me about it later; just got something to write about - and might as well forget about it at present.

"You came, I was alone. I should have known, you were Temptation. You smiled, luring me on. I should have known, you were Temptation." I've been trying to learn that just on account of I'd like to be able to sing it to you sometime–any time –all the time.

Look, Miss, save this letter and I'll tell you why when I have it to remind me of the islands. Double talk, I know I shouldn't worry you at all–and you needn't worry - but right this minute give God your sincere thanks that he has been so good to us. Please! He deserves more than that every day–and any way that we can show him that we appreciate His help is still too small to repay his generosity.

Please don't think that I've really gone a bit off because I don't believe that's true. I've often asked if there wasn't some way that would prove to me there really was a God and that He answered my prayers. Today He did–very concrete evidence, too–though it was shown more than two hundred miles away from me, it definitely proves without the slightest wisp of a doubt that He has helped me more than any human help on the face of the earth could have. All this news reached me just before the beginning of the second paragraph counting this as the first–counting backwards.

I hope I haven't caused you undue worry by all that but this time I believe I should let you know about it, simply because I need your help in giving (not showing by words alone) thanks to God for helping me.

Kitty, sorta hard to get half the news and then expect you to forget it but that's about the way it stands at present. What troubles me is not being able to express enough thanks to ever repay this one time when it should be repaid. This one time is an error on my part, there are countless other times that deserve thanks.

Now all this will be cleared up when I see you, so there, too!

Let's see now–last letter was postmarked Feb. 15–speaking of Harold this time. 'Bout time he wrote another, however I believe now that he'll be O.K. Faith has stopped the worrying that I used to have about him. Still I hope he'll be rotated soon. 'Bout time, don't you think?

So near and yet so far. There are still too many hidden factors to really say when I think we might finish up. However two more months before we do is wishful thinking. Wishful thinking isn't so hard on a guy, at that, is it? O.K.–then I'll continue hoping–in a sober way–on account it's still wishful thinking–and then how long would it take us to get situated for shipment–two weeks at least–and then the boat ride. Long time no see–but there's a great day coming someday. We'd have to beat the monthly average to finish within two months. Rough, ain't it?

Well–whatta you say. Let's call it a day. Time to investigate those five blankets and the dream they might hold. Funny thing though, I don't average one dream a month–however the last one had you as it's star.

LOTS of love,

Jack

[Editor's note: The March 19 target was Neuberg, Germany.]

[Editor's note: Jack wrote this to his mother and family.]

March 22, 1945

Hi Folks,

Looks like these letters are getting about as frequent as missions, doesn't it?

Funny how sometimes it's easy to write a letter and then again you just don't feel up to making a mark on paper. When you're really busy, though, everything falls into a rut and somehow you can't write about a rut when it's the same one you wrote about last week.

Sho, things are happening over here but as a rule it seems like we seldom get in on those things. Now should we take that as being good or bad? When things do happen either we can't write it–or else feel it would be a lot easier to tell about them sometime when there isn't much else to do.

Tiring of all that routine–and the routine training flights, I decided I'd treat the crew and myself to something a bit different. Consequently I've gotten into the habit of hugging ole mother earth when it isn't required that we go way up yonder in the blue–or gray (whichever) where there's nothing but cold, thin air and sometimes soup. So, in other words, I've been doing some sightseeing from the air–not buzzing now–but just lumbering along down close where you can see what's going on. When I was over to see Harp I realized there were parts of England that were a bit fair to the eye after all. Well, anyway we were in that neck of the woods and it's mighty refreshing and livable looking. Creeks, pastures, meadows, pretty towns and houses, hills and all that. Saw a pub today that looked mighty inviting –not that I go around looking for pubs. This one was stuck on a hill with a road as a yard–and a small, sheer drop to the winding river beneath. The road forked at the door and went across a small bridge–nice ain't it? The whole countryside was like that–houses, individual, instead of row on row and left to rot there a few generations back. Clean and neat. Why, there were guys actually lolling around along the river, fishing. We went by a hospital on a hillside–we were in a valley so we could look up to watch them sail by–oh well, different, anyway.

Last time I heard from Harold he was doing O.K. Been keeping sorta close track on his location and it's pretty definite that he's in the outfit–of the outfits that are carrying the biggest part of the job–and the hopes of the Allies. With that guy–that outfit–goes the end of the war. They've got it with them but when they'll be able to prove it is anybody's guess–watch 'em though. They'll tell you when you can start celebrating. For the first time I'm beginning to get mad at those simpleton senators, etc., back in the States. The ones that keep saying the war will be over in Europe before such and such a date. They must be a pretty muddle-headed bunch not to learn from experience. In the first place they know not one whit more than you do–probably less–but they're in a position to draw attention–and use their position to tell everybody what they would do–or how smart they are. I'd like to see a list kept of their names–and predictions–and when the day rolls around when the prediction is up–be made to eat the paper it's written on. 'Nough of that, I guess.

Say, what's the latest news on Roy Edgar? Huh? Man, it would be good to get all the guys together again. Now that brings up "Harp." Got a letter from him just before he was scheduled for home. How did it turn out? Is he back yet and how's he coming along? Sorta scattered out–the guys, I mean.

Here we piddle and poke–in one day–loafing the next. Like turning on a light to write a letter and then having someone switch it off every time you think you'll be able to jot down a paragraph or two. Rough in the E.T.O., ain't it? Oh well, 'bout time we started picking up the stitches we dropped in the rush. We could and almost have hollowed out the inner Germany–however it's the wall around the outer side–the army that has to be licked. I believe they have quite a supply of all the essentials tucked away in bombproof, hidden storage. Consequently they can pretty well keep up a full-scale war–even though there are periods when the manufacturers of those essentials are pretty well stopped. There's one more important factor that probably carries a lot of weight–but rather than mention it, I'd bet-

ter just keep quiet–it might be too important to mention–and then again it might be that I have a higher opinion of what I think is going on–than actually is. Or some such–you know. Anyway we'll see just whether I'm on the right track or not, pretty soon–maybe. What's happened the past couple of weeks–from the time you get this letter? O.K. what's next?

There I go–prattling.

Feels good to relax, doesn't it? Just sitting on the sidelines trying to call the plays, for a change. Somehow tonight I feel a bit more relaxed than is usually the case. Now, was it the flight around the country side or am I getting used to this 'run a mile, rest for five' business?

Tell John and Red that I still haven't forgotten the camping trip–then rush over and tell Kitty all about it–maybe between the six (?) of us we'll be able to work something out. I promised John and Red I'd take them down on Mr. Harris' pond for a weekend camping trip this summer. Think it's possible? Let's see–we'll have to bring a crib along, too–eh what? Just how is all this going to be arranged? Huh?

That's me!

Lots of love

Be seeing you,

Jack

P.S. This thing sounds like I'm about finished, which isn't so. Still looks like a couple of months OR SO to go.

Well this time,
Be seeing you

The Generals (and other powers that be) were planning a massive attack, which they named "Operation Varsity." This was to be the biggest strike, so far, against Germany and perhaps the turning point of the war.

The Allied armies would cross the Rhine by amphibious assault at three points. The Air Force gliders would carry troops and paratroopers to be dropped on enemy lines. R.A.F. and U.S. bombers (1,700) would bomb airfields and railroads and cripple the German defense. Two task groups of B-24s (120 each) would drop ammunition and supplies to the ground troops from an altitude of 200 to 400 feet. In addition to the ground troops (Jack's brother, Harold, among them) 40,000 allied airborne and paratroopers would be utilized.

On the evening of March 22, 1945 a secret Teletype message was received, restricting the base until further notice, effective noon March 23rd. Early evening of the 23rd, top-secret classification documents were delivered to the Group Adjutant amplifying previous instructions for the mission in the morning.

9:30 A.M. March 24, 1945 "Operation Varsity" began. The B-24s flew at 3,000 feet, then dropped down to 1,000 feet and crossed the channel heading south. Their goal was the Wesel area of Germany.

They crossed the Rhine and could see the ground battle raging. Gliders (some intact, others not) were scattered on the ground. Many tow planes were on fire. Large caliber enemy ground fire was everywhere. Anti-aircraft guns and flak bombarded them. They couldn't use their guns to retaliate for fear of hitting their own troops. Many paratroopers were shot and killed before they hit the ground.

Twenty American planes were shot down. Of the 27 sent from Tibenham, two were lost. One was Jack's.

A Colonel Arnold was piloting the Lead Plane. Jack was flying the Deputy Lead Plane with Lt. Col. Carl Fleming (Deputy Commander of the base) flying co-pilot. Their job was to take over if anything happened to the Lead

Plane. They were leading the whole 2nd Air Division of 240 B-24s. Col. Fleming had realized the importance of this mission and wanted to be in on it, although he had just finished his tour of 30 missions and was scheduled to go back to the States. He volunteered to fly as Wing Leader.

The Lead Plane always flew at the lowest altitude, with each following plane flying higher. This prevented the ones in back from being hit by the canisters the plane in front of them had dropped. Jack's plane was flying between 50 and 100 feet off the ground. They had successfully dropped their canisters of supplies on target and had turned and were heading back.

Lloyd E. Stone from Roswell, NM, was also a pilot on that mission and he told me he was flying right beside Jack's plane. He was looking directly into their cockpit and saw both Jack and Col. Fleming get shot by ground machine gun fire and slump over their instrument panel. Their plane crashed immediately.

Tom Campbell, from Warwick, RI, told me had had been co-piloting the plane immediately in back of Jack's and saw the plane crash. He said as soon as it hit the ground it went up in huge ball of fire and smoke which, of necessity, they had to fly through. A tire on Lt. Stone's plane was shot out by machine gun fire and he did not know it until they came in to land at Tibenham.

Jack's brother, Harold, saw the plane go down although at that time he did not know that it was his brother's.

701ST BOMBARDMENT SQUADRON (H)
445TH BOMBARDMENT GROUP (H)
APO 558 Sta 124

24 March, 1945.

LOADING LISTS

SHIP # 525-B (700th)

P	Moebius, K.D.	Capt.
CA	Arnold, M.W.	Col.
CP	Newton, L.W.	1st Lt.
N	Coleman, P.W.	1st Lt.
B	Aarvig, R.J.	1st Lt.
NT	Ricks, W.J.	2nd Lt.
E	Wiley, F.T.	T/Sgt.
RO	Morgan, T.V.	T/Sgt.
WG	Bolek, A.J.	S/Sgt.
WG	Scourby, J.	S/Sgt.
TG	Sebold, J.T.	S/Sgt.

SHIP # 245-P (700th)

P	Strickland, J.M.	1st Lt.
CP	Fleming, C.	Lt. Col.
N	Weingartner, H.F.	2nd Lt.
B	Wegeil, W.F.	2nd Lt.
NT	Golub, E.E.	2nd Lt.
WG	Gillette, H.A.	2nd Lt.
E	Oaks, W.	T/Sgt.
RO	Edward, R.L.	T/Sgt.
WG	Del Pero, O.D.	S/Sgt.
TG	Schultz, E.W.	Sgt.

SHIP # 574-V (702nd)

P	Dewey, W.R.	Capt.
CP	Griswold, T.L.	2nd Lt.
N	West, B.S.	Capt.
B	Mitchell, W.E.	1st Lt.
NT	Alberghini, R.E.	1st Lt.
E	Craig, C.O.	T/Sgt.
RO	Ellson, J.E.	T/Sgt.
WG	Medlock, L.I.	S/Sgt.
WG	Springer, R.V.	Sgt.
TG	Montanez, R.A.	S/Sgt.

SHIP # 811-E (703rd)

P	Davis, F.	1st Lt.
CP	Milo, C.	2nd Lt.
A	Freeman, G.H.	2nd Lt.
B	Hamrick, H.T.	1st Lt.
NT	Pohner, W.H.	2nd Lt.
E	Durant, M.D.	T/Sgt.
RO	Cobb, R.M.	S/Sgt.
WG	Rausch, K.M.	S/Sgt.
TG	Yagley, A.J.	S/Sgt.
TT	Frant, A.R.	S/Sgt.

CERTIFIED CORRECT:

CHARLES L. TORPEY,
Capt., Air Corps,
Operations Officer.

Cargo Mission — 24 March 1945

Gas load: 2300

Bomb load: —

Fusing: X

700

Moebios 525-B
Strickland 245-P
Hines 509-M
Keith 882-K
Haynes 525-A
Alexander 639-O
Curry 521-C
Sholty 620-J
Shafer 565-Q

702

Dewey 574-V
Whitcomb 319-T
Kilburn 710-G
Taylor 280-B
Trombly 985-N
Simonson 020-F
Meehan 664-X
Johnson 572-C
Scott 375-U

MB – 0615
TO – 0920
At Ships 0745!!
Taxitime 0900
27 crews

701

Moebios 525-B — 700
Strickland 245-P — 700
Dewey 574-V — 702
(Lt.) Davis 811-E — 703

703

Davis 811-E
Dunay 544-N
Stone 545-B
Fagerquist 749-L
Adams 506-F
Belcher 228-I
→ Coyle 464-H
Fishman 759-M
Smith 855-A

WING WASH

No. 112 Saturday, 24 March 1945

Saturday the 24th of March was the D-Day of 1945. In a combined effort with units of the 21st Army Group under Field Marshall Montgomery, Eight Air Force Liberators performed a double role in the assault of the Rhine. Operating under clear, sunny skies, 240 B-24's (of which 80 were from this Wing) dropped 600 tons of supplies to the American 17th and the British 6th Airborne Divisions which had parachuted out earlier in the morning. Flying at minimum altitudes, crews were over disputed territory but a few minutes. Even so, the fire from the small arms and automatic weapons was intense enough to cause more than 50% battle damage. Two Tib Libs went down east of the Rhine and two Hathel aircraft are believed lost with two others still unreported. Most felt would be the loss of Lt. Col. Carl Fleming, popular 445th Air Executive whose plane burst into flames as it crashed; Col. Fleming was acting as Deputy Division Air Commander at the time and had already completed a tour of operations.

Commanding the Division while flying as 445th leader was Col. Milton W. Arnold, Commanding Officer, 2d Wing. Crews report dropping of assorted bundles containing ammunition, food and medical supplies was almost entirely effective. First news indicated that progess eastward was satisfactory; 2nd Division combat and ground crews could now watch that progress in the realization that they had played a strong supporting role in the year's greatest drama on the Western Front. The boxscore;

Group	Aircraft Disp't'd	Aircraft Abor'v's	Aircraft Att'k'ng	Results
389th	26	0	26	All
445th	27	0	27	Units
453rd	27	0	27	Effective
2nd Wing	80	0	80	

The morning of April 13, 1945 I turned on the radio and heard that Franklin Delano Roosevelt had died the night before. The whole world was in a state of shock.

On that same day I got a telephone call from Blanche. She had just received a telegram from the War Department saying that Jack was "missing in action" as of March 24th. Because I had no permanent address, Jack has listed his mother as the one to notify in case of an emergency.

We consoled each other with the thought that "missing in action" could very well mean that he had been forced down over friendly territory–or at worst, was captured by the Germans and was a Prisoner of War. I called Harvey and he contacted his father to see if he could get any more information. He was unable to find out any details.

So, we waited–wanting to know what had happened and at the same time, terrified of knowing.

The next telegram arrived on April 28th. It said that Jack had been killed on March 26th. No details. The discrepancy in dates gave us a shred of hope that the reports were inaccurate and that he might still be alive.

This was not to be.

A few days later my parents invited me over to their apartment. "The boy" and I had not been there long when Blanche and Karl arrived. I knew immediately that this had been prearranged. Blanche showed me the telegram that confirmed Jack's death on March 24, 1945.

There are no words to describe how I felt. I did not cry because I knew if I ever started, I would never stop.

My folks and Blanche and Karl wanted desperately to comfort me. For their sakes, I wish I had let them, but my hurt was too deep, too intense and too private to share.

I said, "Well, that's that." I do not remember what was said that evening except my parents suggested they buy a house big enough so my children and I could live with them. I refused. I had grown up and was a mother and there was no way I could go back and be a child again in my mother and father's home.

I returned to Mrs. Beckerman's and continued with my

established routine.

(I've often wondered if it was Standard Operating Procedure in the Army, when someone was killed, to send a "missing in action" telegram to soften the blow.

It would seem a logical thing to do rather than letting survivors receive a stark telegram informing them of their loved one's death.)

WESTERN UNION

CLASS OF SERVICE: This is a full-rate Telegram or Cablegram unless its deferred character is indicated by a suitable symbol above or preceding the address.

A. N. WILLIAMS, PRESIDENT

SYMBOLS: DL=Day Letter; NL=Night Letter; LC=Deferred Cable; NLT=Cable Night Letter; Ship Radiogram

1201 (44)

The filing time shown in the date line on telegrams and day letters is STANDARD TIME at point of origin. Time of receipt is STANDARD TIME at point of destination

WK93 42 GOVT=WUX WASHINGTON DC 13 124P 1945 APR 13 PM 1 43

MRS BLANCHE H BYRON=

313 HIGHVIEW AVE SILVERSPRINGS MD=

THE SECRETARY OF WAR DESIRES ME TO EXPRESS HIS DEEP REGRET THAT YOUR SON 1/LT STRICKLAND JENNIS M HAS BEEN MISSING IN ACTION IN GERMANY SINCE 24 MAR 45 IF FURTHER DETAILS OR OTHER INFORMATION ARE RECEIVED YOU WILLBE PROMPTLY NOTIFIED=

J A ULIO THE ADJUTANT GENERAL.

1/LT 24 45.

WESTERN UNION

CLASS OF SERVICE: This is a full-rate Telegram or Cablegram unless its deferred character is indicated by a suitable symbol above or preceding the address.

A. N. WILLIAMS, PRESIDENT

SYMBOLS: DL=Day Letter; NL=Night Letter; LC=Deferred Cable; NLT=Cable Night Letter; Ship Radiogram

1201 (35)

The filing time shown in the date line on telegrams and day letters is STANDARD TIME at point of origin. Time of receipt is STANDARD TIME at point of destination

WL144 36 GOVT=WUX WASHINGTON DC 28 818P 1945 APR 28 PM 8 36

MRS BLANCHE H BYRON=

313 HIGHVIEW AVE S=

THE SECRETARY OF WAR DESIRES ME TO EXPRESS HIS DEEP REGRET THAT YOUR SON 1ST/LST STRICKLAND JENNIS M WAS KILLED IN ACTION 26 MAR 45 HE HAD PREVIOUSLY BEEN REPORTED MISSING IN ACTION CONFIRMING LETTER FOLLOWS=

J A ULIO THE ADJUTANT GENERAL.

1 26 45.

THE COMPANY WILL APPRECIATE SUGGESTIONS FROM ITS PATRONS CONCERNING ITS SERVICE

Worst

I received numerous letters of condolence from high ranking military personnel, Senators, and others expressing their sympathy, reiterating the fact that Jack had made the supreme sacrifice for his country and assuring me that if there were any way they could help me, to let them know.

Meanwhile my allotment had come to a halt and the survivors' pension I was entitled to had not been started. My parents were ready to loan me any money I needed, however I wanted to maintain my independence and I decided to see just how much in earnest these letters were. So I started making phone calls. I learned that nowhere was there a fund set up for the purpose of helping widows of men killed in action.

I finally called the Air Transport Command, which was at National Airport, and they told me to come and see them. Jack had no connection with them, other than the encounter he mentioned in his letter of December 1, 1944, but they, too, had sent me a condolence letter. I kept the appointment and told the young man with whom I had talked on the phone what the situation was. He asked how much money I needed. When I told him $300, he made out a check for that amount. I asked him when and how they wanted it paid back. He said. "Whenever you can is fine." I asked if he wanted me to sign anything and he said it wasn't necessary. The money tided me over until my pension started and I paid it back promptly.

I can only repeat what Jack said in his December 1st letter, "Makes you like those guys!!!"

WAR DEPARTMENT
THE ADJUTANT GENERAL'S OFFICE
WASHINGTON 25, D. C.

IN REPLY REFER TO:
AGPC-6 Strickland, Jennis M. *28 June 1945*
ETO 129 0797634

Mrs. J. M. Strickland
221 Normandy Drive
Silver Spring, Maryland

Dear Mrs. Strickland:

Since my last communication to you in which you were informed that your husband, First Lieutenant Jennis M. Strickland, was killed in action in the European Area, a corrected report has been received which states that he was killed in action on 24 March 1945 in Germany. No other information was given.

My continued sympathy is extended to you in your bereavement.

Sincerely yours,

J. A. ULIO
Major General
The Adjutant General of the Army

April 23, 1945

Dear Kitty,

I have not written to express my condolences before this time for fear of anticipating news of Jack's crash. There aren't words to express my very deep sympathy for you and your family who loved him. I can only assure you that those of us, who knew him but slightly, miss not only his warmth and smile but his ability and conscientiousness as well.

The Group Commander expressed some of the feelings of all of us when he said, "I have seldom met a fellow who was admired for his ability and liked for his friendliness as much as Strickland was by everyone who knew him." It was this ability, of which the Colonel spoke, that made Jack the Deputy Command of the whole Eight Air Force when he flew the low level cargo mission on which he went down. His plane was seen hit by ground fire and then dive to the ground. It exploded immediately upon striking.

If during the course of this letter I have blunderingly grieved you again, I am truly sorry and hope you will forgive me.

I am returning to the United States in several weeks and if there is anything I can do, please let me know.

With deepest sympathy, I remain,

Bernie Sugarman

On May 20th I went into labor. I called my father and he took me to Walter Reed Army Hospital where I had received my prenatal care.

This was not the quick labor I had experienced with Jennis. I did not know at the time that the doctors, aware of the shock I had just had, were very concerned about the baby. They were afraid to anesthetize me. So, once again, I was being *vocal* in a *quiet* hospital.

I thought my dad had gone home but a nurse informed me that he was right outside the labor room door. I asked her to please tell him to go home. She did–he refused. I tried not to yell, knowing he could hear me, but I could not control it.

My perfectly healthy daughter, Lynne Murray Strickland, was born on May 20, 1945, after a 7-hour labor.

My father went home and told my mother, "If you think it's rough to listen to your wife having a baby, you ought to listen to your BABY have a baby."

Poor man! He and I were always very close and I'm sure that must have been a horrible experience for him to go through.

The next morning Harvey, who had gotten leave from Maguire Hopital in Richmond, came to see me at Walter Reed. He had two bunches of flowers. One was a lovely spring bouquet–the other, a dozen beautiful red roses. He said the spring bouquet was from him and that when he saw Jack in England, Jack had made him promise that if he, Jack, could not be here with me when the baby was born, Harvey was to bring me roses from him.

I had a picture of Jack on the table beside my hospital bed. One day a lovely young nurse came in and saw it. She asked if that was my husband. I said, "Yes."

She said, "Oh, he's an ANGEL. Where is he now?"

I'm sure that that was one question and answer that neither one of us has ever forgotten.

Several months later I took my baby, Lynne, to Walter Reed Hospital for a routine checkup. I was informed that because Jack had been "Reserve" instead of "Regular" Army, the children and I were not entitled to any medical care and that the commissary privileges were revoked, also. I was irate. They condescended to give her that examination but said that regulations were regulations and there was nothing else they could do.

The pension we were getting was not very big and medical treatment and commissary privileges helped a lot. I was fortunate because Jack had taken out an insurance policy (this had been optional for officers) that I had collected on. I also had some savings. Then I thought about the thousands of young women like myself all over the U.S. who were not in as good financial shape as I and who were being told the same thing. There was nothing they could do about it. However *I* was in Washington, D.C., and had the time and determination to pursue the issue. I could understand why the Government could not continue to offer these benefits to the veterans who had returned and were mustered out of the Service–but to deny them to widows and families of men killed in action was absurd, cruel and certainly not to be considered justice. The regulations needed changing.

I made dozens of phone calls to any agency that I thought might be able to help. The answer was always the same, "It's a shame but regulations are regulations and there's nothing we can do about it."

Finally I wrote my Senator, Millard Tydings. You can read his reply and follow up letters on the next page. The letter from The Surgeon General made me see red. I called Senator Tydings office to try and get an appointment with him. His secretary said, "Senator Tydings makes his own appointments." I asked her how one *saw* Senator Tydings to make an appointment to *see* Senator Tydings. She wasn't very helpful–so I sent him another letter wherein I stated, in re Major General Kirk's suggestion I go to the Red Cross, "If a recommendation to a charitable institution is the only answer I get to what I believe is a reasonable request, then I am beginning to wonder if the United States was worth fighting for, much less dying for."

I got a telegram from the Senator asking me to come to his office. We did have our meeting and he told me that he had talked with his friend, General Omar Bradley, about this and they agreed that the regulations should be changed. General Bradley said he would look into it.

Nothing was ever done about it and I had no idea how to pursue it further–but at least I had tried my best.

To this day I do not know if this "oversight" was ever corrected. I certainly hope it has been.

United States Senate

COMMITTEE ON
TERRITORIES AND INSULAR AFFAIRS

October 23, 1945

Mrs. Kitty M. Strickland
701 Flower Ave.
Takoma Park
Maryland

Dear Mrs. Strickland:

I have your letter of recent date and note what you say in connection with your efforts to have your baby daughter given a medical examination at Walter Reed Hospital.

I shall be glad to look into the matter to see what the situation is, and to let you hear further from me.

Please let me extend to you my deepest sympathy in the loss of your husband, and to assure you that I shall do all that I can to be helpful to you in any possible way.

With best wishes, I am

Sincerely yours,

M E Tydings

MILLARD E. TYDINGS, MD., CHAIRMAN

CARL HAYDEN, ARIZ. · ARTHUR H. VANDENBERG, MICH.
BURTON K. WHEELER, MONT. · WARREN R. AUSTIN, VT.
PETER G. GERRY, R. I. · ROBERT A. TAFT, OHIO
DENNIS CHAVEZ, N. MEX. · OWEN BREWSTER, MAINE
ABE MURDOCK, UTAH · HUGH BUTLER, NEBR.
ALLEN J. ELLENDER, LA. · CHARLES W. TOBEY, N. H.
JAMES O. EASTLAND, MISS. · C. WAYLAND BROOKS, ILL.
FRANK P. BRIGGS, MO.
WARREN G. MAGNUSON, WASH.

MISS CORINNE BARGER, CLERK

United States Senate

COMMITTEE ON
TERRITORIES AND INSULAR AFFAIRS

November 8, 1945

Maj. Gen. N. T. Kirk
The Surgeon General
War Department
Washington, D. C.

Dear General Kirk:

Enclosed herewith is a very appealing letter I have received from Mrs. Kitty M. Strickland, 701 Flower Avenue, Takoma Park, Maryland, relative to her experience in endeavoring to have her baby girl given a medical examination at Walter Reed.

You will note she states the child was born at Walter Reed Hospital two months after her husband was killed in a raid over Germany.

I have had the matter up with Walter Reed but am advised that the regulations there do not permit the admission to that Hospital of the children or other dependents of deceased personnel.

I am not sure if there is any aid that the Army can extend to Mrs. Strickland but I am writing with the thought that she might be eligible for medical attention to her children at an Army Dispensary in the City. I shall greatly appreciate your advices.

Thanking you, and with best wishes, I am

Sincerely yours,

2-dk
c-Mrs. Strickl nd
c-Col. Lee
Enc.

Copy to Mrs. Strickland 11-19-45 M. E. Tydings.

SPMCH 705.

Walter Reed General Hospital (K)

16 November 1945

Honorable Millard E. Tydings

United States Senate

Dear Senator Tydings:

Reference is made to your letter of 8 November 1945, with its inclosure, a letter from Mrs. Kitty M. Strickland, 701 Flower Avenue, Takoma Park, Maryland, concerning hospitalization for her infant daughter at Walter Reed Hospital.

The policy of furnishing medical care for dependents of Army personnel is directed by existing Army Regulations based on executive orders. These regulations do not direct that medical care will be furnished dependents of Army personnel, living or deceased. These regulations provide for hospitalization only in case of emergency.

The American Red Cross has facilities for aiding in the hospitalization and securing of medical care for Army personnel. It is recommended that Mrs. Strickland contact her nearest field office of the Red Cross, citing the circumstances surrounding her case and request assistance in obtaining medical care required.

It is regretted that this office cannot assist further in this instance. However, it is felt that the information contained in the above paragraph will guide Mrs. Strickland in obtaining the medical care required.

Sincerely yours,

1 Incl
Ltr from Mrs. Strickland
(16 Oct 45)

NORMAN T. KIRK
Major General
The Surgeon General

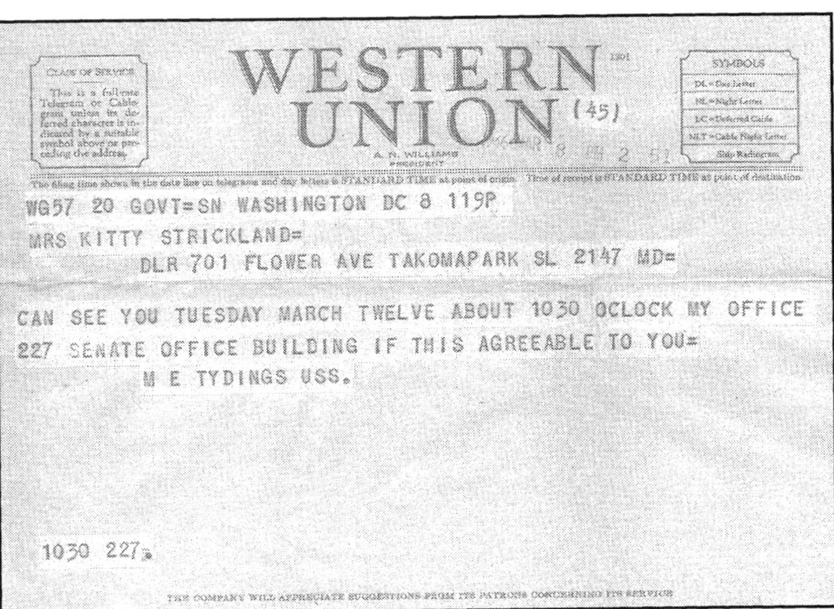

WESTERN UNION (45)

WG57 20 GOVT=SN WASHINGTON DC 8 119P

MRS KITTY STRICKLAND=

DLR 701 FLOWER AVE TAKOMAPARK SL 2147 MD=

CAN SEE YOU TUESDAY MARCH TWELVE ABOUT 1030 OCLOCK MY OFFICE 227 SENATE OFFICE BUILDING IF THIS AGREEABLE TO YOU=

M E TYDINGS USS.

1030 227.

THE COMPANY WILL APPRECIATE SUGGESTIONS FROM ITS PATRONS CONCERNING ITS SERVICE

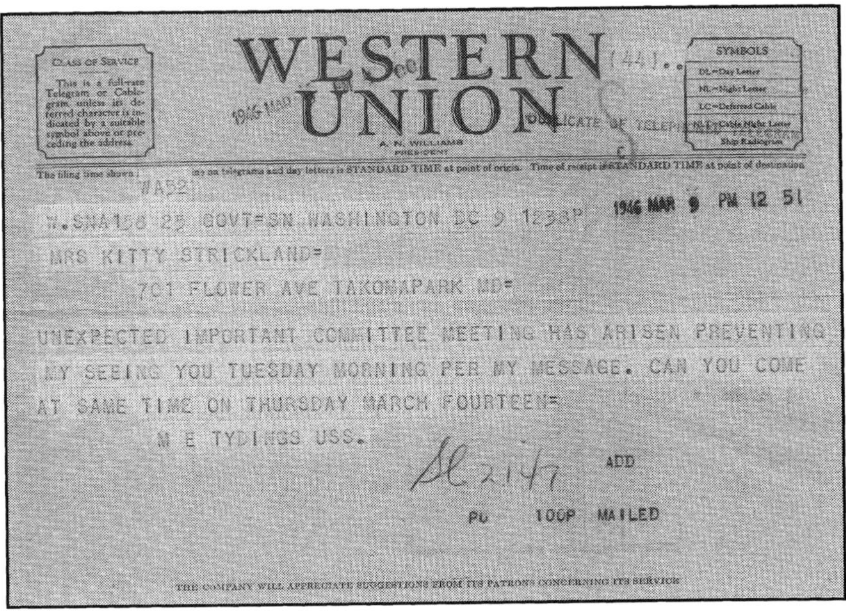

WESTERN UNION (44)

WA52

W.SNA158 25 GOVT=SN WASHINGTON DC 9 1238P 1946 MAR 9 PM 12 51

MRS KITTY STRICKLAND=

701 FLOWER AVE TAKOMAPARK MD=

UNEXPECTED IMPORTANT COMMITTEE MEETING HAS ARISEN PREVENTING MY SEEING YOU TUESDAY MORNING PER MY MESSAGE. CAN YOU COME AT SAME TIME ON THURSDAY MARCH FOURTEEN=

M E TYDINGS USS.

SL 2147 ADD

PU 100P MAILED

THE COMPANY WILL APPRECIATE SUGGESTIONS FROM ITS PATRONS CONCERNING ITS SERVICE

After Jack died there were many times I wanted to give into my grief, crawl into a hole and pull the top in after me. But I could not allow depression to take over as it would not be fair to my little boy and girl. When I told Jack that I could not bear his death if I didn't have his children, I did not know how very true those words were. Our children literally saved my life and my sanity.

Jack had always set very high standards for himself and expected me to do the same. I felt that I had been given a sacred trust to try and live up to his expectations. We certainly had often discussed how he wanted the children raised.

So with this in mind and with Dr. Spock's book, *Baby and Child Care* as my bible, I proceeded to devote my time, love and energy into raising the kind of children he would have been proud of. He had often told me not to spoil "the Boy." This was not an easy job. My maternal instincts had to be soft-pedaled since I felt I had to be both mother and father to them. There were times when my son would come in crying; saying that another child had hit him. Instead of consoling him, which was my natural reaction, I would tell him to go back and fight his own battles. I loved them with all my heart but I was very strict. I made a lot of mistakes but I did the best I could with the knowledge I had then, as all parents do. Of course, in any case, most parents try to make their first child the "perfect" child and are more demanding with that one than they are with subsequent ones. Since a book of rules on child raising doesn't follow the baby out of the womb, the first child must endure the mistakes of first-time parents.

However they managed to survive, in spite of my firm discipline and are both talented and intelligent–and wonderful parents to their children.

Fortunately most of us learn from our mistakes and my other children had a much easier time of it. No two of my children were alike and I respected and encouraged their individuality. I believed, as Jack did, that they should be allowed to follow their own instincts and that the only lessons that are meaningful are those one learns for oneself.

(One day, years later, my mother paid me a compliment that I've always treasured. She said, "Kitty, you're the only person I know who had six *'only'* children.")

On May 7, 1945, Germany surrendered and May 8th was declared V-E Day. That was probably the saddest and loneliest day of my life. People all over the U.S.A. were celebrating the victory, dancing in the streets and eagerly looking forward to the return of their loved ones from overseas. More than anything else that had happened, this brought home to me the knowledge that the man I dearly loved was never coming back.

But life goes on.

I moved to an apartment complex in Silver Spring where there were numerous young neighbors with children. I made many friends. On weekdays the other mothers and I lived pretty much the same kind of life style but in the evenings their husbands would come home to dinner while I had dinner with my little ones. I think I missed Jack most of all on the weekends when all the other Dads were there. That was a pleasure my kids and I would never experience.

United States
Army Air Forces

Leonia, N.J.
28 Aug., 1945

Dear Mrs. Strickland,

At the outset–allow me to introduce myself. I was a buddy, friend and crewmember on your husband's lead crew. I was the "Mickey" or radar navigator.

I do not know what the War Department has told you or who, of his many friends, may have written to you. But I think I can tell you a few things that may in some measure be of comfort.

Though not allowed to fly on the day that Jack and the crew went down, I am thoroughly acquainted with the details of the tragic occurrence. Without going into detail, I would like to tell you this: it was quick, clean and decisive. I am positive that neither Jack nor any member of the crew suffered or knew what was happening until it was all over. This fact alone has been of singular comfort to me and therefore I cling to it and pass it on to you, hoping that you, too, may derive some relief from the realization.

Jack was one of the finest men I have ever known. No one could be more clean cut, thoughtful or considerate of others. He was very much in love with you and above all–completely faithful. I realize that you must be aware of this but perhaps you don't know how others admired him for it.

He was also brave and self-giving above and beyond the call of duty. He led his crew, which was deputy lead for the entire bomber stream, on a very important mission. After the mission was accomplished–Jack and the crew died. It was as clean as the word.

It goes without saying that I commiserate with you and your family. I do know how you feel and though this is a tardy letter I want you to know my deepest sympathy has been and is yours. My sincere wish is that this letter will accomplish its purpose and bring you some peace of mind.

Please call on me if I can in any way be of service.

Sincerely,

James Fluhr

P.S. If you have in your possession the addresses of the other crewmembers, I would be more than grateful if you would send them to me.

J.

Jack was given a temporary burial overseas. Later an official letter informed me that for permanent interment I could elect to have him buried in Arlington Cemetery in Virginia or any cemetery of my choice, including Maargraten, Holland.

I firmly believe that when someone dies, no part of the spirit remains in the corporeal body. I attend funerals out of respect for the survivors and have never otherwise visited cemeteries.

Knowing that my beliefs were not necessarily the same as those of others, I talked it over with Blanche, telling her I would abide by whatever she preferred. She said she felt the same way I did. I authorized his burial in Holland.

The kind Dutch citizens adopted graves of the American soldiers and visited them from time to time and left flowers. A lovely family named Roubroeks, who lived in Terwinselen, Holland, adopted Jack's grave and wrote me letters and sent me pictures of it.

I did not realize how much importance people in the South place on family cemeteries. To this day they often take picnic lunches and have family reunions at the family cemetery. All of Jack's deceased relatives are buried at one cemetery in Nashville, NC.

Jack's sister, Justine, wanted me to have him brought back and buried with them. I vetoed the idea and so she had a marker installed there for him.

A few months after his interment a box arrived at my apartment. I opened it and there was the flag that had been used to cover Jack's coffin at the burial. It came as a complete shock to me and I started crying. My very young son was there and had never seen his mother cry. He didn't know what it was, but he was so upset that he yelled, "Make them take it back, Mommy–make them take it back!"

Years later Harold took a trip to Germany to see the places where he had fought during the war and to visit Maargraten and his brother's grave.

He brought back some beautiful pictures and it reassured me that I had made the right decision.

Maargraten, Holland

Jack's brother, Harold, joined the Army in February 1943 -one week after Jack received his "wings." Although he entered from Maryland he was allowed to join the 30th Division (Old Hickory) which had originated in the South. He was in the 119th Infantry Regiment. These men participated in some of the most grueling battles of the war in Northern France, Holland, Belgium and Germany. (Normandy, St. Lo, the Seigfried Line, Mortain, St. Barthely, Malmedy and many more.)

He was awarded:

- The Bronze Star for action in Holland on September 15, 1944
- The first Oak Leaf Cluster for action in Holland and Germany in November 1944
- The second Oak Leaf Cluster for action in Germany on April 9, 1945
- The third Oak Leaf Cluster for action in Germany on Feb. 23, 1945.

He also was awarded the coveted Infantryman Badge.

He came back to the United States on the *Queen Mary* on August 21, 1945. He and his "Old Hickory" comrades were greeted in New York by bands, rockets, flares and thousands of people cheering and waving.

This country knew the vital part the 30th Division played in bringing the war to a close and was joyfully expressing its eternal gratitude to these brave men.

On April 10, 1946, Harold married Ellen Smith, also from Silver Spring. They had four daughters, Sallie, Martha, Joan, and Amy.

Ellen loaned me Harold's scrapbook, which was filled with newspaper articles, citations, pictures and souvenirs from the war. Jack had been aware of just how arduous and horrible the ground war was. As you have read in his letters, he worried about Harold all the time. It defies the imagination to try and picture what a living Hell those young Infantrymen must have experienced.

I wish I could recount what Harold's "war" was like but that would fill another book.

Suffice is to say, he was truly a HERO.

Harold died in September 1983.

Harold Strickland in Germany

HEADQUARTERS 30TH INFANTRY DIVISION

APO #30
3 November 1944

C I T A T I O N

Private First Class Harold W. Strickland, 33562034, Infantry, United States Army, is awarded the Bronze Star for meritorious conduct in action on 15 September 1944, in Holland. During an extremely heavy attack by his company against the enemy, it became evident that more ammunition would be needed if the attack was to continue with success. Private Strickland, together with five comrades, volunteered to attempt this hazardous mission. With complete disregard for their own safety, these men made more than twelve trips wading across a river which was under excellent enemy observation and heavy enemy fire. Through their tenacity of purpose and determination, they made it possible for this important attack to continue successfully. The outstanding courage and devotion to duty displayed by Private Strickland reflect high credit on himself and the Armed Forces. Entered military service from Maryland.

L. S. HOBBS
Major General - U. S. Army
Commanding

HEADQUARTERS 30TH INFANTRY DIVISION

OFFICE OF THE COMMANDING GENERAL

OLD HICKORY

Battle Honors

The First Battalion, 119th Infantry Regiment, United States Army, reinforced, is cited for outstanding performance of duty in action against the enemy from 19 December 1944 to 21 December 1944, in Belgium. The Battalion occupied positions along a route through which a strong German armored infantry column was attempting to pass, having overrun all organized resistance which had blocked their advance. Despite numerically superior enemy forces and badly depleted personnel of their own companies, the men of the Battalion, realizing that theirs was the last line of resistance, fought heroically. During three fanatical and furious enemy counterattacks the Battalion, with two companies accounting for approximately only sixty men each, and using clerks, messengers, and drivers as riflemen, fought heroically and drove the enemy back. Noncommissioned officers and privates assumed command unhesitatingly after their leaders had been killed or wounded, and though the Battalion suffered 148 casualties during this engagement, the men never faltered. After repulsing an attack and though suffering heavy losses they immediately reorganized under paralyzing enemy fire to successfully withstand subsequent attacks by the enemy in this all out effort. All participants fought with the dogged determination of giving no ground and in the face of almost continuous heavy fire, stood firm, doing their duty unhesitatingly and with unexcelled individual courage.

JAMES M. LEWIS
Brigadier General — U. S. Army
Commanding

Extract of General Order 96, Hq. 30th Inf. Div., 3 May 1945

HEADQUARTERS 30TH INFANTRY DIVISION

OFFICE OF THE COMMANDING GENERAL

OLD HICKORY

Award of the Bronze Star Medal

Citation

Private First Class Harold W. Strickland, 33562034, 119th Infantry Regiment, United States Army, is awarded the third bronze Oak Leaf Cluster, for wear with the Bronze Star previously awarded, for heroic achievement in action on 23 February 1945, in Germany. Private Strickland and a comrade volunteered to carry a radio to another company across an area covered by the fire of a battalion of the enemy. Moving over the hazardous area for five hundred yards, they were able to bring the radio to the company and then they returned to their company. Private Strickland's heroic action aided in the coordination which enabled the assault force to successfully complete its mission. Entered military service from Maryland.

James M. Lewis

JAMES M. LEWIS
Brigadier General - U. S. Army
Commanding

HEADQUARTERS
THIRTIETH INFANTRY DIVISION

OFFICE OF
COMMANDING GENERAL

AWARD OF THE BRONZE STAR MEDAL

CITATION

Private First Class Harold W. Strickland, 33562034, 119th Infantry Regiment, United States Army, is awarded a second Oak Leaf Cluster, for wear with the Bronze Star previously awarded, for heroic achievement in action on 9 April 1945, in Germany. Upon receiving information that one of the assault companies of his Battalion was short of vital types of ammunition, Private Strickland volunteered to carry this ammunition to them, even though it meant traveling over dangerous terrain, crossing a small stream in a boat under enemy artillery fire, and at all times under enemy observation. Upon completing the trip and finding another company in the same dire need of ammunition, Private Strickland unhesitatingly repeated this courageous act. His actions and devotion to duty reflect great credit upon himself and the Armed Forces. Entered military service from Maryland.

James M. Lewis
JAMES M. LEWIS
Brigadier General - U. S. Army
Commanding

The Bridge
Manningford Abbas
Marlborough, Wilts,
England

5th January, 1946

Dear Mr. Strickland,

I am writing you this letter in the hope that it will find you fit and well and back once again in your native land.

On reading your letter again I find that is it almost exactly a year since we casually met in the train. A very great deal has happened since then and I hope you are able to take up more peaceful pursuits once again.

Most of your comrades now have left us and we are returning once more to the hubbub of English ways and habits. It was not until the war was over did most of us realize how very much we owed to the men from the States and although politicians will wrangle over financial details, I am sure most of us are still very grateful for the help so spontaneously given by your country. The death of President Roosevelt was a very great shock to us all–he was a very great gentleman.

I do not suppose I shall ever have the pleasure of visiting your country so I am hoping I may keep in touch with you and so learn a small bit of what I should imagine, is a very beautiful country. During the past year I have had little time for leisure owing to pressure of work at the office. Although my wife and I have had some very enjoyable days cycling in the country. I spent one or two days during June hunting on the downs for orchids and found about ten varieties. Orchid hunting is quite a favorite pastime for the local naturalists and we compare notes on what we have found. Bird life in my garden has been scarce this year owing to the wife's cat. The past year I had more than a dozen nests in the garden.

I am now looking forward to the spring for the awakening of the countryside. Already I have heard the Missel Thrush, although we do not get our real winter until the end of this month or the beginning of next.

I am sending you a specimen copy of our Geographical Magazine and although it deals with a variety of subjects and countries, occasionally there are some really good articles about this country. It would give me great pleasure to send you this each month, that is, if you would like it.

I hope these few lines will eventually find you and that I may hear something of you once again.

With my kindest regards and best wishes,

Sincerely yours,

F.W.C. Merritt

[Editor's note: Mr. Merritt is the Englishman whom Jack mentioned meeting in his letter of January 27, 1945.]

The Bridge
Manningford Abbas
Marlborough
Wilts, England

22nd April, 1946

Dear Mrs. Strickland

It was with profound regret that I read your letter and while I have no desire or wish to open the wound, may I simply offer you my sincere sympathies.

During the course of the war I met many hundreds of your fellow county men and yet your husband was the only one I felt bound to ask for his address in the hope we might at least correspond, and I did have a faint hope that I might one day visit your wonderful country. However those pleasant dreams have been rudely shattered. But that fleeting friendship will always be treasured by me and I feel that I met and knew an American gentleman.

If it were possible it would give my wife and myself very great pleasure to invite you to stay with us, but unfortunately, like so many others at the present time, we have no house of our own and have to shift with in-laws until something can be built or purchased.

It is extremely difficult for me to write with any fluency, as I am sure you will appreciate, I have no idea to whom I am writing, and it becomes more difficult when I venture to think why I'm writing to you. I am sending a snap of my wife and myself and from this you will be able to get some idea of what we look like. We have been married nearly eight years, most of them under war conditions. I, like most of us, have to work for my living and this is in a lawyer's office at Dwizis. My wife has for some three or four years worked on the land, planting and gathering potatoes, etc. We have a good deal in common and in the spring and summer spend our spare time wandering over the downs.

We shall be delighted to meet your friends when they return to this country and I hope that we, too, may have the very great pleasure of meeting you and your children.

I will write you from time to time and if there is anything in particular you would like to know of the places your husband visited it would be a great honour for me to help.

This is a rather scrappy letter but I am labouring under great difficulties but I hope you will understand.

Yours very sincerely,

F.W.C. Merritt

Memorial Day Just Another Day for D.C. Widows of World War II

Three little boys and a baby girl whose daddies will never come back from the war symbolize for Washington today the aching void which Memorial Day, 1946, emphasizes in countless homes. Yesterday they presented floral wreaths and flowers to Brig. Gen. Burton M. Hovey, Bolling Field commandant (right), in memory of Air Force personnel who gave their lives in both wars. From left they are, Edward and Allen Ducher, son of Flight Officer Edward H. Ducher, whose widow lives at 1530 N. Longfellow-av, Arlington, and Jennis and Lynne Strickland, children of First Lieut. Jennis M. Strickland II, whose widow lives at 701 Flower-av, Takoma Park.

Sundown—Three bombers, led by Capt. Richard L. Ramer, a veteran of the European theater, will leave Bolling Field and fly over Arlington National Cemetery to drop flowers in a salute to the air war dead. The flowers yesterday were presented to Brig. Gen. Burton M. Hovey jr., commander of Bolling Field, by Col. Willis Fitch, executive director of the Air Force Association, and four children of airmen who died in the last war.

The latter were: Lynne, 1, and Jennis Strickland 3d, 2½, children of Mrs. Kitty M. Strickland, 700 block Florida Ave., Takoma Park, Md., and the late Lt. J. M. Strickland 2d, of the 8th air force, and Edward 3d, 3, and Allen S. Ducher, 2, sons of Mrs. Ruth Ducher, 1500 block North Longfellow Ave., Arlington, and the late Flight Officer E. H. Ducher, of the 15th air force.

8:30 P.M.—Organ recital by Paul Callaway in Washington Cathedral.

Thousands Pay Honor to Dead At Ceremonies

WASHINGTON NEWS
FRIDAY, MAY 31, 194

Truman Puts Wreath Of White Roses on Arlington Tomb

A brightly dressed crowd, interspersed here and there with women in mourning black, wandered among white crosses in the hot sunlight at Arlington National Cemetery yesterday, as the Nation paid tribute to its war dead.

On hillside after hillside, the well-kept graves were decorated with tiny American flags and bunches of red poppies.

President Truman was one of the first to stand bareheaded before the Tomb of the Unknown Soldier. Opening the observance of Memorial Day in the Nation's Capital, he placed a wreath of white roses there at 9 a.m. in silent homage to each man who has given his life for his country.

Today multi-colored floral offerings decorated the graves of hundreds of soldiers and sailors at Arlington and in Battle Ground National Cemetery. Words of humble respect and words of warning echoed in the ears of thousands who had listened to Memorial Day speakers asking the living to make sure that the dead shall not have died in vain.

In the colorful ceremonies at Arlington, veterans and other patriotic groups placed scores of wreaths on the Tomb of the Unknown Soldier.

Gen. Bradley Speaks.

At noon, approximately 3,000, including Gen. and Mrs. Dwight Eisenhower, gathered in the flag-bedecked amphitheater nearby for exercises under the auspices of the GAR Memorial Day Corp. Shielding themselves from the blistering sun with their programs, they listened in thoughtful solemnity to the measured words of Gen. Omar N. Bradley, veterans' administrator:

"We come to learn, if we can, how men might live as charitably together in peace as they died for each other in war * * *"

As the Marine Corps Band played taps at the conclusion of the ceremony, a black-clad woman in the audience broke suddenly into audible sobs.

One of the few wreaths already on the Unknown's Tomb when President Truman placed his wreath was put there at 8 a.m. by three children of Army flyers killed in action in World War II. They were Jennis M. Strickland III of 701 Flower avenue, Takoma Park, Md., son of First Lt. Jennis M. Strickland II, and Edward and Alan Ducher of 1530 North Longfellow street, Arlington, sons of Flight Officer Edward H. Ducher.

At sunset last night, flowers in the presentation of which these children took part Wednesday were dropped over the cemetery from three Army bombers.

Jennis and Lynne at Bolling Field Memorial Day, 1946

The Tomb of the Unknown Soldier, Memorial Day, 1946
Kitty and Jennis on right

Years ago I read a book called *The Reluctant Messiah.* In it was said–in essence, "If you ever ask yourself if you have done every thing you were put here on Earth to do and you are still alive, the answer is, No."

Jack was 22 years old when he died. He had known love. He had sired two children. He had realized just who he was and recognized his own strengths and weaknesses. He had found his God. He had accepted responsibility and had strived to be the best person he could be. He had lived his life with integrity and kindness and he thoroughly believed in the cause for which he willingly gave his life.

I believe he had done what God put him here to do.

I often had one-sided conversations with Jack. I remember the day I decided that this was not a good thing. If there were a life after death, perhaps my clinging to him was preventing him from getting on with his spiritual growth. So, regretfully, I told him I would let him go. I seldom had dreams about him, much to my disappointment, but that night I had a vivid dream that I was holding him in my arms as he died.

In 1950 I married Francis (Frank) M. Shore, Jr. He had served in the Navy as a Lieutenant during World War II. Frank was a "plank owner" of the destroyer, *U.S.S. Barton.*

The ship was commissioned in December 1943 and participated in the landings at Normandy on D-Day, the battles at Leyte Gulf, Ormac, Mindoro Island, Lingayen Gulf, the invasion of Iwo Jima, and–from March through June of 1945–the horrendous battle at Okinawa, to name a few. As a result of her action at Okinawa she was awarded the Navy Commendation for "Outstanding Heroism."

One month before we were married Frank instigated and organized a reunion of his *Barton* shipmates. Over 100 people attended. I was amazed at the obvious bond all of these men had formed. Everyone had a wonderful time and the reunions have continued every year since then. This year was the 49th reunion. This must set a Navy record.

The *Barton* was considered a "lucky ship" by everyone who served aboard her. While many ships were lost in the battles, the closest the *Barton* came to being hurt was when a kamikaze plane aimed at her and missed her bow by a few feet and exploded as it hit the water. Parts of the airplane were scattered all over the deck. Another time a torpedo did hit her but it lodged in the side of the ship and did not explode. Some of the men had to push it back out.

When she was decommissioned at Norfolk, VA, the number of former crew members attending was quite impressive. It was a moving and very sad occasion. The Navy took her out and used her for target practice. They were unable to sink her (her "luck" was holding) so they put explosives on board and sunk her outside of Norfolk.

Frank died in 1987 and was given a military burial at sea by the Navy and his ashes were scattered over the spot where the *Barton* had finally gone down.

When we married, Frank had one child, Frank III, who was 2 months younger than Jennis (who is now called Jack) and I, of course, had Jack and Lynne. Together we had three more children, Kitty (KC), Anthony (Tony), and Donald.

Frank was born in Washington, D.C. and was 11 years older than I. He was an excellent tennis player in his youth and was nationally ranked in the boys' division by the U.S. Lawn Tennis Association.

A few years after we married we bought a home in Chevy Chase, Md., and joined a nearby country club. Frank had a host of friends from his childhood, his "Barber Shop" singing group, his American Legion Post (of which he had served as Commander), his work at the U.S. Tariff Commission, his tennis-playing friends, and his ex-shipmates.

We had an active social life. Although this was not the lifestyle I had anticipated, I accepted and enjoyed it. I slowly, but surely, relegated my memories of World War II to a far corner of my mind and got on with the present. I busied myself with my large family. Our youngest child was born when Jack and Frankie were in college. When I finally had all the children in school and had some spare time I pursued a dream I had always had of taking art lessons.

I found a wonderful art teacher, Guy Fairlamb, and have enjoyed some success with my oil paintings. I led a normal, happy life.

Meanwhile, Lynne went over to England to visit. There she met an Englishman named Jeffrey Grace. They fell in love and married. She now has five children: Jeff, Jr., Cherie, Hillary, John Mark, and Natalie. She also has twin grandchildren, Sebastian and Jessica. They all live in England but have visited me from time to time. Jack has four children: Marisa, Felicia, Jennis, and Adam and lives nearby. Frankie and his wife have one daughter, Jennifer, and live in Florida. Tony and his wife, Lorain, have four children: Victoria, Anthony (who is called "Spike"), Michaela, and Melissa. They live a few blocks from me. KC and Donald live fairly close by and I see them frequently.

Frank loved me very much and there was no time when

it would have been appropriate for me to dredge up the long buried memories of my life with Jack. As you read in the beginning of this story, Cherie and her husband, Tim Williamson, sent me the lovely booklet that they had constructed about Cherie's grandfather. Once I found and started reading the wartime letters, all of the memories came flooding back. In reliving those long ago events I began to realize how much effect they had on me. For one thing, when you lose someone you love, you learn to appreciate every minute you're given with the loved ones who are still here. You also learn that the saying, "Love never dies," is not a *platitude* but a God-given *fact.*

Like the vast majority of people who lived through those days, I learned that I could "do the un-doable, bear the unbearable, run the gamut of emotions" and survive–and be stronger for it. That knowledge has stood me in good stead over the years and I give thanks for it. I also shall be eternally grateful that I was allowed to experience a deep love at that young age.

As I started writing the book, miraculously, more and more information from various sources began to come my way. The bare outline, in my mind, of what had happened so long ago, began to fill out.

When the book was almost finished, I had the opportunity of going to England with my daughter, KC, and her fiance, Tom Blankenship.

Tim and Cherie took us to see the fabulous Imperial War Museum at Duxford (which had been an Eighth Air Force Fighter base from 1943 to 1945.) In 1997 a new wing was dedicated at the museum. It is called, 'The American Air Museum of Britain.' It is a huge, beautiful hanger filled with U.S. planes from World War I up to the present. Among dozens of other planes, they have a B-17 but only a part of a B-24. For some unknown reason, very few B-24s are still in existence. The British have been trying to locate one and it is my understanding that they've finally been successful and one should be in the museum soon.

After seeing Duxford we went to Norwich where

the 8th Air Force Museum was located. The original museum was destroyed by fire a few years ago. It is being rebuilt and is scheduled to open in the year 2001. It is now temporarily housed in the town library in Norwich.

It was a cold, rainy, windy, typical March day when we went to Tibenham, the base where Jack had been stationed. The airfield is about 5 miles from the little town of Tibenham and is in the middle of the quiet countryside. It is now being used as a glider school but most of the huge original runways are still intact. Because of the bad weather the day we were there, the gliders could not fly and the field was deserted. We were able to drive and walk across all the runways. It was quite an emotional experience. The present seemed to disappear and it could have been a day in 1945. I felt that all that had happened since I started writing the book had been leading me to this day.

I looked at the trees at the end of the runway over which heavily loaded bombers had taken off. There was a little house in back of the trees. I could imagine its occupants listening to the planes flying overhead, so low that their tires almost touched the roof, and praying that they would gain altitude in time to miss the house. I saw the old church that the men used for a landmark to tell them that once again they had made it back safely. In my mind I saw the young American airmen rushing to the B-24s that were lined up on the runways, ready to start another mission. I could picture Jack, sitting in the cockpit, checking instruments, his mind on the job that lay ahead. As he glanced out of the window he saw exactly what I was seeing then.

I felt his presence and had the distinct impression that, at that moment, he was watching his granddaughter and me and was pleased.

Tibenham memorial

Kitty at memorial

View from runway at Tibenham

After we left the airfield at Tibenham we drove around the surrounding little roads. There wasn't much there except a few houses. We saw the railroad tracks that Jack mentioned and then we came to a pub called "Greyhound Pub." It was open, so we went in. Although a few changes had been made over the years, it was basically as it had been during the war. There was a dart board on the wall-several fireplaces-low ceilings-cozy but sturdy tables and chairs and pictures of B-24s on the wall that I later learned had been painted on pieces of B-24 fuselage by an American airman stationed there in the early '40s. The woman who ran it, Margaret Franks, had only been there three years. She was very friendly and told me that she had been a child during the war and remembered the Americans giving her chewing gum and chocolate. She said there was a man who lived down the road who was an expert on that part of history. He came into the pub frequently and would be very disappointed that he missed us. She said that he could probably give me more information about those days. While we were sitting there, she made a phone call to him and told us he was on his way over.

In a few minutes I looked up to see a young man in a leather pilot's jacket (with an 8th Air Force patch on the arm) and a crumpled pilot's hat. His name was Roland Bridge and he had been in the process of making tea (dinner) for his daughters when Margaret called him. His wife knew his obsession with the airfield and was not surprised when he dashed out of the house. He assured me that he was perfectly normal in every other facet of his life but that everyone who knew him knew how he felt about this subject. He said that as a teenager his father would let him drive on the runways while his father and a friend shot at rabbits from the back window of the car. Sometimes the two men would get out of the car and go into the fields to hunt. Roly, as he is called, said that he would then wander around the field by himself. He could not explain the attachment he felt but said he had the most wonderful feeling of peace when he was there. He still walks there often and always senses a feeling of belonging.

In my research I've often come across the rumor that the tower, which has since been torn down, was haunted. Many different people have said they saw an American pilot walking around it. Apparently it was a benevolent ghost. I do not know if Roly had heard of this but he said that once when he was wandering on the runways he saw a man come out of the trees and walk toward him. He was wearing a strange uniform that Roly didn't recognize. (From his description it was a heavy, fleece-lined bomber jacket.) When he got closer, the man disappeared. Roly said he never told anyone, other than his wife, about seeing this. He didn't want anyone to think he was crazy.

Over the years on his walks, Roly has picked up numerous artifacts. He says he has a garage full of them. He brought me the cartridge end of a bullet flare that was used from the tower to signal the squadrons to take off; a starter release panel from the side of a B-24; a rack and pinion for the steering flaps; an ID plate on a component part–stamped with Bendix Aviation Corporation, New Jersey, USA; a metal clip, made in Chicago, that was used on one of the hoses of the plane; a plastic spark plug cylinder that was inserted in the B-24 engine for shipping purposes and replaced when it arrived in England; and, lastly, two shells from the AA guns used on board the B-24. (I had an interesting time getting them aboard the airplane coming home–security checks, police, X-rays, etc.–but all ended well and they made it). He gave me all of these to take home.

When we were at the airfield we noticed an edifice that had been torn down at the end of one runway. We had picked up some pieces of slate and cement from the rubble. We asked Roly what the building was. He said that bunkers had been built at the end of the runways so that Headquarters could operate from them in case the field was bombed by Germans. The bunkers were crumbling and they had to tear them down to prevent someone from falling in them and getting hurt.

It was wonderful talking with him. Before we left he confided that he has often felt that he had actually been there–maybe in a past life–because he identified so much with those young men he had only heard about. And I'm not so sure he's wrong.

ADDENDA

When I started writing this book, I was amazed at the things I remembered. But there were other things of which I was either unaware or which I had forgotten. I tried to get Jack's records from the National Personnel Record Center in St. Louis. After a lengthy period, they wrote me that his records had been lost in the fire they had in 1973. I was quite frustrated, as I had no idea whom to contact to solicit information. Then, by chance, I met Ben Olsen who had been in the ETO at that time. He was a B-17 pilot and lives nearby. He put me in touch with his friend, David Patterson, a former B-24 pilot who was editor of the *Second Air Division Association Journal*. When Dave found out about my endeavors, he wrote me several letters offering his help. He sent me an excerpt from Rudolph Brisic's *The History of the 445th Bombardment Group (H)* in which he describes the raid on Wesel on March 24, 1945. He also gave me Fred Dale's address. Fred was editor for the 445th B.G. section in the *2ADA Journal*. I became a member of the 2ADA.

I also found out there was another association called the B-24 Liberator Club. They, too, put out a publication. It is called *Briefing*. I sent an application to them and received a wonderful packet from George Welsh, "Manager, Editor, Publisher and Chief Bottle Washer," containing newspaper articles, pictures of the B-24, cartoons, copies of B*riefing*, and a magnificent Certificate–gold seal and all–to attest to my membership in the association.

I wrote Fred Dale and he in turn wrote me a very encouraging letter. He had been a Link Trainer Instructor for the 445th. He gave me Ray Pytel's name and address. Ray is also an editor for the *Journal.* I contacted Ray and he wrote and offered to send me 10 years of back issues of the *Journal,* an offer I gratefully acepted. He also gave me the address of Mary Beth Barnard, who is the Historian for the 8th AF museum in Savannah, Ga. Mary Beth's father had been a member of the 445th B.G. She, too, was most helpful. She sent me some of Jack's flight orders. At her request I sent her a picture of Jack's original crew for the museum.

In reading the *2ADA Journals,* I came across an article that Chuck Walker had written about trying to get someone to fly the "Bunnie" on its 99th mission. Chuck, too, had been a pilot at Tibenham and he and his crew had flown the "Bunnie" numerous times. The Air Force was planning on sending the plane back to the U.S. after its 100th mission and displaying it at Bond Rallies. Chuck and crew were told that if they flew it on its 100th mission, they could accompany it. As it turned out, when the 99th mission came up, they had only one more mission to fly to end their tour. He beat the bushes trying to get some crew to fly its 99th. When I read this, I wrote him and enclosed a copy of the letter Jack had written about flying the "Bunnie." I figured he might like to know how the guy who did fly it felt about it. Chuck wrote me a most interesting letter and, when I asked, gave me permission to print it in this book.

R.F. Gelvin heard about my quest and wrote that he had flown two missions with Jack–one on the 1st of October, 1944, and one on the 17th. He had been acting Squadron Navigator assigned to check out Bernie Sugarman for a lead crew. He also had been trying to locate some of his old buddies and was having difficulty. He realized that no one had ever put together a spreadsheet format that would allow sorting by whatever and for wherever. So he took it upon himself to correct this oversight. He has spent more than a year gathering information and putting it on several spreadsheets. (It includes aircraft inventory; a complete roster, now totaling more than 5,000 persons; the pilots by squadron; their crews; where they went; and when they went.)

In April 1998 he flew from Arizona to Washington, D.C., along with Ed Zobac. Ed was interested in finding information about his father who was a B-24 gunner and was also stationed at Tibenham. They graciously let me tag along with them to the National Archives at College Park, Md., where we were given access to boxes and boxes of original Army Air Force records. Some of the documents in this book are copies that we obtained there.

Ray Pytel and Fred Dale put a notice in the winter issue of the *2ADA Journal* that I was seeking information about Jack and would like to hear from anyone who might have been on the March 24, 1945, raid.

Two days after the *Journal* came out, the calls started coming in.

The first call was from Lloyd Stone in Roswell, N.M. As I reported earlier, he was flying on Jack's left wing and saw Jack and Col. Fleming when they were shot down. He sent me two videos of actual B-24 raids.

Then John Napolitano in New Jersey called me. He had been on Jack's original crew and was at Westover, Mass., and Savannah, Ga., with him. He told me the name of the liner they sailed overseas on–the *Ile de France.* He also sent me the record of the targets and the dates of the 12 missions he had flown with Jack. He, too, had originally been assigned to the 93rd Bomb Group at Hardwick, England, and went to Tibenham with Jack to replace the B-24s that had been shot down at Kassel.

Tom Campbell called from Rhode Island. He had been the co-pilot for Lt. Art Keith on the plane flying directly behind Jack at the time he was hit. He sent me a long letter and enclosed a copy of the Pilot's Flimsy Sheet for the 3/24/45 raid. These sheets were handed out before a mission. He also send a copy of his personal notes which he wrote after each raid, a photo of his crew taken on the morning of the raid, and a copy of *Target Magazine,* a confidential publication distributed weekly to groups in their Wing. It acknowleged their significant achievements for the week. It contained two articles about the March 24 mission. He also sent a copy of the *Providence Evening Bulletin* newspaper for March 24, 1945, that his mother had saved for him.

Later Donald Croft called from Pennsylvania. He was a pilot who was also on that raid. He told me that the planes had dropped their loads and were heading home when they had to fly between two hillocks. Because they were so low, they could not see that between these hillocks there were numerous Germans with rifles and machine guns. As they flew through, they were bombarded with ground fire–as he said, they were "sitting ducks."

John Goffe wrote and enclosed pages from his Mission Diary detailing the raid. He gave me permission to include them in the book.

Dr. Richard Howell called from Michigan. He had been a tail gunner and was on the Wesel raid. He, also, was able to describe that day in minute detail.

Karl Rausch called from Illinois. He was in the lead squadron at Tibenham on 3/24/45. He offered any assistance I might need.

Tom Shafer wrote from Rochester, Pa. He was a pilot on the Wesel raid. He saw Jack's plane pitch slightly down and a few seconds later strike the ground and disintegrate.

All of these men have total recall about their parts in the war. Their stories are fascinating and each one could write a book about the events in which they participated. Fortunately some of them kept journals and have printed them for their children.

Their interest, help, kindness, and encouragement have been a revelation to me and have certainly had a great impact on my life. So to all of them, with my heartfelt thanks, I dedicate this book.

[Letter from Chuck Walker Nov. 5, 1997]

Dear Mrs. Shore,

What a pleasant surprise to hear from you and to learn of your efforts to write a book about Jack Strickland.

I remember Jack very well. He was an excellent pilot who was dedicated to the service of his country. I believe I may have given him and his crew their first orientation ride after he joined the 445th Bomb Group. In any case I am very familiar with his command of the B-24.

Of course I somewhat resent his referring to my beloved "Bunnie" as a pile of junk, although I must admit in all fairness that he wasn't far off target. My crew had been assigned to the "Bunnie" full time after the disastrous Kassel mission on Sept. 27, 1944. I complained bitterly that my crew was the oldest, from the point of longevity, in the squadron and thus should be given one of the new planes being flown in to replace all those we lost on the Kassel mission. The response was that the new crews wouldn't be able to fly that old plane, as they had no experience with battle-weary airplanes. As consolation, we were promised we would get to fly the "Bunnie" back to the States and on a bond selling tour if we indeed got the 100th mission on the bird.

As it evolved, my crew had only one mission to go when the "Bunnie" reached 98, thus necessitating another crew flying the "Bunnie's" 99th. I coaxed, begged and pleaded with many crews to fly that 99th. Most aborted on the hardstand before even running the engines up. As I recall, after 11 other crews failed, Jack Strickland and his crew completed the "Bunnie's" 99th for which we were most grateful. We put the 100th on that proud old bird on Jan. 6, 1945–thus completing our tour. Of course by then plans had been changed and a decision was made not to return the "Bunnie" to the States as had been promised. My crew was very disappointed as we had dreams of appearing with all the Hollywood stars at bond rallies.

Over the course of the next couple of months, other crews were able to put 9 additional missions on the "Bunnie" before it crashed on takeoff and was totally wrecked. As a matter of fact, in 1993 on a trip back to Tibenham, the farmer in whose field the airplane crashed, gave Mary Beth Barnard several small pieces of the plane that he had unearthed. Mary Beth had them framed and they are now on the wall of my office. I have since met the farmer who had several larger pieces I would like to have had but he wouldn't part with them.

Again my memory is not too keen after these 52 years but I believe I briefed the mission that Jack and Col. Fleming went down on. (I stayed on after I finished my tour and served as the Group check pilot and Briefing Officer.) It was a low level (on the deck) mission to drop supplies to our ground forces at the river crossing into Germany. Both Jack and Col. Fleming (Command Pilot) were extremely competent pilots so it was a direct hit from ground fire that brought them down. Everyone at the base was shocked and had a difficult time coping with the loss of these two fine men.

I hope I've answered some of your questions. If you wish, call or contact me any time if I can be of assistance. You've embarked on a very worthy project and I wish you well.

Kindest regards

Chuck Walker

[Excerpt from John Goffe's Mission Journal]

Mission #7 Wesel, Ger. 3/24/45; 5:40 hours

It was obvious that this was going to be different when one of the briefing officers was a Lt. Col. Paratrooper. Another difference was the doors were locked with Military Police at each one. After the briefing had begun, no one could enter or leave. The secrecy was due to the fact that the American and British Armies were poised to cross the Rhine River near the small German town of Wesel. The plan called for 14,000 paratroopers and glider infantry to land northeast of Wesel. This drop would consist of the U.S. 17th Airborne Division and the British 6th Airborne Division (XVIII Corps, Allied 1st Airborne Army.) The British XXX Corps, consisting of the 15th Infantry Division and the 51st Highland Division, would cross near Wesel. The British units were part of the British 2nd Army commanded by Gen. Sir Miles Dempsey. The overall operation was code named Plunder. Farther up the Rhine the crossing was to be made by the XVI Corps of the U.S. 9th Army under the command of Lt. Gen. William H. Simpson. The German units on the east bank of the Rhine were some of the best German troops on the entire Western Front, consisting of the 1st Parachute Army commanded by Gen. Kurt Student. Our contribution would be to drop, by parachutes, supplies to the Airborne troops. This would include food, gasoline and ammunition to be dropped from 300 feet at an air speed of 135 mph. It seemed obvious that the primary problem would be to locate the drop area since the British had laid down a smoke screen for several days.

The command pilot for the 2nd Combat Wing was scheduled to be Col. Carl Fleming, Deputy Commanding Officer of the 445th, who was flying his 31st mission - his first mission after completing a regular tour of duty. Col. Fleming contested the air speed as being too close to stall speed, especially if a plane lost an engine. The Paratrooper Col. thought the parachutes would be ripped apart at any higher speed. It was finally decided that 145 mph would get the job done. Each plane would carry a reduced crew consisting of a pilot, co-pilot, navigator, radio operator, engineer and three gunners. Some of the supplies would be pushed out the camera hatch in the rear of the plane and I would salvo the remainder out the bomb bay.

I lined the floor of the Navigator's compartment with flack suits since most enemy opposition was expected to be small arms fire. A flack suit looks like a sleeveless jacket with thin stripes of steel sewn into the material. This acts as some protection from nearby exploding flack shells. The assembly was at a relatively low altitude and then the entire formation let down across the North Sea. The 445th dispatched 27 aircraft and all dropped their supplies in the designated area. While flying at 300 feet over Southern Holland it was difficult to pilotage checkpoints. As we approached the Rhine the smoke was very thick and at times I couldn't see the ground. I had to hope the lead navigator was doing a better job than I was. The formation made more turns than on a bombardment mission in order to confuse the enemy of our intentions. When we crossed the Rhine we could see what was left of Wesel on our right. We flew directly over a pontoon bridge that was being used by Infantrymen running as fast as they could. I also saw several landing craft been piloted by sailors of the U.S. Navy wearing white sailor hats. From the river to the drop zone, which was 8 miles northeast, I could see many gun flashes on the ground and hoped they were aimed at someone other than us. There were paratroopers and supplies all over the ground and we could see paratroopers carrying canisters from the fields into the woods. There were a few wrecked gliders in one particular field. Almost the entire 8 miles was active on the ground. The most fighting was taking place right in our drop zone and there were many parachutes and canisters that had not been retrieved. I don't believe we were over 100 feet when we dropped our supplies. The formation immediately made a right turn and increased speed to 210 knots and then made another right turn crossing the Rhine into friendly territory. Two planes from the 445th were shot down in the drop zone including Col. Fleming's. He was declared KIA that afternoon since his plane was seen to hit the ground and explode. This was the Group's 262nd mission and a sad one since Col. Fleming was a very popular figure among the officers and the men. He came from a prominent Virginia family that apparently thought he would return home after a normal 30 missions. He was killed on his 31st. I heard later that on orders from Washington General Doolittle came to

Tibenham to personally question Group officers on just why Col. Fleming was flying his extra mission. It seems the importance of the supply drop convinced Col. Fleming to volunteer to fly as Wing Leader.

The Group was given good results but had 16 men KIA. After we landed there were about 20 small arms holes in the wings and fuselage; luckily no one was injured. The overall results to the 2nd Air Div. were severe. The supply drop was completed by 240 B-24s with 14 being shot down. There were 5 KIA, 30 WIA and 116 MIA. Four planes were so badly damaged that they had to be junked and 130 other planes received battle damage, including ours. The loss was 6%, which was very high this late in the European war. Thus ended my most dangerous mission.

[Except from Frank Russo's Mission Journal]

Mission #19 3/24/45

Mission was to carry supplies across Rhine River to Airborne troops near Wesel, Germany. Flew over front lines at tree top level to drop cargoes of ammunition and other supplies in prearranged zones where newly landed paratroopers and glider borne Infantrymen were awaiting them. This I must say was a most unorthodox mission for a B-24 to fly, however we dropped our load of 5,000 pounds at the designated spot. It will more than likely be the most important mission I'll fly during my tour. We were too low for the Jerries to shoot up any heavy flak. So we caught light flak What scared me most were the tracers whizzing by my turret. We were flying in the lead squadron and lost two ships to small arms fire. We were really sitting ducks at that altitude! Got a real good view of the German countryside. Could almost see the people's faces down there. We gunners were given strict orders not to do any strafing - too many of our own troops in the area, I guess. Passing over the Rhine we could see our troops massed along the banks with all sorts of armored equipment, waiting for the word to attack - a wonderful sight to see. Enroute to the dropping area we passed directly over the town of Wesel which was just newly captured. It could hardly be called a town anymore. Couldn't even see so much as a wall left standing - oh boy, what a mess!

Dear Mrs. Shore,

I have reproduced all the material that I have on the March 24, 1945 mission to Wesel, Germany where we lost your husband, Lt. Strickland. I hope this does not open up any old wounds as I recall the traumatic event. The reason I'm sending so much material is to give you an idea of how involved this operation was and how our small part contributed to the overall success.

Prior to the Mar. 24 operation we were stood down on standby with no indication of what we were going to do there than it was very important and they estimated we might suffer a 25% loss.

The briefing time was quite late in the morning as we were usually airborne before dawn. The 9:30 take off time explained the late briefing hour. Our fuel load of 2,300 gals. was 400 gals. less than our maximum. When they laid out the route with the red string on the war map it did not appear to be too bad. The unusual part of the mission would be dropping supplies at very low altitude and we would not have any of our defensive 50 calibers operational.

On the mission we were leading the whole 2nd Air Division of 240 B-24s. That being the case, a Col. Arnold from the wing would be in the lead Aircraft with our lead crew from the 445th. Your husband was Deputy Head with Lt. Col. Fleming, designated to take over should anything happen to the lead ship. Whenever a Wing or Group person flew in the lead ship the co-pilot was displaced to the Tail Gunner Turret to report any problems with the rear of the flight. On the Strickland crew Lt. Gillette was displaced to the rear.

After the briefing we went to our aircraft to prepare for the mission. Since it was so late in the morning we had the rare opportunity for a crew photo (enclosed) so we took advange of it. As I recall it was a nice spring day and we were able to take off and meet all our scheduled times wihtout a problem. It was a pleasure to fly over France without any worry about anti-aircraft guns. The unusual part of the mission was the supply drop where the lead ships had to be at the lowest altitude and all following aircraft flew above so no one would run into the leader's supply drop. Since our flight was in the lead we were at tree top level to allow reasonable drop altitude for the following flights. So as we approached the target area we continued to let down to our tree top level as required. As we approached the designated drop area we could see a tremendous line of men and equipment all heading in the same direction toward the Rhine River. The smell of cordite was very strong as we approached the battle area and the smoke partially obscured our vision. Suddenly two tall radio towers appeared directly in our flight path. The supporting guy wires left little room to maneuver since we were in formation at very low altitude. This broke up our reasonably tight formation as some aircraft went right and left and some through the middle. I recall slipping through the middle with one wing low to avoid the guy wires. At this point we were flying directly behind Lt. Strickland.

The River was a beehive of activity with a great many boats sculling men and equipment across the staging area. On the other side we ran into the large blue and yellow panels indicating our drop zone. We could feel the plane rise as we unloaded the 5,000 lbs. of supplies.

With all the supplies delivered all we had to do was make a right turn and head back across the river. As directed everyone was to turn right to avoid other aircraft. On our right side was a large hill which we had to go around as it was above our altitude. We were still directly behind Lt. Strickland. As we went around the back side of the hill we encountered a large concentration of German Infantry. All the troops began firing their rifles at the aircraft. Every where you looked there was someone firing.

Now we were in trail of Lt. Strickland and headed for the river. Suddenly out of nowhere these shells came up to Lt. Strickland. The slow speed and color looked like something from a Roman Candle. From my vantagepoint I could not see them impact or any indication of a fire or damage to the engines. Without any indication of trouble the nose of the ship went down slowly and they flew into the ground with all engines running and no visible damage to the aircraft. Upon impact the ship exploded in a tremendous fireball high in the air. We were so close behind we flew through the fireball. We never observed any shells being fired at our aircraft.

Shortly after, we crossed the river and rejoined our group for an uneventful flight back to the base.

At the after mission briefing we learned of another casualty in our flight–Lt. Shultz. Later we found out our overall losses to be 25 aircraft out of 240, which was well below the 25% estimate and most all of the supplies were recovered. This was the biggest operation since D-Day and the last major combined effort of the war.

Our crew survived the war with only one loss–our bombardier. We flew home in our aircraft.

I continued to fly with the R.I. Air Guard in fighters and a number of other aircraft for 35 years. This was the most traumatic thing that ever happened to me in all my years of flying. I can never forget what happened even to the last detail.

When I saw your request in the 2ADA Journal I could not believe it. I sincerely felt a responsibility to respond and let you know what happened and hopefully can put it to rest.

If I can be of any further help don't hesitate to call or write.

Sincerely

Tom Campbell

GROUP COMBAT MISSION HISTORY -- Jennis M. Strickland

Mn No	Date	Grp Mssn No	City	Country	Target	Types Of Bombs Used	Results	A/C Over Target	No. of Acft L:ost
1	10/12/44	178	Osnabruck	Germany	Marshalling Yards	500# Gp 500# lb	Good	30	
2	10/14/44	180	Koln	Germany	Marshaling Yars	250# Gp 500# lb	Unobserved	13	
3	10/17/44	182	Koln	Germany	Ford Motor Works	0# Gp 500# lb 500# Mk1	Unobserved	34	
4	10/18/44	183	Leverkusen	Germany	Industrial Complex	0# Gp 500# Gb 500# Mk	Unobserved	10	
5	10/22/44	185	Hamm	Germany	Marshaling Yars	250# Gp 500# Gp 500# ll	Unobserved	33	
6	11/27/44	195	Offenberg	Germany	Marshallling Yards	500 lp	Good	14	
7	11/30/44	197	Homburg	Germany	Marshallling Yards	100# lp	Unobserved	20	1
8	12/05/44	199	Munster	Germany	Marshallling Yards	500# Gp	Unobserved	34	
9	12/11/44	201	Hanau	Germany	Marshalling Yards	100# lp	Unobserved	37	2
10	12/19/44	203	Ehrang	Germany	Marshalling Yards	100# Gp 500# lb	Unob.	7	
11	12/24/44	205	Bitburg	Germany	Comm. Center	250# Gp 500# Gp	Excellent	18	1
12	12/28/44	207	Homburg	Germany	Marshalling Yards	250# Gp 500# lp	Unobserved	9	
13	12/30/44	209	Auskirchen	Germany	Railroad Bridge	500# Gp	Unobserved	30	
14	01/02/45	212	Glush	Germany	Railroad Bridge	1000# Gp	Unobserved	28	
15	01/03/45	213	Pirmasens	Germany	Rail Head	500# Gp	Unobserved	27	
16	01/05/45	214	Somernheim	Germany	Marshalling Yards	500# Gp 500# lp	Good	29	
17	01/31/45	225	Hallendorf	Germany		1000# Gp	Unobserved	0	
18	02/26/45	239	Berlin	Germany	Marshalling Yards	500# Gp 500# lb	Unobserved	31	
19	02/27/45	240	Halle	Germany	Marshalling Yards	500# Gp	Unobserved	40	2
20	03/01/45	242	Ingolstadt	Germany	Marshalling Yards	500# Gp 500# lb	Unobserved	29	
21	03/03/45	244	Magdeburg	Germany	Oil Refinery	500# Gp	Unobserved	22	2
22	03/19/45	256	Neuberg	Germany	Air Base	500# Gp 500# lb	Good	21	
23	03/24/45	262	Wesel	Germany	Air Base	Cargo only	Good	27	2